QUALITATIVE METHODS
for
MARKETPLACE RESEARCH

SOCIAL & BEHAVIORAL SCIENCES   *Business, Management & Labor*

39-0413   HF5415   00-12352 CIP

Sayre, Shay. **Qualitative methods for marketplace research.** Sage
Publications, CA, 2001. 255p bibl index afp ISBN 0-7619-2269-5, $72.00

This work is designed for marketing practitioners and students who have a basic
understanding of statistical data collection and analysis as it relates to various research processes. While much of the current literature in this area is concerned with quantitative analysis, this book emphasizes the collection and use of qualitative methods as they relate to
marketing research methods. Sayre (California State Univ., Fullerton) intends not to coach
the reader in how to conduct marketplace research, but to point out the kind of information
available for developing market strategies and planning. The text is divided into five parts:
"Approaching Qualitative Methods," "Getting Ready to Research," "Choosing a Research
Model," "Data Collection: Techniques and Tools," and "Text Analysis and Reporting."
The author offers carefully crafted explanations of how to apply popular concepts to
develop realistic plans of action. Through the use of practical and successful examples,
Sayre provides the reader with a detailed roadmap for developing, executing, and analyzing
current market research. This very applied approach to qualitative market research is rec-
ommended for upper-division undergraduate students through professionals.—*W. G. Ellis,
Concordia University*

To Aubyn, Ryan, and Sean.

QUALITATIVE METHODS
for
MARKETPLACE
RESEARCH

SHAY SAYRE

Sage Publications
International Educational and Professional Publisher
Thousand Oaks ▪ London ▪ New Delhi

For information:

Sage Publications, Inc.
2455 Teller Road
Thousand Oaks, California 91320
E-mail: order@sagepub.com

Sage Publications Ltd.
6 Bonhill Street
London EC2A 4PU
United Kingdom

Sage Publications India Pvt. Ltd.
M-32 Market
Greater Kailash I
New Delhi 110 048 India

Printed in the United States of America

Library of Congress Cataloging-in-Publication Data

Sayre, Shay.
  Qualitative methods for marketplace research / by Shay Sayre.
    p. cm.
  Includes bibliographical references and index.
  ISBN 0-7619-2269-5 — ISBN 0-7619-2270-9 (pbk.)
  1. Marketing research—Methodology. I. Title.
  HF5415.2 .S29 2001
  658.8'3—dc21   00-012352

This book is printed on acid-free paper.

01   02   03   04   05   06   07   7   6   5   4   3   2   1

Acquiring Editor:	Marquita Flemming
Editorial Assistant:	MaryAnn Vail
Production Editor:	Diane S. Foster
Editorial Assistant:	Kathryn Journey
Typesetter/Designer:	Rebecca Evans
Indexer:	Molly Hall
Cover Designer:	Michelle Lee

Contents

�\| PART IV

Foreword

What It Is

This book is an introduction to the role of qualitative research methods for marketing research, a discipline that has traditionally relied on quantitative tools. The text combines explanations, examples, and occasions when these methods are appropriate to marketplace research. It advocates multiple techniques and tools to achieve answers to research questions; it presents alternatives to theoretical testing. It provides sources for more in-depth presentations of each technique discussed, so when you're faced with executing these principles, you can get help. And it's the only text appropriate for scholars and students of marketing, advertising, public relations, communications, and entertainment studies on the market today.

What It Isn't

This book is *not* a "how-to" on methods. It is not the single answer to every research problem nor is it intended to be. It is not a panacea for research solutions.

And it's not wise to pass off these methods as inconsequential for developing market strategy and planning activities.

How It Works

The book is divided into five sections and 16 chapters. In three chapters of Part I, I present the differences between *positivist* (quantitative) and *naturalistic* (qualitative) approaches to research. Five structural models are explained, and I suggest their relevance for application to studying marketplace consumption experiences. Part II contains two chapters that describe the planning process of qualitative research. Study designs and proposal writing are outlined, and a brief discussion of issues and ethical concerns will get you started on your study.

Part III provides an in-depth look at each structural model in four chapters, beginning with the narrowest focus we use: history, living biography, and self-narratives. The case method, phenomenology and grounded theory, and ethnographic approaches to research get progressively less focused, taking on a cultural rather than an individualistic approach.

In Part IV, data collection techniques and tools are explained in four chapters, including observation and fieldwork, field interviews, structured interviews that are conducted in off-site locations, and projective techniques. Part V covers methods of analyzing visual and written text and presents a guide for writing narrative reports.

Chapters have similar formats, beginning with an introduction to and discussion of the topic. A chapter summary reviews the discussion. Activities intended for practical application of chapter principles are presented as Stretching Exercises. I also recommend texts on the topic. Finally, examples or Cases in Point of actual studies are included (except in Part I) to dramatize their integration into marketplace research.

Readerly Expectations

As readers, you will approach research from a variety of marketplace disciplines. I use the term *marketplace* to represent cultural *scenes* where consumption activity takes place. Scenes include commercial, mass mediated, and entertainment cultures. And I apply the label *consumer* to all members of a cultural scene. Shoppers, audiences, and travelers are among the consumers of cultural scenes. You can expect to understand these terms and labels to reflect disciplines where the study of individuals is situated within a communication system of signs and symbols.

Your job, as a marketplace researcher, is to interpret those signs and symbols for others who need to understand specific consumption cultures and consumer segments. You will be concerned with meanings as they emerge from marketplace *text*. As readers of text (action), you collect observational notes, interviews, and artifacts from the *field* (where the action takes place). You analyze text collected in the field for patterns and themes, similarities and differences, and surprises. Your study revelations are presented to others as a narrative report for use in problem solving or for illumination on a scholarly topic.

Writerly Assumptions

As an author, I make several assumptions about you, the reader of this textbook. One is that you have a basic understanding of the research process, particularly as it relates to statistical data collection and analysis. Another is that you will supplement this text with others when additional detail is necessary for your study requirements. And I also assume that you are interested in understanding how to apply qualitative methods to marketing, communication, or consumer research.

Last

As author and reader, we strive to make sense out of human activity. To that purpose, I send you on a journey into the pages that follow in anticipation of a mutually delightful experience. As you venture into marketplace research, allow the methods, techniques, and tools provided in this book to be your guide.

Acknowledgments

Interpretive consumer research owes a great debt to scholars who have challenged tradition through their advocacy of qualitative techniques for marketing purposes. Seven such researchers are recognized here for their profound influence on the field: Eric Arnould, Russ Belk, Beth Hirschman, Sid Levy, Grant McCracken, Barbara Stern, and Craig Thompson. This author wishes to thank them and all the members of the Association for Consumer Research for their input and support.

Part I

APPROACHING QUALITATIVE METHODS

The three chapters in this section establish the why and what of qualitative methods for marketing purposes. The first chapter introduces the subject, comparing and contrasting qualitative and quantitative methods, and advocating the integration of both for a thorough research approach to problem solving. Four parameters for qualitative investigation are established: (a) an understanding of the consumer culture being studied, (b) a naturalistic approach to study, (c) thematic and conceptual analysis of consumer narratives, and (d) bringing a subjective point of view to the research.

Chapter 2 introduces five models for approaching qualitative research: biography, case study, phenomenology, grounded theory, and ethnography. As researchers of the human condition, we refer to all information collected as *text*, including the words contained in consumer dialogue. Words enable us to focus on the meanings shared and understood by the members of a single consumption culture.

Chapter 3 characterizes the audiences we study using qualitative techniques. We see audiences as active interpretive communities that include media users, entertainment audiences, sports and music fans, tourists, investors, shoppers, and other types of consuming publics. We learn that objects are embraced for their meaning and are very important for our personal identities in this postmodern consumer culture. We see how anthropologists bring their methods to marketing and advertising agencies in the form of account planners who act as consumer advocates.

This section provides a thorough introduction for students and marketing practitioners who wish to gain an understanding of the role qualitative methods play in marketplace research.

1 Why Qualitative Research?

As a psychologist who has turned his interest and attention to the study of marketing problems, I believe the preferred way to bring behavioral science to bear on marketing management and study might be to train people within the behavioral science disciplines, then to let them go into business.

—Sidney J. Levy, 1974

When asked to "defend" the use of qualitative research for business and marketing applications for this book, I became both defensive and irritated at the notion of defending a legitimate approach for the sake of appeasing marketing traditionalists. Qualitative methods, I believe, need no defense. So what follows is more of a rationale for using a variety of methods, including quantitative ones, to arrive at the more encompassing answer to a research question. Notice I did *not* say to prove a hypothesis. That's because informative research is not about proving anything.

Therein lies the difference between what has traditionally been considered the only appropriate measure of marketing information (quantitative data) and the recent acceptance of consumer testimony (qualitative data) as valuable guidance for market planning. Rather than proving, qualitative techniques help us *understand* consumer motivations and *illuminate* creative concepts.

So, we will leave "the proof in the puddin'" and focus on understanding and illumination to answer our marketing questions. That's not to say we ignore the facts. On the contrary, we use the facts to direct our inquiry and substantiate our hunches. And we always incorporate quantitative data into our thinking about how to formulate questions and identify problems.

What about replication, you ask? Not applicable here. We use qualitative methods to gather insight that may or may not be absolutely typical of another group of folks who inform the research. Our results are not intended to be an absolute answer.

3

And we're not the first folks to take this view. Qualitative research has been around for a half century. It's my guess it will gain complete acceptance by the marketing community as it has by the Association of Consumer Research, a leading group of researchers located around the world.

This chapter deals with differences between qualitative and quantitative methods. But if you're looking for a defense, read the one by Sidney Levy, thinker extrordinaire and former marketing professor at the Kellogg Graduate School of Management.[1]

Qualitative and Quantitative Approaches

Positivism is a philosophy that denies our knowledge of the Real and affirms our ignorance of the Apparent.

—Ambrose Bierce, 1911

Gathering intelligence about the marketplace is the purpose of conducting research of all types. Determining what research methods to use comes during the objective-forming stages of planning. Market data (who, when, where, and how) are best achieved numerically; market understanding (why) comes from penetrating the minds of those who are in that market. We choose qualitative methods because of its emphasis on processes and meanings; we choose quantitative methods because they substantiate. We combine both methodologies to provide a comprehensive approach to problem solving.

Let's think about research as a *mode of inquiry,* a way to learn answers to questions about the marketplace. To conceptualize these modes, we can compare four aspects of inquiry: assumptions about the market, purpose of the research, approach to data gathering, and the role of the researcher. We'll use the case of Peet's Coffee, a San Francisco roaster, to illustrate the aspects of each method.

Assumptions About the Market

Here's where bipolarity comes into the research arena. Each of the two methodological paradigms views reality from a different perspective. Quantitative data are social data with a reality based on objectivity. Its perspective is one of an outsider, called an *etic* view. At the other end of the spectrum, qualitative data result from a socially constructed reality with an insider's perspective or *emic* view. This view is exemplified in Peet's positioning dilemma: After selling off Starbucks and finding itself in the role of competitor for expanding retail operations, Peet's is faced with the problem of how to position itself among the plethora of coffee brands. If we assume the marketplace consists of X number of coffee drinkers in Y places who consume an average of 3 cups per day for a gross annual product of Z, we have characterized the coffee market from an etic, objective perspective. From this data, we know what is bought, where consumers buy it, and how often, but we don't know why they buy from Peet's rather than from Starbucks.

To discover how consumers perceive one product among the competition, we must watch them select, ask them about their preferences, and understand the role of coffee in their social interactions. This is an emic, insider perspective; we learn that Peet's dark-roasted taste is what distinguishes it in the minds of consumers. Maybe we also find out that Starbucks's clusters of tables permit more social interactivity than Peet's linear seating, and that's why consumers prefer Starbucks, even if the coffee's taste is inferior to Peet's.

Purpose of the Research

Research begins with objectives. What do we want to know? For concrete answers to market questions, we use reliable and valid data that can be generalized to the entire marketplace. We use this information to predict sales and profits or to forecast the need for expansion or consolidation. We use quantitative methods to give us explanations of cause and effect so that we can approach planning from a bottom-line approach. If, on the other hand, we want to understand how the product fits into the lives of consumers, we use a contextualized approach. We stress interpretation of consumer testimony and behavior. We rely on situational and circumstantial information that has limited geographic and demographic application and that is subjective in nature because it incorporates biases from both consumer and researcher into the results. We research humans, so we call ourselves *human science researchers.*

Peet's uses quantitative data to identify locations for its proposed expansion and to predict business based on street traffic numbers that can be generalized from one location to another. They also use qualitative techniques to understand how consumers interact with retail space during their coffee consumption. They learn the importance of aggregated tables that facilitate the social interaction consumers expect from coffeehouses. And they adapt preferences of local users based on specific needs and wants, such as outdoor versus indoor space for climatized socializing.

Approaches to Conducting the Research

To determine the extent of a relationship between cause and effect, quantitative researchers form hypotheses and theories that can be applied to multiple situations. Facts can be manipulated and controlled to yield favorable or unfavorable results. Usually, experiments are conducted with control and experimental groups, and the results are deductive. They conduct component analysis and seek consensus so the data make sense in a consistent fashion. We use a different approach.

To understand the relationship that exists between consumers and a product or service, qualitative researchers develop a question and expect the answer to emerge from transcripts or observational data collected in a natural setting without experimental groups. Inductive results yield patterns, and researchers seek pluralism to explore difference.

Back to Peet's: A quantitative approach to selecting a retail location is to hypothesize that an outlet's success is based on traffic. To test the hypothesis, we compare traffic numbers at two locations until the results point to the store generating the most traffic. A qualitative approach asks, "Why this location?" We watch how shoppers interact with the street, and we inquire about their expectations for stopping for coffee during their shopping routine. Traffic patterns are observed as they occur naturally, and consumer narrative is analyzed for themes of preference, choice, and rationale. The variety of shopping motivations revealed during the study determines what consumers want in a location. Peet's opens a retail outlet to provide those consumers' needs.

The Role of the Researcher

> *Study what you must affect.*
> —Shakespeare, *Taming of the Shrew*

Quantitative researchers, like newspaper reporters, strive for objectivity free from bias to gather and analyze their data. With detached impartiality, they portray the research situation as an objective third person with no investment in either the data or the outcome. Conversely, personal involvement and partiality are trademarks of qualitative researchers. The researcher becomes the instrument, interpreting through empathetic understanding of consumer revelations. Life experience and background play directly into the researcher's understanding of a situation and cannot be overlooked in the resulting subjective interpretation.

If Peet's wants market data to justify selecting a specific retail location, they rely on syndicated data, surveys, tallies, economic forecasts, and traffic reports collected by outside services. But if what they need are data to characterize consumers and identify the role of a coffee house location in their lives, Peet's will hire researchers who are comfortable with humanistic methods to answer research questions.

What Qualitative Research Does and What It Doesn't

In case you don't get the idea, this summary should help clarify some of the misunderstanding about the nature of qualitative methods. In this text, we won't talk about theories because they imply abstraction. We discard a positivist philosophy (which says that all knowledge derives from observational experience) for a humanistic approach. *We don't measure, we interpret.* We advocate using inductive reasoning—proceeding from particulars to more general statements—to offer an alternative to the scientific model. We begin with this assumption: Studying consumers is examining the creative process whereby people produce and maintain forms of life and society and systems of meaning and value.

We're not opposed to statistics, math, or counting. We just use them as starting points or to strengthen our findings. We incorporate, combine, and integrate data-gathering methods for an in-depth understanding of our research question. We won't prove or disprove, and we won't generalize. But we will bring meaningful interpretation of consumer behavior to the table for consideration in strategic decision-making or creative conceptualization.

Borrowing From the Social and Human Sciences

Qualitative marketplace researchers believe that the consumer's view is the key to gathering intelligence about the marketplace. And to understand a consumer's perspective, we borrow methods from humanistic researchers. Among them are psychologists who provide probing and projective techniques for understanding individuals' motivations. We use methods developed by anthropologists who look to artifacts for characterizations of ancient peoples. Spears, pots, and animal statues provide clues about ancient Egyptians in much the same way as the contents of a consumer's refrigerator reveal purchase choices. And sociologists provide methods for understanding how people interact, which enable market researchers to reveal how consumers influence one another.

In his brief history of the origin of qualitative methods for marketing research, Levy[2] suggests that the growth of surveying to measure audience characteristics led to asking "why," a task that cannot be accomplished using traditional polling methods. Advertising agencies, noticing the types of inquiry practiced in the communications field, began looking to consumers to gather brand preferences, product likes and dislikes, and reasons for buying or not buying.

Early work on social-psychological aspects of consumer behavior appeared in the late 1940s in trade publications, such as *Advertising Age* and *Harvard Business Review*. Marketers began to make the association between the usual rational explanations for behavior and unconscious motivations. Acknowledging that direct answers to direct questions might not be the panacea previously awarded surveys, researchers began to emulate the projective techniques popular with psychologists and social research. Thematic apperception tests (visual projection) and word association techniques were modified to assess what products meant to consumers. The infamous Haire[3] experiment used two versions of a grocery list to understand perceptions about users of instant coffee.

In the 1950s, interviewing techniques became nondirective to encourage free and lengthy consumer narratives. Motivational research was determined to be appropriate for studying a variety of marketing aspects, including factors that influence product consumption, the content of print and broadcast advertising, media audiences, media content, public images or corporations, and public conceptions of retail stores and brands. Personality studies were used by advertising agencies to correlate personality variables with marketing behavior.[4]

The following decade (1960s), buyer behavior theory and textbooks were introduced, giving rise to the use of focus groups for all aspects of business research. As we begin the 21st century, marketplace researchers invoke few humanistic techniques other than focus groups.

Some instances where qualitative methods are especially helpful occur when little is known about a topic, such as why consumers shop and browse online or when consumers belong to a culture that is closed or secretive, such as teen gangs that hang out in the food courts of shopping malls or stay in the shadows of tall buildings in urban areas. In both instances, skilled researchers can use qualitative methods to understand what meaning consumers attach to products and buying environments. Researchers get to the heart of consumer concerns by sharing their experiences and understanding their perspectives.

Becoming Humanistic Researchers

Humanistic inquiry differs from scientific or positivist research because it advocates the indwelling of the researcher.[5] The outcome of humanistic research is *interpretation*. According to four noted researchers,[6] the six fundamental beliefs of humanistic inquiry are as follows:

1. Human beings construct multiple realities.

2. A researcher and the phenomenon under study are mutually interactive.

3. A researcher should strive to construct a "thick description" of the phenomenon under study.[7] If "man is an animal suspended in webs of significance he himself has spun,"[8] the job of the researcher is to achieve a *thick* description of those webs.

4. Because they are dynamic rather than static entities, phenomenological aspects cannot be considered either causes or effects.

5. Research inquiry is inherently value laden.

6. Inquiry is a social construction between researcher and phenomenon, and knowledge is subjectively attained; knowledge is constructed, not discovered.

Contrast these beliefs with the scientific mode of inquiry—a single reality, researcher independence from phenomenon, generalizable statements of truth, cause-and-effect-based reality, and value-free knowledge—and the differences loom large. Researchers must choose between the positivist or humanist view of reality and design their methods appropriately. Hirschman[9] suggests a series of four steps useful for implementing humanistic research that differ in both form and content from those followed by positivist science. These steps emphasize a researcher's immersion in a phenomenon and constructing an interpretation of it. We'll talk more about this later.

Roots

Four perspectives used in marketing research come from other disciplines. Table 1.1 identifies the method's root and a typical research question posed for marketing purposes, using Vans shoes as an example.

Brave marketing researchers acknowledge that projective techniques enable consumers to apply stories to products, to match pictures of coffee drinkers with people, and to communicate their shopping fantasies. Some of them even embrace ethnographic approaches to learn about consumer cultures. But not enough of us are comfortable with the diversity and variety of qualitative methods. To that end, this text exists.

The choice of method, then, is an emphasis on either proof or discovery—and whether or not to rely on a single technique or integrate techniques for depth of understanding. Although no text advocates a "best" method, traditional marketing research experts direct students toward quantitative, measurable techniques for data collection, casting off qualitative research as "focus groups." After reading this text, I hope you will agree that there is more to research than a survey, a definitive answer, or a proven hypothesis. I invite you to take a look at just

Table 1.1 Methodological Roots

Perspective	Root	Question for Marketing Use
Ethnography	Anthropology	What is the culture of Vans wearers?
Phenomenology	Philosophy	What is the essence and structure of wearing sneakers for skateboarders?
Heuristics	Psychology	What is my experience with wearing Vans sneakers? What are the experiences of other wearers of Vans?
Ethnomethodology	Sociology	How do Vans wearers integrate skateboarding into their lives so that it is a socially acceptable behavior?

how well creative research design yields insight, discovery, and understanding of the consumer marketplace.

Data Collection Methods and Checks

Once the research question or hypothesis is determined, researchers using either qualitative or quantitative methods must decide how to gather the information; we call this *data collection*. Data can be collected in a variety of ways according to the type of information needed. Collected data are characterized by quantitative researchers as *numeric units;* humanistic researchers think of data as *word units*.

Although the nature of the data being collected differs, researchers using both qualitative and quantitative methods employ similar data-gathering techniques, including observation, document analysis, and interviews. Differences, as explained next, occur during technique execution.

Observational techniques are appropriate for counting and for understanding. Marketers wanting to learn the purchase habits of convenience store shoppers can approach observation in one of two ways:

1. Count the number of consumption activities taking place using preestablished categories, such as "purchase cold beverages only," "play lottery and make a purchase," "retrieve cash from the ATM machine," "purchase a money order," and so

forth. The totals will provide an accounting of the numbers and types of transactions made during a particular period of time.

or

2. Observe and record the activities taking place in the store as they occur, letting the events drive the data. Note behavior, dress, mood, and physical appearance of patrons. Listen to their conversations and social interactions with other patrons and with the clerk. The outcome yields a portrait of a convenience store culture.

In the first instance, positivist researchers gather statistical facts concerning purchase types and amounts to determine traffic and purchase patterns. The second, humanistic approach helps us to learn about consumer habits and preferences, decision-making steps, and attitudes toward the environment to understand how to provide consumer satisfaction.

Content or document analysis is also viewed differently, depending on the research objective. Advertisers interested in measuring the commercial clutter of a particular magazine under consideration for a full-page insertion look at the competition's ad content in one of two ways:

1. They identify ad types, such as product in use, product alone, product in setting, and so forth, and count them.

or

2. They look at the magazine as text and allow categories to emerge on their own. Placement, color, camera angle, resolution, language, and design are conceptualized for their fit within the editorial context of the publication.

Positivists use numbers of established categories, a process that often excludes important competitive data. Categories emerging naturally from the text provide a richer and more detailed understanding of the advertising message.

Interviewing one or numerous respondents is used extensively in marketplace research. A perfume manufacturer is interested in consumer reaction to its new product's scent. Once again, the approach to interviewing differs in structure:

1. Surveys are delivered, sent, or handed out with samples to query representatives in the demographics of perfume wearers. Numbers yield statistically significant results.

or

2. Open-ended questions are posed to a representative group of perfume users, and their answers are analyzed for patterns and themes. Respondents are probed with elaboration questions ("Can you tell more?" or "What else do you remember?") for

additional information that might help the manufacturer refine the product or marketing approach.

Quantitative surveys yield numbers of responses to predetermined questions that leave no room for misinterpretation. Humanists use open-ended questions to shed light on aspects not included in surveys, such as quality of the packaging, similarity to other perfumes, or price. Often more costly than surveys, personally posed questions reveal consumer preferences that manufacturers value.

Collected on audio or video recordings, interview transcripts provide valuable testimony for analysis. Consumers often share private thoughts and attitudes about a product or consumption experience during interviews, and their quotes provide powerful evidence for research sponsors. Captured on video, facial expression and other nonverbal communication expressed indirectly is vivid evidence of attitudes that often contradict actual narrative. Audiotapes reveal fluctuations in voice pitch, which help researchers determine opinions and attitudes not overtly expressed. Transcript analysis is a time-consuming task unless computer software is used.[10] Analysis also provides researchers with patterns of verbal organization and content useful for meaning interpretation.

For these reasons, qualitative researchers rely heavily on transcript data to understand a phenomenon. Conversely, transcripts, when collected, simply provide a means of validating or checking numerical survey data for quantitative researchers.

Quality of data collected is measurable to a degree. *Validity* (measuring what is intended to be measured) and *reliability* (response consistency) are important factors for quantitative accountability. Pretested survey instruments ensure high validity and reliability marks. For qualitative data, *authenticity* is an important measure. Avoiding biased questions and responses, checking respondent identification, and using informants to confirm assumptions are a few tactics researchers use to authenticate data.

Summary

1. Qualitative and quantitative research methods provide answers to different questions. A positivist approach is hypothesis driven and uses empirical research to prove or disprove hypotheses. It operates on a belief in single truth, objective testing, and an etic approach. Humanistic, interpretive research, on the other hand, is conducted to understand a lived experience, a phenomenon.

2. Qualitative methods are appropriate for marketing because statistical measures ignore meaning creation and because we believe in multiple truths, not a single one.

And because we believe the individual's point of view is key to understanding the marketplace, we are committed to an emic position.

3. Although data are gathered differently, three techniques dominate both methods. Quantitative researchers count units in observations and in content analyses, prefer survey instruments for interviewing, and use transcripts as a check.

4. Qualitative researchers observe to understand culture, view content to understand categories, use open-ended questions during interviews, and employ transcripts to understand verbal organization.

5. To be useful, quantitative data must be reliable and valid; qualitative data must be authentic.

Stretching Exercises

1. Conduct a miniresearch project to learn about female consumer preferences for Coke and Pepsi. First, design a five-question survey to prove the hypothesis "More women prefer Coke than Pepsi." Have 20 women take the survey. Now, ask 10 women to characterize Coke and Pepsi according to film stars that they would cast to endorse each beverage. Record their answers on audiotape. What conclusions can you make about each method's ability to inform the question?

2. Go online and locate a marketing research firm that uses the Internet to gather information about products or services. What kind of data do they provide clients? Would you classify their methods as qualitative or quantitative?

Recommended Readings About the Qualitative-Quantitative Debate

Creswell, J. W. (1994). *Research design: Qualitative & quantitative approaches.* Thousand Oaks, CA: Sage.

Hirschman, E., & Holbrook, M. (1992). *Postmodern consumer research.* Thousand Oaks, CA: Sage.

Morgan, G., & Smirsich, L. (1980, October). A case for qualitative research. *Academy of Management Review, 5,* 491-500.

Rook, D. (1999). *Brands, consumers, symbols and research: Sidney J. Levy on marketing.* Thousand Oaks, CA: Sage.

Sherry, J. (Ed.). (1995). *Contemporary marketing and consumer behavior: An anthropological sourcebook.* Thousand Oaks, CA: Sage.

Notes

1. Levy's best defense of qualitative methodology was presented to the International Research Seminar at La Londe les Maures in June, 1999. However, you can read most of his work in Rook (1999).

2. Rook (1999, p. 455). See Note 1.

3. Haire, M. (1950). Projective techniques in marketing research. *Journal of Marketing, 145,* 649-656.

4. See Kassarjian, H., & Sheffet, J. E. (1975). Personality and consumer behavior: One more time. In E. Mazze (Ed.), *Combined proceedings* (pp. 324-327). Chicago: American Marketing Association.

5. Hirschman, E. (1986). Humanistic inquiry in marketing research: Philosophy, method and criteria. *Journal of Marketing Research, 23,* 237-249.

6. Denzin, N. (1984). *The research act.* Englewood Cliffs, NJ: Prentice Hall; Lincoln, Y., & Guba, E. (1985). *Naturalistic inquiry.* Beverly Hills, CA: Sage; & Morgan, G. (1983). *Beyond method: Strategies for social research.* Beverly Hills, CA: Sage.

7. See Geertz, C. (1973). Deep play: Notes on a Balinese cock fight. In C. Geertz (Ed.), *The interpretations of cultures: Selected essays.* New York: Basic Books.

8. From Geertz (1973). See Note 7.

9. Hirschman (1986). See Note 5.

10. Nud*ist and Ethnograph are two examples of text analysis software. For details, see Tesch, R. (1990). *Qualitative research: Analysis types and software tools.* New York: Falmer.

2 Five Models of Qualitative Research

Metaphorically, qualitative research is an intricate fabric composed of minute threads, many colors, different textures, and various blends of material . . . . With the complexity of qualitative research, its terms and its traditions, what common ground exists for qualitative research?

—John Creswell (1998)

In the foregoing quote, John Creswell (1998) addresses the question of common grounds by characterizing qualitative research as a group of "distinct methodological traditions of inquiry that explore a social or human problem. The researcher builds a complex, holistic picture, analyzes works, reports detailed views of informants, and conducts the study in a natural setting" (p. 17). Five models of qualitative inquire—biography, case study, phenomenology, grounded theory, and ethnography—provide the foundation for his research traditions. The following brief grounding in the traditions will enable readers to understand specific approaches to qualitative methods as they apply to marketing research. Each model is explained according to the guidelines established by Creswell.

Biographical Life History

In the biographical genre, an author tells a story of self or another person as the central focus for study. Conversations of the author or his or her subject provide data in the form of transcripts for analysis about a single phenomenon. Included in this genre are biographies, autobiographies, life histories, and oral histories.

Each form constructs the history of a life using a variety of data or text: archival documents,[1] writings about self,[2] reports on an individual life and how it reflects cultural themes of society,[3] and personal recollections of events from one or several individuals in narrative or fictionalized accounts.[4] Biographies are either *classical* (conclusions drawn from the researcher's perspective) or *interpretive,* blurring the lines between fact and fiction.

Marketplace researchers use this genre of research to explore consumer-product story meanings. Here, a consumer brings the self into the narrative by acknowledging a specific standpoint. Harley-Davidson uses biographies to detail the lives of motorcycle riders for a better understanding of the relationship between bike and biker. This knowledge manifests itself in retail merchandise offered to consumers and "wannabees" of the biker lifestyle.

Example of Biographical Life History: Self-Narrative as Consumer Research

Objective: Understand the experience of alcohol consumption and recovery for its contribution to consumer behavior research

Method: Narrative

In a detailed account of alcohol consumption, the author uses narrative to:

Recall the social and emotional conditions that led to compulsive consumption

Explain the process of selecting a treatment center

Present the actual treatment experience

Reflect on the effect of being in recovery

Artifacts used for memory elicitation:

Photographs

Letters

Vodka bottle

Getting Straight film documentary

Results: Understanding of the consumption process

The author characterizes her addiction as a possession acquired as part of society's expectations for women as mother, teacher, wife, cleaner, ballast, and captain.

Implications for marketing and advertising strategy: Experiences of a single consumer contribute to an understanding of the acquisition process, which enables marketers to approach the subject with delicacy and understanding. Implications can be drawn for marketing, advertising, and public relations campaigns.

Case Study

Most business school graduates are familiar with the method of learning by case study analysis. In addition to being a learning tool, this model is used as a mode of research. By understanding a single system of consumption, researchers may better understand similar instances and address the problems and issues identified in one case. Bounded systems of time and space, cases rely on multiple sources of information to provide an in-depth portrait of an organization or situation under study. Observations, interviews, collateral materials, corporate documents, and financial statements are collected for analysis. Case studies can be intrinsic (uniqueness oriented) or instrumental (issue oriented) and may also involve multiple cases for a collective perspective.[5] Analysis is made within the case or across cases and usually features a specific problem or incident.

Studying a specific case enables the researcher to become acquainted with an organization and its conduct, procedures, and products and to produce an analytical document for use by the company under study and similar entities. Students who study the case of IBM learn that brand equity is not always a guarantee for continuing success, as evidenced by the entry of Apple's Macintosh into the computer marketplace in 1984.

Case Study Example: Patagonia[6]

Objective: Understand corporate culture and the impact of gender on leadership style

Method: Document analysis, interviews, observation, survey

> Company archives provided documents such as catalogs, newsletters, publicity, and business plans. Interviews were conducted with the company founder, CEO, CFO, managers, employees, and line workers. Participant observation lasted 3 months. Informants clarified meanings. A survey distributed to all employees following the study validated findings.

Results: The CEO's leadership style and gender determine Patagonia's corporate culture. Communication patterns reflect an open dialogue and consensus decision making. Stories about the founder drive the corporate mythology and create bonding among culture members.

> Case problem statements emerged:
>
> > What training will managers receive to handle company growth?
> >
> > Should Patagonia continue its "closed hiring" policy?
> >
> > Will employees benefit from catalog sales relocation?

Decision options were formulated:

Develop management training for employees or recruit from outside the company.

Recruit qualified applicants to fill positions or accept only enculturated members to join the company.

Keep the company in a single location and risk estrangement, or send a portion to Montana and maintain independent cultures.

Implications for marketing and advertising strategy: This case is an example of how a company was forced to rethink its communication and management policies in the face of expanding product lines and employee numbers. It also shows how gender affects the communication and leadership styles of a corporate culture.

Phenomenology

This model is one used often in business and marketing situations because it identifies and explores a particular occurrence in the market. Here, researchers gather multiple views of an experience to enlighten their perspective of the occurrence. By gathering statements from each person who has experienced the phenomenon, researchers locate meanings and cluster them into themes. Based in psychology, phenomenologies focus on the meaning of individual experiences.

People who have experienced the phenomenon describe their stories to the researcher, and those stories are analyzed for common themes, usually with the aid of computer programs such as Nud*ist and Ethnograph. Typical of the types of phenomena of interest to marketers is the experience of driving an electric car: the excitements, disappointments, problems, benefits, social implications, economics, and so forth encountered by a series of new drivers. Advertising agencies use results of such studies to direct promotional activities and campaign concepts.

Example of Phenomenology: Surfing the Web[7]

Objective: Understand the behavior of Web browsers and its implications for advertising strategy

Method: Observation and interviews

This researcher observed the styles and ways of browsing the Web and queried eight users about their Web navigation and homepage visit experiences. Interview transcripts and observational field notes were analyzed for styles and patterns of interactions that come into play in Web surfing.

Results: Web browsing consists of common behavioral patterns best explained through user quotes:

Reject unless interesting: *"I'll only read something if it's interesting."*

Lead me to it: *"I use Web Crawler and type in whatever I am interested in."*

Back-up button: *"I use the back button all the time because it's the easiest way to get back to the previous page."*

Name it and get it: *"The nice thing about the Web is that you can pretty much find anything you want."*

Determine validity of the site: *"I never go to marketers' pages because their information is one-sided, like a commercial."*

Implications for marketing and advertising strategy: Marketers need to craft their sites to meet user needs. For instance, pictures and graphics held the attention of users, suggesting they should play a primary role in site development. Users' lack of concern for commercial Web sites suggests that marketers should develop sites with nonbiased information for consumer use.

Grounded Theory

Sometimes, researchers use modes of questioning to develop theories rather than to study them. This model is called *grounded theory,* a process of discovery by developing theoretical propositions from interview data and field research. Grounded theory is often accomplished visually, establishing categories, refining them, and revisiting the questions repeatedly until specific propositions are developed for future testing.

Marketers may pose a question, such as "How do we define consumption?" by providing respondents with cameras to conceptualize their views on film. Their photographs are analyzed for similarities and differences, and respondents are questioned about their visuals until explanations are paired with concepts for future testing. Researchers use four types of coding—open, axial, selective, and conditional—to arrive at a substantive-level theory with prescribed categories that are used for testing the theory. This is the most challenging and demanding tradition because of the modification and revision necessary to refine the procedure to arrive at testable propositions.

Example of Grounded Theory: Consumers'
Relationships With Advertising and Mass Media[8]

Objective: Understand how perceived meanings are derived from advertisements, from consumers' relationships with mass media

Method: Semistructured interviews with 28 consumers

These researchers looked for key patterns in transcribed data, found links to the literature, and checked comparisons between observed evidence and theoretical concepts.

Results: Theory development

The major obstacle to shared communication is the reader's or consumer's adoption of a cultural frame of reference that is different from what is desired by the producer. In other words, the intended messages are failing to get across to audiences.

Implications for marketing and advertising strategy: Advertising must make itself meaningful within the larger ideological realm constructed by the mass media. By "singing in harmony" with the prevailing chorus of mass media texts, advertising may become much more potent as a conveyor of consumption preferences.

Ethnography

The researcher in this model tells a story based on in-depth understanding of an organization or consumer culture gathered from observations, interviews, and insider testimony. Once immersed in the culture, researchers study the meanings, behavior, language, and interaction of a particular group. Artifacts, similar to those collected by anthropologists in remote societies, are studied to learn about what the culture produces and values. Fieldwork is holistic in nature because it incorporates all modes of activity and of culture into the final product of understanding.

One problem researchers face in ethnography is "going native" from over-immersion in the culture under study. While conducting an ethnography of the corporate culture of sporting-goods manufacturer Patagonia, this researcher was forced to detach from the situation with regular intervals of absence to maintain the role of a participant observer.[9] In an ethnography of two adjacent fast-food chains, researchers were able to learn that McDonald's was losing out to Quick Restaurants in Brussels because they did not understand Belgian consumers' expectations of "fast" food delivery.[10]

Example of an Ethnography: Social Conventions of a Fast Food Restaurant[11]

Objective: Understand the fast food cultural milieu of Taco Bell, in which people work and consume

Method: Observation, consumer interviews, and informant testimony

Four weekday lunch peaks, five weekday dinner peaks, and three off-peak periods were observed and recorded. Customer behaviors were plotted, seven informants were interviewed, a management training meeting was observed, focus group sessions were reviewed, and the CEO was interviewed and videotaped.

Results: Themes emerged from the data:

Visible employee hierarchy exists.

Routinization and scripting ensure product conformity across locations.

Queue formations are culture and site based.

The counter is a boundary region.

Two dimensions of understanding were highlighted by the study:

Culture members across roles know and understand the local conventions.

Customers are most interested in accuracy of the order and ease of interaction with employees.

Implications for marketing and advertising strategy: This ethnographic exploration of Taco Bell is indicative of the food consumption culture. Marketers may use this information to better understand consumer expectations and to accommodate industry participants who interact within the restaurant's physical structure.

Data as Words

The marketing exchange process is a dialogue in which all actions by sellers or buyers are taken to be symbols that express something about the source of the behavior and the actor's intentions.

—Sidney J. Levy

Studies in each of the foregoing examples incorporate a variety of data-gathering techniques into their research. Qualitative research incorporating all five traditions uses a *variety* of techniques. And most of this data is collected as *words,* not numbers. The best way to think about qualitative research is that it's about *the use and analysis of words.* Words are language, and language, studied as communication, is interpretive. The same narrative read by 10 different people yields as many interpretations of its meaning. Qualitative research emphasizes language, and language is studied by social scientists as narrative data. Language is also studied as the embodiment of culture.[12] As language is culture, culture becomes text for study.

This approach works for marketing cultures and organizational cultures as well. The language of a sales transaction, the dialogue between seller and buyer, and the retail environment yield a rich textual culture for study by marketers. A company's logo, dress, ethics, spatial arrangement, stories, and communications compose its corporate culture, also a rich text for studying meaning in a business setting. So we think about qualitative research as *discovery through the collection and analysis of language used by actors within a specific environment.*

Qualitative researchers *use language to discover regularities:*

Grounded theory research is undertaken to identify and categorize elements and to explore their connections.

Phenomenologists are interested in discerning patterns in conceptualization.

Ethnographers study patterns as culture.

Qualitative researchers also *use language to interpret meaning:*

Phenomenology yields meaning comprehension of text or action by identifying commonalities and uniqueness.

Case study and life history are invoked to interpret meaning situated in a company, a situation, or a life.

Language and meaning are best achieved through what is called *naturalistic inquiry,*[13] which is investigation within the context of its usual interaction, as opposed to controlled situations. Much richer data are collected from consumers in the shopping process than during a focus group where they reconstruct their actions. Companies are better observed during daily activity than from reports about them as told during a depth interview off location. Similarly, commercials' impact on viewers is best understood by observing them watch, not testing their recall at a later date. Chapter 15 deals more extensively with the analysis of verbal data gathered during research in each tradition.

Summary

1. We organize qualitative research into five models with different origins and outcomes:[14]

Biography creates a portrait of an individual, using interviews and documents (psychological origins). It yields stories.

Case study provides understanding of one system under study, using documents, archival records, interviews, observations, and artifacts (social science origins). It yields a description, themes, and assertions.

Phenomenology provides insight into a concept or phenomenon through long interviews with up to 10 people (psychological origins). It yields meaning themes.

Grounded theory yields a theory for future testing, using interviews with 20 to 30 people (sociological origins). It yields codes and conditional matrices.

Ethnography creates a portrait of a cultural group, using observations, interviews, and artifacts for an extended period of time in the "field" (anthropological origins). It yields a description, analysis, and interpretation.

2. Words are the data of collection and analysis in qualitative research. Words enable researchers to focus on understanding meaning as made by members of the culture studied.

Stretching Exercises

1. For each of the five research traditions, tell how you would structure a study to answer the question, "What is day trading?"

2. From a recent volume of the *Journal of Consumer Research,* locate an article that uses one of the research traditions discussed here. What questions were posed? What methods were used to answer it?

3. Up for a challenge? Consider online self-assessment of your qualitative vocabulary. You can work a crossword puzzle or test your knowledge at these Web sites: www.utmem.edu/%7Ecreissell/hotpot/qualcross or www.utmem.edu/%Ecreissell/hotpot/qualresterm. Good luck!

Recommended Readings About Models of Qualitative Inquiry

Creswell, J. (1998). *Qualitative inquiry and research design.* Thousand Oaks, CA: Sage.

Denzin, N. (1989). *Interpretive biography.* Newbury Park, CA: Sage.

Fetterman, D. M. (1989). *Ethnography step by step.* Newbury Park, CA: Sage.

Moustakas, C. (1994). *Phenomenological research methods.* Thousand Oaks, CA: Sage.

Stake, R. E. (1995). *The art of case study research.* Thousand Oaks, CA: Sage.

Strauss, A. & Corbin, J. (1990). *Basics of qualitative research: Grounded theory procedures and techniques.* Newbury Park, CA: Sage.

Notes

1. Creswell, J. (1998). *Qualitative inquiry and research design: Choosing among five traditions* (p. 15). Newbury Park, CA: Sage.

2. Denzin, N. (1989). *Interpretive biography.* Thousand Oaks, CA: Sage.

3. Angrosino, M. V. (1989). *Documents of interaction: Biography, autobiography and life history in social science perspective.* Gainsville: University of Florida Press.

4. Cole, A. (1994). *Doing life history research in theory and practice.* Paper presented to the American Educational Research Association, New Orleans, LA.

5. Smith, L. M. (1994). Biographical method. In N. K. Denzin & Y. K. Lincoln (Eds.), *Handbook of qualitative research* (pp. 286-305). Thousand Oaks, CA: Sage.

6. Stake, R. E. (1995). *The art of case study.* Thousand Oaks, CA: Sage.

7. Based on field notes collected for a doctoral dissertation: Sayre, S. (1986). *Leader communication and organizational culture: A field study.* Doctoral dissertation, University of San Diego, CA.

8. From Raman, N. (1997). A qualitative investigation of web-browsing behavior. *Advances in Consumer Research, 24,* 511-516.

9. From Hirschman, E., & Thompson, C. (1997). Why media matter: Toward a richer understanding of consumers' relationships with advertising and mass media. *Journal of Advertising, 26*(1), 43-60.

10. From Sayre, S. (1986).See Note 7.

11. This study was conducted by graduate students enrolled in Emerson College's International Advertising Masters Program in Brussels, Belgium, 1998.

12. From Schau, H., & Gilly, M. (1997). Social conventions of a fast food restaurant: An ethnomethodological analysis. *Advances in Consumer Research, 24,* 315-321.

13. For an extensive discussion of working with words, see Tesch, R. (1990). *Qualitative research: Analysis types and software tools.* New York: Falmer.

14. Lincoln, Y., & Guba, E. (1985). *Naturalistic inquiry.* Beverly Hills, CA: Sage.

3 Applications of Qualitative Methods for Marketing

To deal with the marketplace requires an understanding of the people in it, what buyers and sellers do, and why they do it.
—Sidney J. Levy, 1964

Marketing research for the 21st century is taking on many of the characteristics of social and human sciences for a variety of reasons. In this service age, the selling of intangibles—credit, consulting, memberships, travel—requires new insights on markets, consumer groups, publics, or tourists and their changing motivations. No longer Pavlovian in response to promises of a good deal, consumers require sophisticated and credible communications to affect their behavior. There are several reasons for this phenomenon.

Our lives operate at the speed of light. Technology, especially the Internet, is altering the way people communicate, the reasons we buy, and how we are entertained. Innovation begets innovation, pushing competitors to be ever first with a new gismo. Economic fluctuations and a pulsating NASDAC demand immediate action—no one holds your place in line if you leave to take a break.

Our global village repels standardization, requiring instead cultural sensitivity and ethnic diversity. People across national boundaries buy products for different reasons, use them for different purposes, and possess them with varying degrees of loyalty. Godiva Chocolates packages its product differently for sale in Belgium than it does for export: American diet-conscious consumers buy chocolate for gifts or as a reward for good behavior, whereas Europeans incorporate chocolate into their everyday diets. How does Godiva know this? They asked chocolate eaters to talk about chocolate and the role it plays in their lives. Research enabled them to understand the meaning of chocolate in each culture in which they have distribution and to communicate in a meaningful way to their consumers.

This chapter discusses the communication process, consumer research, account planning, and the roles they play in the marketplace.

The Exchange Narrative

Marketing has shifted from macro to micro, from groups to individuals, from global to local. In response, marketing study now focuses on all participants in the sales transaction, including the people who sell and the people who buy products and use services. We pay particular attention to what people need and why people buy, how they search for it and what they do with it, and whether or not they will buy it again. The motives and actions of buyers are primary considerations for all marketers today.

Sid Levy says *marketing is what people do when they want to provide something to, or get something from, someone else.*[1] In other words, what is said between seller and buyer becomes paramount in the marketing transaction. Verbal exchanges taking place between sellers (retailers, doctors, theaters, artists, brokers, banks, media) and buyers (householders, purchasing agents, audiences, patients, tourists, viewers) must complete a successful message transfer to be useful or profitable. So how can that happen?

Communication that anticipates an exchange of meanings always includes feedback in the form of behavioral response. A message sender encodes, the message is delivered in person or through a mass medium, and a receiver decodes. The communication cycle is completed only when an action is taken by the receiver to indicate message comprehension and perhaps compliance. Advertising commercials that entertain without generating brand recall or intention to purchase do not complete the feedback loop.

Meaning is developed from a variety of sources: cultural values, group learning, personal experience, physical appearance, and mass media. Meanings generated by message senders and receivers are the sum total of their respective internal and external influences. Products and logos become symbols in the minds of consumers, and the dialogue between buyer and seller is an exchange of those symbols.

Much of the sales dialogue takes place through mediated communication, especially television. Mass communication research—studying audiences and viewers—provides relevant models for marketing and consumer research. The basis for complex communication models is a Haiku-like question posed by an early communications scholar:[2]

Who
Says what
To whom
In which medium
With what effect?

What this question means for marketing is that *all marketing transactions are communications* that are interpreted (or not) by consumers. Successful communication begins by understanding consumer cultures and the meanings consumers attach to products. Understanding is accomplished by researching consumers and their interactions with products and services within their natural environments.

The Exchange Culture

Culture is environment constructed of signs and symbols made and understood by a group of people. Culture is one way to explain how and why buyers, clients, and publics behave the way they do in the marketing transaction. To illustrate, I'll share a recent experience I had buying produce in a Brussels supermarket. Not understanding why a grocery clerk wouldn't accept my unmarked apple purchase (she spoke rapid French), I purposefully observed a female shopper's actions to understand the problem. Selecting an orange for purchase, she placed it on a scale, pressed a button with a graphic of an orange on it, retrieved a sticker containing the orange's price and weight, and affixed the sticker to the orange before taking it to the checker. I had to learn from other shoppers in order to buy a piece of fruit.

Learning the culture of a supermarket environment expanded my knowledge of shopping in another country. The experience enabled me to take a fresh look at the purchase process. What customs do Americans have that would equally baffle a Belgian shopper, I wondered. How could such nuances be simplified for newcomers? Such questions arose from personal research, similar to the kind now used by marketing researchers to understand the culture-specific purchase process.

Marketers who understand culture can appreciate the social processes of exchange. Another grocery store experience took me to a market in the Marina district of San Francisco. With limited parking and lots of competition, the Safeway studied its customers for innovative ways to keep them coming back. During the evening I shopped, a string quartet played classical music near the wine section, and paté samples were being served in an adjacent aisle. A Napa Valley winery offered tastings of Merlot and Sauvignon Blanc. During a focus group, the Safeway had learned that young professionals would stop on their way home from work to pick up the evening meal and would socialize with neighbors during this stop. To enhance the shopping experience, Safeway provided Thursday evening music and tastings. The results were spectacular. Eventually, they were providing a pianist for senior shoppers on Tuesday afternoons and childcare for mothers on Monday mornings.

Noticing the rise in male grocery shoppers, the Leo Burnett Advertising Agency sent a team of anthropologists to observe men shopping. They talked to them about how they made product decisions and inquired about the influencers of their purchases. The client, Proctor and Gamble, used this information to make profound changes in the way they marketed to male shoppers. For instance, they increased product licensing because men shop more for bargains than brands. And they attached coupon dispensers to shelves because men rarely clip coupons.

These three supermarket examples are evidence that shopping cultures can only be understood within the context of their social and sales environments. Researchers collected narrative, organized the transcribed words into patterns of meaning, and, from them, learned about their customers' needs and motivations. Results of consumption ethnographies enabled these retailers to take specific steps to improve the way they marketed groceries.

Exchange in a Postmodern Culture

If we agree that culture is made up of signs, we are on our way to understanding that consumption is mainly related to a manipulation of those signs.[3] In a consumption culture, goods only exist within a specific symbolic system. A postmodern political economy sees rapid circulation of both consumers and goods until they begin to blur in the minds of marketers. By studying consumption practices, we learn their connections to class and occupation to help us decode the symbolic relationships involved in the commodity system. Postmodern research builds on the familiar lifestyle approach. Lifestyles are defined as shared values, tastes, opinions, interests, and ways of behavior as they are expressed through consumption practices. Safeway capitalized on lifestyle research to present new shopping experiences for each consumer lifestyle they served.

The focus of postmodern consumer research is based on the different ways in which people use goods to create social bonds or distinctions. We need to understand the emotional pleasures of consumption to make buyers happy with our products. Postmodern research reveals new shopping modes, such as *flanerie*, browsing, sampling, and nonrational, spontaneous purchases, which indicate that individuals are looking for a sense of identity through their consumption practices. In the "you are what you buy" syndrome, consumption becomes a means of expressing identity for consumers and the world around them. We construct ourselves through our purchases, say postmodernists.[4] In the postmodern condition, consumption becomes a way for people to construct selves by purchasing products and rebuilding signs of identity. In the film *American Psycho* (April, 2000), 1980s stock brokers wear Armani suits, drive Mercedes, and compete for the most elegant business card. The acquisition of designer logos and symbols of status depicted in this satire illustrates the postmodern philosophy of symbolic consumption for the construction of identity.

The Human Component of Consumption

We are just statistics, born to consume resources.
—Horace, 68 BC

Psychologists and researchers have found out that people are consuming products for just the reasons suggested by postmodernists—identity building and maintenance. To understand the identity-building process, marketers must understand the motives and needs of consumption stars, best known as human beings: human science research to the rescue. We can use the models presented in Chapter 2 to answer our research questions.

What do the models of humanistic research have in common? Features that distinguish them from traditional, natural science, quantitative research theory and methodologies. Humanistic investigations of all types have commonalities that require the researcher to do the following things:[5]

1. Focus on the wholeness of consumer experiences

2. Search for meanings and the essence of consumer experiences

3. Obtain descriptions of experience through first-person accounts in conversations and interviews

4. Regard the data of experience as crucial for understanding consumer behavior

5. View experience and behavior as the inseparable relationship between consumer and product

Two of the most important ingredients for successful inquiry are a researcher's intuition and imagination. Keeping an open mind, setting aside biases and assumptions, and maintaining curiosity are essential components for gaining understanding of a consumer within his or her shopping and using environment.

Consumer Aliases

Throughout this text, the word *consumer* is used to represent all sorts of people who engage in a consumption process. This list is just the beginning:

Media users consume television drama and magazine features.

Entertainment *audiences* consume film adventure or theater.

Sports and music *fans* consume field conflict and concerts.

Tourists consume souvenirs and trips.

Investors consume stock options.

Diners consume food.

Gamblers consume chances to win.

Worshipers consume religion.

Shoppers consume brands.

We are all consumers in one fashion or another. We all participate in some commodity acquisition process on a daily basis.

The nature and amount of consumption provides us clues to how consumers construct their identity. Wrestling fans who drive Chevy trucks see themselves differently than opera enthusiasts who arrive at the concert in Jaguars. Only by immersion in both consumer cultures can we understand the differences between what guides the behavior of a wrestling fan and an opera buff. If we want to sell one consumer beer and another wine, we need to know more about the folks who consume them than stereotypical images provide. We need intimate insight into what makes them tick. We need to know *why they do what they do.*

Think of humanistic research as answering the *why* question. Then, decide how you will investigate the answer. A phenomenology of wrestling fans or the life history of an opera buff may provide answers. The longer researchers spend observing, interviewing, and participating, the better they understand the why of consumption.

Consumers as Audience

Everything in life is a paid-for experience.
    —Jeremy Rifkin, 2000

One group of consumers of increasing interest to marketers is entertainment audiences. The significance of understanding what fills concert halls, stadiums, and theaters is paramount to producing successful productions. Two communication theories are useful for understanding entertainment audiences: Uses and gratifications theory and reception theory. With uses and gratifications theory, audience members' motivation for attending is a vantage point used to study entertainment appeal. For years, researchers have looked at the influence of gratification seeking on the quality and consequences of people's engagement with media content by observing audience activity before, during, and after exposure to the media.

More recent research focuses on the social and psychological origins of gratification. The newest innovation in audience research is understanding how audiences get pleasure and meaning from entertainment. Two assumptions about audiences drive the research: an audience is always active, and content is always open to interpretation.[6] Although the second assumption seems to resist challenge, media researchers question the "activeness" of audiences, claiming that many audiences are passive to mediated entertainment. Most communication literature agrees that, however active or passive, audiences are actively making meaning of their entertainment. Reception theory is invoked to validate a notion that audiences make sense of what they see by who they are and where they have been, not necessarily as a result of any intention by the producer.

Polling and survey data may tell us that certain groups attend corresponding entertainment venues in various amounts. Qualitative data will help us understand why people attend those venues and under what circumstances the event is enjoyable.[7]

Studying popular culture or entertainment audiences as "interpretive communities" enables us to understand the interplay between people's dimension as "audience" and the meanings, rituals, practices, struggles, and structural roles and realities that make up the rest of their lives.[8] We know how many attend, and we know what regions of the world prefer what type of entertainment. But it's what we don't know that is strategically important for marketing purposes. Entertainment promoters are most interested in how audiences make choices and how they put entertainment into their lives. Audience ethnographies can give them that information.

A growing number of marketing professionals have acknowledged the humanistic approach to research and become consumer and audience advocates during the planning and creative processes. One such advocacy role is executed by *account planners,* a position imported from England by American advertising agencies.

Professional Snoops

Above all, the work of an advertising agency is warmly and immediately human. It deals with human needs, wants, dreams and hopes.

—Leo Burnett, 1961

Insight about consumption and consumers is necessary for almost every aspect of marketing communication. For advertisers, it's making a connection between a product and a corresponding need. When Burnett connected the ethos of cowboy to Marlboro cigarettes, he hit on our fantasy of wild, open spaces—the American expression of freedom. To be a really good consumer detective, we must find out about consumers' dreams and fantasies and give them back as product symbols.

The most important task of an account planner is to bring the philosophy of consumer insight to life.[9] Research is interpreted and advocated by the account planner who actively works to understand the consumer. The Chiat/Day Advertising Agency began using account planners in the early 1980s, and today, the majority of advertising agencies have a person in the account planning function as part of their management teams.

Acting as a liaison between client and creative team, account planners make certain the consumer's point of view is incorporated into the decision-making process. By bringing the consumer to the forefront of the planning process, they help set campaign and often media objectives. Jay Chiat attributes the agency's success to understanding, empathizing with, and speaking the same language as the consumer—integrating the "why" into creative strategy and execution.

Qualitative research has several applications for advertising agencies, among them are these three:[10]

1. Obtaining background information about a problem or target group: Of particular interest to ad agencies today are older groups such as "active seniors."

2. Identifying, developing, and testing creative concepts with consumers: Here, active seniors can participate in creating concepts as well as viewing and critiquing a proposed campaign.

3. Identifying behavioral patterns, beliefs, opinions, and attitudes about brand perceptions: Asking active seniors to talk about their experiences with brands like Cadillac and Timex shed light on their usage and loyalty.

In addition to account planners, professionals from other fields are now being hired by advertising agencies and research companies to investigate consumers' mind-sets and behaviors. For instance, symbolic anthropologists focus on more than just what respondents say—they reveal what their statements and actions mean symbolically. A young dot.com executive may like to drive a Porsche, not just for its design and performance but because it means he is part of the Silicon Valley in-crowd.

Sid Levy was one of the first marketing scholars to use anthropology's symbolic analysis technique to interpret what's going on when Americans eat and drink.[11] His ideas about color and beverage consumption revealed trends toward light alcohol because of a good-bad dichotomy of meanings associated with liquids. For instance, beer is the milk of alcoholic beverages and champagne the ad-

Table 3.1 Alcoholic Beverages and Consumer Meaning

Preparation	Color	Meanings	Segment
Complexity	Dark	Discriminating	Exclusive
Distillation		Sophisticated	
Fermenting		Intoxicating	Mature
Brewing		Relaxing	
Steeping	Deep hues	Addicting	
Carbonation	Colorful	Social	Adult
Squeezing		Autonomous	
		Conventional	
	Light		Young
Heating		Nutritious	
Natural		Dependent	
Simplicity	Colorless	Virtuous	
		Immature	Universal

SOURCE: Adapted from S. Levy (as cited in Rook, 1999).

olescent ginger ale of wines. Red wines are linked to religious symbolism with a kinship to blood, and brandy and liqueurs are the acme of the genre. Vodka is perceived to be more dignified than bourbon, like tea is more genteel than coffee. Levy's structures result from consumer perceptions and preferences that reflect changing values and ways advertising uses a symbolic vocabulary of beverage characteristics, as shown in Table 3.1.[12]

Social psychologists design and interpret marketing research. In a project by Chilton Research Services,[13] a psychologist gave people video cameras to tape themselves in everyday pursuits, such as shopping, eating, driving, and working. In this do-it-yourself version of candid camera, consumers revealed a great deal about their consumption habits. Telling comments were captured: One woman, while talking about the contents of her refrigerator, said, with a can of Reddi Whip: "This is whipped cream. I only like the real stuff. I don't like the Cool Whips." The camera then reveals a tub of Cool Whip on the shelf below to the embarrassment of the woman, who asks, "How did that get in here?"

Bugle Boy Industries and DDB Needham, the apparel marketer's ad agency, tracked young men aged 16 to 19 using a similar video technique called "Right There Research." Although much of what they learned confirmed what they already knew, the research revealed the importance of comfort and price to purchasers. One consumer quote was even used in an ad: "Your closet is where old clothes go to die." The project helped the agency select appropriate models for the ad campaign.

A special issue of *AdWeek* devoted to consumer research explains the predominance of agencies using consumer psychologists.[14] One public relations project completed for Lever Brothers, called "Caress Body Barometer," was used to examine how women view their bodies. What the psychologist learned was contrary to creative executions produced by Lever's ad agency. Ultimately, results of the qualitative study were used to develop a new campaign concept.

Another psychologist studied "sensation transference,"[15] a process by which consumers transfer feelings and sensations received from advertising and packaging to the product itself. Video showing consumers making liquor choices based on packaging rather than brand revealed the importance of product image for purchasing. Realistic research is effective for use with creative teams. Rather than view charts of numbers, writers and art directors see the faces of consumers. Creative teams, who often rebuff research as confining or limiting, better understand a research emphasis and its role for creativity with expressive visual evidence.

Summary

1. The marketplace is an arena of communication between buyers and sellers that results in a change in attitude or behavior.

2. In a postmodern consumer culture, objects are embraced for their meaning, are important for personal identity, and have symbolic significance. The shopping process is enjoyable and exciting.

3. Consumers come in a variety of shapes and designations, and studying them is important for marketing researchers.

4. The role of qualitative research has penetrated advertising and marketing fields, as evidenced by the presence of account planners and humanistic researchers from anthropology and psychology on management teams.

Stretching Exercises

1. Attend a performance or concert and observe the audience (a) prior to the event, (b) during the event, and (c) after the event. What types of activities and interactions take place? How might you use this information to direct a study for further investigation?

2. Use the reception and uses and gratifications theories to explain consumer motivations for purchasing (a) a book, (b) a film ticket, and (c) a fitness club membership.

Recommended Readings About Consumer Culture and Audience Research

Featherstone, M. (1991). *Consumer culture and postmodernism.* London: Sage.

Fortini-Campbell, L. (1992). *Hitting the sweet spot: How consumer insights can inspire better marketing and advertising.* Chicago: The Copy Workshop.

Hay, J., Grossberg, L., & Wartgella, E. (Eds.). (1996). *The audience and its landscape.* Boulder, CO: Westview.

Hirschman, E., & Holbrook, M. (1992). *Postmodern consumer research.* Newbury Park, CA: Sage.

Jones, J. (1998). *How advertising works: The role of research.* Thousand Oaks, CA: Sage.

Underhill, P. (1999). *Why we buy: The science of shopping.* New York: Simon & Schuster.

Notes

1. Levy, S. (1969). Broadening the concept of marketing. *Journal of Marketing, 33,* 10-15.

2. Written by Lasswell, H. (1964). The structure and function of communication in society. In L. Brown (Ed.), *The communication of ideas* (p. 37). New York: Cooper Square Publishers.

3. For a discussion of postmodern consumption, see Beaudrillard, J. (1985). The ecstasy of communication. In H. Foster (Ed.), *Postmodern culture.* London: Pluto.

4. For a discussion of postmodern consumption, see Featherstone, M. (1990, February). Perspectives on consumer culture. *Sociology, 24,* 5-22.

5. Extracted from a list in Moustakas, C. (1994). *Phenomenological research methods.* Thousand Oaks, CA: Sage.

6. See Evans, W. (1990). The interpretive turn in media research. *Critical Studies in Mass Communication, 7*(2), 145-168.

7. For an in-depth discussion of humanistic and social science approaches to audience research, see Vorderer, P., & Groeben, N. (1992). Audience research: What the humanistic and the social science approaches could learn from each other. *Poetics, 21,* 361-376.

8. See Press, A. (1996). Toward a qualitative methodology of audience study: Using ethnography to study the popular culture audience. In J. Hay, L. Grossberg, & E. Wartella (Eds.), *The audience and its landscape.* Boulder CO: Westview.

9. See Fortini-Campbell, L. (1992). *Hitting the sweet spot: How consumer insights can inspire better marketing and advertising.* Chicago: The Copy Workshop.

10. From Jones, J. (1998). *How advertising works: The role of research.* Thousand Oaks, CA: Sage.

11. Levy, S. (1981). Interpreting consumer mythology: A structural approach to consumer behavior. *Journal of Marketing, 45*(3), 49-61.

12. Adapted from Levy as found in Rook (1999), Table 39.2, p. 395.

13. Reported by Stuart Elliott in his regular Advertising Column of the *New York Times,* Monday, August 23, 1993, p. B8.

14. John Motavalli wrote this piece for an *AdWeek* Special Report, Probing Consumers' Minds, December 7, 1987.

15. Motavalli (1987). See Note 14.

■ Part II

GETTING READY
TO RESEARCH

This section presents the preliminary steps researchers take prior to engaging in a study. In Chapter 4, issues of subject selection and subject rights, study location, gaining access to that location, understanding research protocol, and ensuring your study's integrity are addressed. Institutional review boards are introduced, and five modes of triangulation are reviewed so you might incorporate them into your study in the planning process.

Chapter 5 explains the process of topic selection, setting objectives, and grounding research in past studies and relevant theories. Data collection techniques most used for qualitative research are reviewed. We suggest that researchers write proposals as arguments to persuade a specific reader to approve or fund their research. A sample proposal outline is included.

When you complete this section, you should be ready to select a research model and begin your study.

4 Issues and Concerns

To capture the marketplace and consumers in their natural settings, most qualitative research is conducted in the "field." Field studies have a unique set of problems and opportunities, including field ethics and researcher access to the field. This chapter presents some issues relevant for study preparation, including who to study and how to protect those subjects, determining a field site and how to gain access, research ethics, and the criteria for controlling the quality of your study. These prestudy tasks and considerations ensure that your research experience will be a successful one. Before you begin designing your study, give careful thought to these six concerns.

First Concern: Selecting Participants

The first considerations are the participants we involve in our study. With qualitative research, finding participants is not as easy as selecting every *n*th number of folks listed in the phone book or grabbing a passerby. Locating appropriate participants who are willing to be part of your study may be a time-consuming task. After identifying the target audience (media users, coffee drinkers, tourists), you may begin networking to locate willing subjects. Should that avenue be a dead end, a few alternatives remain. Remember *not* to use your family or friends as subjects.

Students often recruit subjects by putting notices on campus billboards or announcements in the college newspaper. Internet chat rooms are also good places to locate participants. Professionals often use research companies to screen and obtain participants. In any case, several questions remain. How many people should you interview? How long should you observe them? Will you conduct long interviews with a few folks or short interviews with many people?

Selecting participants differs from subject sampling because qualitative study intentions differ from those of quantitative research. We don't look for numbers of bodies, we look for people willing to share their thoughts to help us illuminate, interpret, and understand a phenomenon better. And although we don't conduct scientific experiments, we must consider how our interface with subjects will affect their emotional and psychological well-being. Educational institutions and governmental organizations help safeguard the rights of human subjects by establishing review boards to make certain that research participants are aware of what is expected of them and are participating willingly. We need to understand the role of such boards in our research process.

Second Concern: Protecting Participants[1]

Public and private institutions that conduct human or animal research have institutional review boards (IRBs) to articulate and enforce the institution's standards of subjects' protection. IRBs protect subjects against endangerment from a study's procedures or outcomes and support researchers if problems with human or animal subjects arise. Human and animal subject protections are in place to ensure that study participants know the risks involved in research and to reduce risk. IRB members review proposals for evidence of fair treatment of participants, safe handling of data and reports, and fairness of subject protections.

When reviewing qualitative proposals, IRBs addresses four issues:

1. *Informed consent* guarantees that participants (a) participate voluntarily, (b) understand what the study demands, (c) know the risks and benefits, and (d) have the legal capacity to give consent. Participants must also be told they can leave the study at any time without negative consequence. Furthermore, researchers must present these guarantees in the language of the participants. When studies are conducted in a free-access setting, such as a shopping mall, it's usually not necessary to tell shoppers that you're studying their behavior because of the anonymity and public interaction involved. Covert observation, although usually harmless, may afford researchers power or superiority that is detrimental to study outcomes.

2. *Instruments* such as surveys, interview questions, and visuals should be submitted to the IRB for its review of language and content.

3. *Vulnerable populations,* according to FDA guidelines, include the following: "patients with incurable diseases, persons in nursing homes, unemployed or impoverished persons, patients in emergency rooms, ethnic minority groups, homeless persons, nomads, refugees, children and those incapable of giving consent."[2] *Human Research Report,* published monthly, declares that students

and staff also qualify as vulnerable subjects. The IRB usually wants to know why a vulnerable population is needed for a particular project.

4. Subject anonymity must be guaranteed, especially when audiotapes and videotapes or transcripts are used for data analysis. Researchers must ensure that subjects' actual identities will remain unknown to everyone else and that any identifying elements will be removed from reports resulting from the project. The confidentiality of everything that is collected from or about the participants also needs to be ensured.

The role of review boards for qualitative research is still being debated among academics. Although the value of IRB protections in qualitative research is questioned by some scholars, the review process protects both the subjects and the field researcher, who may depend on participants for safety and shelter. Some scholars maintain that discourse collected online is not confidential:

> Public discourse on computer mediated communication is viewed as just that: public. Analysis of such content, where individuals', institutions' and lists' identities are shielded, is not subject to 'Human Subject' restraints. Such study is more akin to the study of tombstone epitaphs, graffiti, or letters to the editor. Personal? Yes. Private? No.[3]

Our advice is that you contact your institution's IRB *prior* to conducting research to consult their guidelines for qualitative class projects and thesis studies.

Third Concern: Field Locations

Where to conduct your study is another important consideration. A few rules are offered here as "good ideas" but certainly are not absolute restrictions.

Don't do your study where you work, go to school, or play. Obvious facilitation ease makes these choices tempting, but problems lurk at every turn in locations where your personal or professional life comes into contact with your research obligations. People have a hard time relating to you in a new role and may treat the research lightly or give you information they think you want to hear. So-called backyard research can also create ethical and political dilemmas that are easily avoided by steering clear of friends and family as study participants.

When possible, conduct your research in the natural setting where the action occurs. Taking respondents to other locations can change the nature of their interaction with the phenomenon. By removing them, you often remove some of the drama provided by the environment. When a study is conducted in the field, the results are more authentic. However, some techniques require special situations. Focus groups, for instance, are often conducted in specially designed facilities equipped with cameras, microphones, and two-way mirrors. No one conducts an entire study as a focus group, but groups may be useful for generating concepts, posttesting creative strategies, and extracting information from hard-to-reach populations in a comfortable setting.

Places where you do fieldwork can be convenient. Mall interventions can take place in your town, certainly. And although you don't always have to go on the road for research, it's a good idea to put some physical and emotional distance between yourself and the site you select.

Fourth Concern: Gaining Access

Gaining access to a research site (or *field entry*) involves getting permission to go where you want, observe what you want, obtain documents you need, and talk with whomever you wish. Access can be unqualified or restricted and is site specific. In *action research,* a client engages the researcher to study organizational procedures or use of a new product. The researcher will diagnose problems, engage in collaborative analysis of data, and develop problem-solving activities for the organization.

When an agency, company, or organization is involved, we suggest you locate the person who acts as the location gatekeeper to obtain consent. Begin with the guy at the top and work down; if you start at the bottom, you end up climbing the ladder to the top, anyhow. An insider helps you identify the proper gatekeeper and sometimes even assists with access negotiations. We suggest ascertaining the possibility of access *prior* to preparing the proposal to avoid having to abort the study when you've completed much of the groundwork for conducting it.

Qualitative methods, such as participant observation and interviewing, are preferred for understanding the often hidden and at-risk populations, such as AIDS victims, prostitutes, unwed mothers, and criminals. However, gaining access to settings where at-risk populations live or work is often difficult, even impossible. Gaining access in situations where research is potentially threatening involves the "politics of distrust."[4] Trust is facilitated because those within a relationship have information about each other arising from self-disclosure and observations of past actions. Any breach of trust in these situations has a high emotional cost to everyone involved. Employing the assistance of an informant or member of the at-risk population may be necessary to gain access.

While researching disaster victims, this researcher was assisted by a friend's grandmother who had access to portions of the population who were evacuated prior to a firestorm. Acting as a *sponsor,* her phone calls and introductions facilitated my access to survivors already mistrusting media and marketers who constantly invaded their grief.

Information sharing is a result of trust, a bond formed between interviewer and respondent. By establishing access through a gatekeeper, a community of at-risk subjects can begin to develop trust in the outsider-researcher. Once in a while, when access is denied, researchers choose another path—covert entry. This situation compromises any trust, for once deception has been uncovered, the research must cease.

Overt research allows the researcher to study with permission. Research is *covert* when participants or consumers are not aware that they are being studied. Although covert study provides a researcher with an insider's view, ethical questions arise about data collection and its efficacy. Covert studies ignore a principle of informed consent and may involve deception and invasion of subject privacy. A fine line exists between the need to obtain information and compromising the welfare of subjects. Consensual access is always preferred; when this is not possible, researchers should define those studied as political adversaries or allies and adopt a conflict-based or collaborative fieldwork style accordingly.

The drawbacks of using covert research, aside from the ethical issue, include the inability to ask probing questions for fear of compromising the researcher's false identity. And the researcher risks being discovered, discrediting all previously established trust. For example, researchers studying Amway's layered marketing techniques entered a local group as new members, attending meetings, selling merchandise, and recruiting new sales people. At the end of their data collection period, researchers disclosed their identities to Amway who, in anger over breech of privacy, initiated legal action against the researchers. To avoid prosecution, researchers handed over transcripts and other materials collected during the field study and were unable to report their findings officially for fear of recrimination.

Issues of motive, method, and morality are intertwined in field studies. Researchers inevitably face contradictions while doing naturalistic research. When developing relationships is not easily accomplished, a researcher may consider deception in the name of understanding and truth. Regardless of pressure, marketplace research must respect the rights of individuals over client profits if a choice between them must be made.

Fifth Concern: Research Do's and Don'ts

Most often, our subjects are consumers of products or media who willingly participate in our studies. Occasionally, our interests or clients involve unique populations or circumstances. Assuming the responsibilities involved with such

situations requires skills beyond what most students and marketing professionals possess. Sensitive research topics and reluctant subjects present special challenges for researchers. Rarely trained as psychologists, marketplace researchers
may confront sensitive issues, such as alcoholism, incontinence, contraception,
and the like. *Socially sensitive research* has been defined as "studies in which
there are potential consequences or implications, either directly for the participants or for the group represented by the research."[5] Such a definition has limitations because it can be extended to most types of field research not intended to
deal with sensitive issues.

An alternative to thinking about sensitive research as adverse to participants
is to assume a view that certain topics involve a level of threat or risk to those
studied that may cause problems for collecting, holding, or disseminating the research data.[6] In other words, the research may pose a threat to researchers as well
as respondents. Studies may impose demands on a subject or a researcher that
yield unintentional consequences. One instance where this might happen is
when research poses an *intrusive threat* by dealing with private, stressful, or sacred matters; survivors of natural disaster consider invasion into their grief as intrusive. Another instance of invasion occurs while studying *deviance,* which
may yield incriminating results. Consumer behavior research on alcoholism,
drug addiction, and theft are examples of deviant studies.

In a national study of campus drinking, students—concerned with recriminations from school officials—were reluctant to divulge information to anyone but
peers. Researchers finally developed a video-elicitation technique to ensure privacy (see Chapter 13) and elicit meaningful responses. For many years, AIDS
victims kept secrets from those trying to study the spread of the disease, in fear
of recriminations. Those who engage in deviant behavior make up *hidden populations* of varying sizes. Although often significant in number, these populations
are characterized as hidden because of their anonymity and reluctance to self-
identify.

For marketplace researchers, situations must be carefully assessed prior to
fieldwork to avoid intrusive threats. Intrusion can be construed differently depending on culture, gender, and situation. Women are considered more easily
approached on personal topics, whereas their male counterparts are unwilling to
disclose personal information. Questions directed at finance or sexual behavior
are cited by subjects of both sexes as particularly intrusive;[7] people often worry
that they might be "found out."

Similarly, the questioners themselves may feel compromised. Conducting
marketplace research of people in power or another social class is often difficult.
Interviewing poses a problem for researchers reluctant to invade the privacy of
so-called elite people, such as doctors or politicians who are already sensitive to
the way they're portrayed to the public. Physical danger may also threaten

researchers whose studies require them to test equipment, vehicles, or diets or who enter war zones to collect data.

Final Concern: Ensuring Quality[8]

One of the problems of validating qualitative research is that we do not use tested instruments or replicate studies, which is standard procedure in quantitative research. Concepts of validity and reliability are standard checking criteria for quantitative methods—they evaluate a study's ability to consistently measure what it purports to measure. However, when a study contains no measures and cannot be duplicated, validation consists of other criteria to determine the authenticity, correctness, or credibility of description and interpretation.

Threats to validity in qualitative research are found in description, interpretation, and theories. Description is threatened by accuracy, interpretation by researcher bias, and theory by omission of discrepant data. We give specific emphasis to explaining researcher bias for the following two reasons:

1. Researchers often have preconceptions that alter research. Or, they bias the selection of material included in the study. It is up to you as a researcher to explain how you will deal with these threats to validity. Integrity is the key to validity in qualitative research.

2. The influence of the researcher on the setting or study subjects is another threat to validity. Recognizing that researcher influence cannot be eliminated, study proposers must understand those influences and use them productively. Reactivity is almost a given during interviews, but you can minimize your effect by avoiding leading questions and understanding how subjects react to you personally.

Rather than using reliability and validity constructs based on a positivist tradition, humanistic research evaluation is based on other criteria. Four criteria appropriate for evaluating humanistic inquiry are presented here with their positivist inquiry equivalencies:[9]

Credibility—accurately representing multiple realities of the people under investigation. This involves the successful exchange of mutual trust between researcher and subject and presumes an honesty of discourse. This is equivalent to internal validity in positivist research.

Transferability—"the ability of one manifestation of a phenomenon to a second manifestation of the phenomenon, recognizing that no two social contexts are ever identical."[10] This is equivalent to external validity in positivist research.

Dependability—the use of multiple human investigators enhances the dependability of humanistic inquiry. Because all humans are different, no two construals of the same phenomenon are expected to be identical. This is equivalent to reliability in positivist studies.

Confirmability—information is supportable from the data, as gathered by the inquirer, to "represent a logical set of conclusions, and to be non-prejudiced and non-judgmental renderings of observed reality."[11] The researcher is expected to be involved with the topic and personally immersed in interpreting its meaning. This is equivalent to a notion of neutrality and objectivity in positivist research, where the researcher is presumed to be emotionally neutral.

In the absence of positivist tactics, such as control groups, statistical control of variables, randomized sampling, hypothesis testing, and statistical significance, qualitative studies rely on *triangulation* to authenticate data gathering and analysis tactics. Triangulation is collecting information from a diverse range of individuals and settings and using a variety of methods.[12] The most effective way to combat threats to validity is to triangulate using one or more of the five types explained here:

1. *Data triangulation*—using a variety of data sources in a study

   Example: Multiple sources of data for a researcher studying the culture of a health spa are interviews, census data, journal articles, and artifacts.

2. *Investigator triangulation*—using several researchers to gather data

   Example: Research teams interview members of one organization to compile a biography of the CEO.

3. *Theory triangulation*—using multiple perspectives to interpret the data set

   Example: A study grounded in persuasion theory from communications and personality theory from psychology is conducted to analyze campaign speeches prior to a senatorial election.

4. *Methodological triangulation*—using multiple methods to study a single problem[13]

   Example: To study an attendance problem for a professional football team, we conduct a phenomenology of tailgate parties among football fans, the biography of a lifelong team fan, and a case study of the team's involvement with its hometown.

5. *Interdisciplinary triangulation*—using other disciplines to inform the research process

   Example: A study involving consumer perceptions of brands borrows projective methods of data collection from psychology and narrative analysis techniques from linguistic tradition.

Triangulation is an insurance policy that protects you from questions of credibility and bias. Experienced researchers anticipate problems by building multiple sources of data collection, researchers, theories, disciplines. and data analysis into their research designs.

Can We Assume the Results Are Typical of All Similar Situations?

The issue of external generalization, important for quantitative validity and reliability, is a moot point for qualitative studies. The point is mute because we study a single setting and a small number of individuals. And we use purposive sampling that cannot be generalized to the population at large. Internal generalizability—generalizing a conclusion within the setting or group studied—is important for case studies, however. The descriptive, interpretive, and theoretical validity of the conclusions all depend on their internal relationship to the case as a whole. Although results cannot be extrapolated from one study to another, results are indicative of what might be expected from similar studies under similar circumstances.

In the next section, we take a look at the qualitative models from which to choose to conduct research, as outlined in Chapter 2. There is no one right model for all studies, but there should be a model that is appropriate for your study based on the research question or study objective.

Summary

1. Study participants may be easier to locate than to engage in the research process. Friends and family who relate to you in a nonprofessional way are not recommended for inclusion in your study.

2. Institutional review boards protect research subjects from psychological and physical harm by requiring adherence to human subjects' standards. Consent forms and guarantees of anonymity are most important for qualitative researchers who conduct experiments that might compromise their subjects.

3. Researchers often need the assistance of a gatekeeper to gain access to a population for study. Initiated by a sponsor who takes an active role in the study, mutual trust between researcher and subject is essential for successful qualitative inquiry to take place.

4. Researcher integrity is paramount to ensure high ethical research standards.

5. Issues of validation criteria include accurate data and authenticity testimony. Five types of triangulation help researchers obtain credible research results.

Stretching Exercises

1. In each of the following situations, identify and explain your choice of a gate-keeper for gaining access to each field location described:
   a. *A multinational corporation* with an office in your city, for a case study of international marketing
   b. *A local hardware store,* for a study to investigate how women shop for repair and improvement products
   c. *A shopping mall* with four anchor stores, for a study of how their employees use the mall's open spaces during work and nonwork hours
   d. *A hospital maternity ward,* to study the role of fathers in the birthing process
2. Recommend the best triangulation tactic for the following research situations:
   a. An ethnography of a video game arcade or gaming venue
   b. A motivational study of football fans
   c. A phenomenology of serial dieting
   d. Transcript data describing the effects of watching violence on television
   e. A national study on the impact of negative political advertising

Recommended Readings
About Issues and Concerns

Crabtree, B., & Miller, W. (1992). *Doing qualitative research.* Newbury Park, CA: Sage.
Kirk, J. (1986). *Reliability and validity in qualitative research.* Beverly Hills, CA: Sage.
Lee, R. (1993). *Doing research on sensitive topics.* Newbury Park, CA: Sage.
Lindlof, T. (1995). *Qualitative communication research methods.* Thousand Oaks, CA: Sage.
Mitchell, R., Jr. (1993). *Secrecy and fieldwork.* Newbury Park, CA: Sage.

Case in Point: Triangulating
Approaches to Tourism Research

Client: City of Laguna Beach

Laguna Beach is a California coastal town of 40,000 residents, located between Los Angeles and San Diego, that serves as both a destination spot for vacationers and a stopover for day-trippers. Boasting over 500 artist residents, Laguna Beach is home of the nationally acclaimed Pageant of the Masters, a stage presentation depicting paintings and sculpture using volunteer actors. Over 500,000 people visit Laguna Beach each year to see the Pageant and shop for art in three judged venues adjacent to the performance grounds.

Problem: Tourism

Faced with making decisions about traffic, parking, and retail franchises, Laguna Beach asked us to conduct research on several aspects of the city, including its tourism management, city image, promotion tactics, assets, and resident complaints.

RQ1: *What is the tourist experience in a small beach vacation town?*

Method: Life history

Data collection: Four foreign students who had not previously been to Laguna Beach were asked to spend one day visiting and touring the city, taking photographs of interesting places, and keeping a diary of what they saw and where they went. On their second visit, our "tourists" were instructed to visit the city's Web site, then return to Laguna to collect momentos, send postcards to their friends and relatives, and purchase at least one souvenir that would symbolize their experience. Lastly, tourists wrote up their experiences as narrative, including photos, anecdotes, observations, recollections, preferences, and problems.

Data analysis: Thematic clustering

While analyzing the visual and verbal text collected, the group developed descriptors for each researcher to reflect common tourist approaches: Historian, Explorer, Wanderer, and Shopper.

Results: The text suggests that tourists encounter heavy traffic and parking problems, but they are pleased with retail experience, thrilled by the ocean vistas, and delighted by artistic treasures. The bad news is that our tourists opted to visit another spot rather than encounter the congestion of Laguna Beach a third time. This report was directed to the city's tourist bureau.

RQ2: *How do residents deal with living in a tourist town?*

Method: Ethnography

Data collection: Five researchers conducted in-depth interviews with residents who had lived in Laguna Beach for at least 5 years, city officials, shop owners, and high school students to investigate the effects of tourism on their everyday lives. Observations of summer activity were recorded, using a lifelong resident as informant. Story narratives were transcribed from audio, analyzed by subjective interpretation, and used to build a composite explanation of the phenomenon.

Data analysis: Thematic clustering

From the data, common themes emerged. Transcripts were coded by category of subject discussed. Categories were then analyzed for themes and quotes to characterize each theme.

Results: Evidence of positive feelings existed about tourists but less enthusiasm for tourism itself. Claiming that in summers, "It's a pain in the butt to get around town," one resident echoed the sentiments of most respondents. A list of resident concerns was expanded on in the final report prepared for the city council.

RQ3: *How does a resort town promote itself as a tourist venue?*

Method: Case study

Data collection: Four researchers conducted an audit of collateral materials, logo, design, Web page, and maps intended for tourist use. They interviewed the mayor, director of the tourist office, county clerk, and three staff members who handled tourist-related business.

Data analysis: Collateral materials were evaluated for design, readability, and consistency. Findings of a hospitality study conducted at area hotels the previous season were evaluated for their usefulness and validity.

Results: Shortages in personnel and funds contributed the a lack of effective marketing research needed to properly analyze visitor demographics and travel motivations. Web pages were not user-friendly.

Solution recommended to client: Implement new marketing strategies, conduct more research, and update the Web pages.

Benefit of method integration: Three approaches to this single research focus yielded different perspectives, bringing dimension and depth to the marketing study. No single method was comprehensive enough to stand on its own, yet the combined results fit together like pieces of a tightly crafted puzzle. The study identified problems and gave city officials suggestions for appropriate solutions to the city's marketing problems.

Notes

1. From Chapter 4 in Lindlof, T. R. (1995). *Qualitative communication research methods.* Thousand Oaks, CA: Sage.

2. See the *Human Research Report, 10* (10), p. 2, October 1995.

3. Quoted from Sudweeks, F., & Rafaeli, S. (1995). How do you get a hundred strangers to agree? Computer mediated communication and collaboration. In T. M. Harrison & T. D. Stephen (Eds.), *Computer networking and scholarship in the 21st-century university* (pp. 115-136). New York: SUNY Press.

4. See Form, W. (1973). Field problems in comparative research: The politics of distrust. In M. Armer & A. Grimshaw (Eds.), *Comparative social research: Methodological problems and strategies.* New York: John Wiley.

5. See Sieber, J., & Stanley, B. (1988). Ethical and professional dimensions of socially sensitive research. *American Psychologist, 43,* 49-55.

6. See Lee, R., & Renzetti, C. (1990). The problems of researching sensitive topics: An overview and Introduction. *American Behavioral Scientist, 33,* 510-528.

7. Boyder, J. (1987). *The silent minority: Non-respondents on sample surveys* (p. 143). Cambridge, MA: Polity.

8. From a discussion in Maxwell, J. (1996). *Qualitative research design: An interpretive approach.* Thousand Oaks, CA: Sage.

9. From Hirschman, E. (1986). Humanistic inquiry in marketing research: Philosophy, method and criteria. *Journal of Marketing Research, 23,* 237-249.

10. Hirschman (1986), p. 244. See Note 9.

11. Hirschman (1986), p. 246. See Note 9.

12. See Denzin, N. (1970). *The research act.* Chicago: Aldine.

13. For an interesting approach to multimethod consumer research, see Arnould, E., & Price, L. (1996). Conducting the choir: A strategy for multimethod consumer research. *Advances in Consumer Research, 13.*

5 Designing a Study and Writing a Proposal

Our delight in any particular study rises and improves in proportion to the application which we bestow upon it. Thus, what was at first an exercise becomes at length an entertainment.

—Joseph Addison

Qualitative research has often been characterized as "conducting a focus group or two." Certainly, focus groups are used quite often to collect qualitative data, but data-gathering techniques are only a minor part of conducting a complete study. This chapter provides some basic guidelines for beginning the research process, namely, deciding on a topic and putting together a research proposal.

Four Steps to Study Design

Deciding what to study and how to approach the topic are questions students face before every research effort. With practitioners, however, research objectives are usually provided by the client. Four steps to study design are presented here to help both students and marketing practitioners craft a plan and develop a proposal.

Step 1: Decide on a Topic or Formulate a Definitive Research Objective

A research project is an effort to eliminate the doubt that exists about something. Research begins with the selection of a topic of study (often, a student's most difficult task) or identifying a client's problem. For students and scholars, topics of research usually fall within the boundaries of subjects studied in departmental disciplines. Communications students research effects of media, whereas business students look at consumer issues. For practitioners, research begins by formulating a research question that accurately and concisely defines the research objective.

The specific objectives for developing a research focus are (a) to explain what you are writing about (*topic*), (b) state what you don't know about it (*question*), and (c) explain why we need to know about it (*rationale*). This tripartite structure, which was developed to motivate the research question (RQ), works well for students and practitioners using qualitative methods:[1]

1. *Name your topic:*

    I am researching _____

2. *Imply your question:*

    because I want to find out who/how/why _____

3. *State the rationale for the question and the project:*

    to understand how/why/what _____.

A completed research question to study the lottery phenomenon to develop the creative concept for an advertising campaign might be something like this:

I am researching *lottery playing* because I want to know *why people spend money on games of chance* in order to understand *what motivates ticket purchase.*

A research question developed for a client who asks, "Why aren't people buying art supplies at my picture framing chain?" is more purposeful:

We will research *purchasers of art supplies* because we want to know *how they make shopping decisions* in order to understand *why they shop elsewhere.*

Process-oriented research questions such as these serve two study design functions: they help refine focus and suggest ways to conduct the research. In the lottery study, the RQ suggests studying the phenomenon of playing the lottery and using interviews and observation techniques to focus on purchase motivations. For the framing chain, a case study may be appropriate for investigating local shoppers and their interaction with this retailer.

The prevailing types of research questions posed by qualitative researchers are (a) situation-specific questions about the *meaning* of events and activities for the people involved in them or (b) research questions about the influence of the physical and social *context* of events and activities.

Step 2: Explain the Research Context

This section is often referred to as a "literature review." I like to think of it as grounding your topic. In proposals, this section provides an argument for conducting the study; in the final thesis or report, the context section functions more as a pyramid on which to build your study. It's analogous to downloading MapQuest prior to taking a trip; you benefit from those who have gone before you, those who have plotted a course. That's not to say you need to follow it, but at least you know what has been accomplished (rational directions) and how (by car). You also have other options: take a plane or discover a new route.

Back to the research context, of which there are two parts: literature and theory. We'll begin with literature. If you're trying to understand the motivations behind corporate philanthropy, you consult public relations journals and texts to locate previous studies. Suppose you find a study that surveyed 50 Fortune 500 companies about their philanthropic practices—to whom, how much, and how often they give money—a perfect starting point. All other studies conducted on philanthropy that you find provide statistical data and policy discussion, nothing else. You want to know how corporate officers make their allocation and recipient decisions, the *why* of giving. Previous research attests to the worth of your study, and the lack of qualitative investigation gives you a rationale for revisiting the subject.

Past research will also identify *theories* and propositions used by other researchers to approach your topic, making your job easier than starting from scratch. Perhaps a balance theory is mentioned, suggesting that as you profit, you give back. Social justification theory, which purports that image is a primary concern with giving, may inform your study. If neither of these theories quite fits, perhaps you turn to psychology for motivation theory and the decision-making process. Why are the ways people make decisions important to your study? Because you will likely discover that most of your participants make decisions using one of the processes presented by persuasion literature.

Interpretivists (that's what we call ourselves because we interpret information from people) use theory to provide understanding of direct *lived experience* instead of abstract generalizations. As interpretivists, we attempt to capture the core of meanings and contradictions involved in human experiences.[2]

Four types of theory (a theory is essentially the latest version of truth to be tested and proven) are used to inform research:[3]

1. *Empirical generalizations* are outcomes and function to raise questions or provide rationale for new studies, such as empirical data provided in our earlier philanthropy example.

2. *Models* contain more variables than empirical research and are primarily results of quantitative research. Models can provide a basis for qualitative studies, however.

3. *Propositions* deal with a variety of applications and are broader in scope than the previous two types. Qualitative researchers can also use propositions as frameworks for asking questions in their studies and discussing aspects of their findings.

4. *Conceptual frameworks*[4] use descriptive categories within a broad structure to inform both method and substantive aspects of qualitative studies.

By this point, researchers should have had a few epiphanies or "ahas" from doing some detective work. Armed with lists of relevant articles and theories, researchers can organize them to provide a logical discussion about what they will do, grounded on a great pyramid of past research and theoretical application opportunities.

Step 3: Select Collection Techniques and Tools

After identifying the relevant research model (from Chapter 2), consider the available options for data collection. Three techniques used most often for qualitative studies are (a) participant observation, (b) interviewing (individual and focus group), and (c) document collection (explained in detail in Part 4). Observations are facilitated by using videotapes that can be replayed and electronic note taking and field logs to eliminate fumbling with pen and paper. Likewise, interviews can be taped and transcribed later for analysis or gathered on the Internet and saved as text. Scanners, cameras, and copy machines enable researchers to carry away documents and photos of artifacts for later analysis.

Ideally, researchers draw from a variety of techniques to triangulate data sources (see Chapter 4). Decisions about which ones to use are based on your research objectives and what you want to learn or understand. They involve knowledge of how to apply your personal expertise to collecting data, especially during interactivity. Gathering in-depth information requires *elicitation* skills, discussed in detail in conjunction with interviewing guidelines.

For our corporate philanthropy study, a phenomenology might be chosen, invoking personal interviews and document collection as the primary data-gathering vehicles. A focus group or follow-up survey could be included to provide another perspective and validate our findings.

Step 4: Choose Who and Where to Study

Identifying and recruiting subjects, locating a place to collect data, and getting permission to access that place are the next issues of consideration. Chapter 4 deals in depth with these topics, but they are mentioned here to give an idea of the logical steps you'll take to reach the stage where you're ready to write your proposal.

At this point, you may decide to do a short pilot study to pretest some of your ideas prior to committing them to paper. For our corporate philanthropy study, we could develop a list of questions and hold a mock interview with someone willing to participate. This experience will illuminate unclear or redundant questions and will provide an opportunity to revise the questions prior to asking the actual subjects. Pilot studies also substantiate the effectiveness of the questions you select when they appear in your proposal.

Determining the time it will take to locate corporations, locate subjects, schedule and conduct interviews, collect documents, and perhaps conduct a focus group is not a simple task. But it is one you will need to do prior to proposing the research. Factor in enough time to account for problems—such as equipment failure, broken appointments, and underestimating the number of interviews needed—which inevitably arise during the research process. Be very liberal with your time frame. Delays frustrate clients and advisers, but researchers are rarely penalized for finishing ahead of schedule!

Preparing the Proposal

Students and practitioners submit proposals of their research objectives, which are usually directed at resolving an existing problem in the marketplace. Students write proposals for university review committees, researchers write them for funding bodies and foundations, and professionals write them for commercial clients. In all cases, the proposal must persuade the reader of the project's value.

Proposals can be developed in a variety of ways, as explained and presented in the Locke and Punch volumes in the Recommended Reading section at the end of this chapter. Rather than duplicate these texts, this chapter explains proposal ingredients and presents the outline of a research proposal to do qualitative research on supermarket club cards as an example.

Developing Your Argument

> We must never assume that which is incapable of proof.
> —G. H. Lewis, 1859

When developing your argument, remember that the readers of your proposal will probably want answers to at least seven questions. Here are the questions and how you respond:[5]

Their Question	*Your Answer*
What is your point?	I claim that . . .
What is the scope of your claim?	I limit it to . . .
What evidence do you have?	I offer as evidence . . .
What links evidence to claim?	I offer this principle . . .
But what about . . .?	I can rebut that. First, . . .
But what if . . .?	Under these circumstances, . . .
What are the problems?	Certain limitations exist . . .

After the topic or problems is presented, a proposal must build a case for conducting the study. *Evidence* is the most important section of the entire proposal because it gives your argument credibility. Like a lawyer trying to convince a jury, a proposer must supply readers with evidence that their study is necessary for answering the RQ or solving the problem. When offering evidence, make certain that you include past research conducted on the topic in a logical fashion. The following is an outline of how evidence for research on how women purchase cars might be presented:

   I. Claim: Women's motivations for buying cars is uncertain.

     A. Buyers of different sexes require different marketing strategies.

     B. Marketing targets needs and wants of users.

     C. Needs and wants differ according to demographics and lifestyle.

  II. *RQ:* What drives women's motivations for purchasing cars?

 III. *Evidence:* Studies show that women and men have different purchase motivations.

     A. Study A: women's purchases are based on emotion, men's on objective criteria.

 IV. *Evidence:* Research indicates that women's roles in the purchase process are changing.

     A. Study A: Women are often cast in the role of influencer rather than buyer.

     B. Census data: Women are now primary wage earners with new buying power.

  V. *Evidence:* Studies ignore aesthetic and performance variables of women's purchase decisions.

 VI. *Study Rationale:* More research is necessary to properly market to women.

     A. Too few reliable empirical studies exist on female car buying.

     B. Too little "why" research is available on gender-based purchasing.

     C. Most research to determine basic motivations for car purchasing has been conducted with men.

This kind of outline shows the relationships among your claims and where evidence is needed to support those claims. Evidence is usually presented by reviewing the literature on past research conducted on your topic. Your discussion of past research should expose an existing gap that can be filled by your study; your rationale is justified through this review process.

Organizing Your Proposal[6]

The following model, one of many ways to organize a qualitative proposal, lends itself well to the design of a qualitative study. However, universities and funding sources have their own requirements regarding proposal structure. Explanations for each section will make more sense if you read them in conjunction with the proposal outline example at the conclusion of this chapter.

1. Abstract: Clients usually like a "road map" of what the proposal will contain. Sometimes, graduate forms also require a synopsis of the argument, topic, and method of study in the form of an abstract. Although it appears first, it is written after the proposal is finished and in essence is a summary.

2. Introduction: Setting the stage for your research, the introduction tells what you want to do and why. It must present the purposes of the study and a general overview of the research questions and the model of study you are proposing.

3. Research Context: In this section, you should show how your proposed research fits into what is already known about the topic and how it makes a contribution to the understanding of the subject. It should also explain the theoretical framework that informs your study. By grounding your study in relevant previous work, you give the reader a clear sense of your approach to answering the research question. Your personal experience and knowledge about the subject can be included here when useful for providing credibility as to the importance of your topic.

4. Research Question: Pose one or a few clearly focused questions that flow naturally from the research context section.

5. Research Methods: Justify and describe the particular methods you will use with an explanation as to why they are reasonable choices. A description of the research setting will be helpful in justifying your choice of methods. Budgets may be included here when clients are the audience for the proposal. Sampling, data collection, and data analysis sections should also be included here; ethics issues appear when appropriate.

6. Validity: Address this issue by discussing ways in which your study incorporates checks such as triangulation and coding procedures.

7. Expected Outcomes: You should have some idea of your expectations for the study after developing the research context section. Your intuition about study results may motivate foundations or clients to fund the research.

8. Implications: This is the "so what?" section of your proposal. It provides an indication of the study's contribution to the field of knowledge or its usefulness for solving the client's problem.

9. References: Limit this section to the references cited in your proposal; it is not intended as a bibliography of texts on the topic.

10. Appendixes: Suggested documents include timetable, questionnaires or interview guides, and interview schedules.

Having organized and prepared your argument, you're ready to think about particular aspects and issues, such as whom you will research, where you'll conduct the study, and how you'll ensure the study's quality. Begin by consulting the next chapter.

Summary

1. Topics and research objectives are best formed using a four-step format to begin your focus and limit the scope of your research.

2. Grounding your research using past studies and relevant theories provides a stable platform on which to build a case for conducting your study.

3. Individual and group interviews, observation, and document collection are the three main methods of gathering data in qualitative methods.

4. Proposals are written as arguments to persuade a specific audience to approve or fund a research study. Although formats vary, contents remain consistent. Research context, evidence, and "so what" sections require the most preparation attention.

Stretching Exercises

1. Using the four-step procedure presented in this chapter, develop topic statements for proposals directed to the following people:

K-Mart senior executives, to research a perceived image problem

A school superintendent, to research the ramifications of naming high schools for brand donors to educational programs

A transit authority board, to research train rider motivations and dissatisfactions

2. With the Internet as your research tool, locate three edu.-domain Web sites that can provide you with evidence to build an argument for a qualitative study to understand the effects of television violence on children.

Recommended Readings for Proposal Design

Locke, L., Spirduso, W., & Silverman, S. (1999). *Proposals that work.* Thousand Oaks, CA: Sage.

Marshall, C., & Rossman, G. (1995). *Designing qualitative research* (2nd ed.). Thousand Oaks, CA: Sage.

Maxwell, J. (1996). *Qualitative research design: An interpretive approach.* Thousand Oaks, CA: Sage.

Punch, K. (2000). *Developing effective research proposals.* Thousand Oaks, CA: Sage.

Example: Study Proposal Outline

The problem: How concerned are consumers about supermarket club cards as a privacy threat?[7]

I. Introduction

A. The media report that corporate America is starting to collect information on what customers buy and how much they spend.

B. California law makers introduced a dozen bills in 1999 aimed at curtailing the threat that high technology poses to personal privacy, one of which is intended to curb the gathering of personal consumer information from supermarket shoppers who use "club cards" to gain special discounts.

C. Public interest groups declare that popular club card systems pose a potential invasion of privacy.

D. Little evidence exists addressing this specific issue.

II. Context

A. Existing literature on privacy

1. Studies show Americans feel they have less and less privacy.

2. Research suggests that consumer segments emerge with different levels of concern about privacy.
3. One study showed that consumers are more likely to protest invasions of their privacy in domains deemed important to self-image than incursions into other domains, which they feel are less critical to the protection of self-image.
4. A privacy survey indicates that fear of medical record disclosure heads the list of perceived dangers faced by consumers.
5. The theory of operant conditioning is applicable to the club card phenomenon because card behavior is instrumental in determining whether one gets a reward (savings) or avoids a punishment (higher prices).
6. A study shows that customers are willing to share information if they receive something in return.
7. Another study reports that card users are willing to have information on them gathered and possibly used if they see benefits and some safeguards.

B. What is needed

1. Efforts to learn more about consumers' concerns with regard to frequent shopper club cards should help clarify the need for legislation in this area.
2. Information on consumer fears may help grocery store chains make decisions related to privacy policies and card usage.

C. Personal interest

1. The researcher is interested in the ethics involved and their ramifications for business and consumer behavior.
2. The researcher is a club card user experiencing doubts about the intended use of personal information for market solicitations.

III. Proposed Research

A. Research goals

1. Discover the relationship between card usage and shopping behavior.
2. Identify the harmful effects of club cards as perceived by users.
3. Understand the concerns of consumers about club cards.

B. Research questions

1. How concerned are consumers about club cards as a privacy threat?
2. Should legislators pass privacy violation regulations for grocers?

C. Research models

1. Ethnography
2. Phenomenology

D. Implications for marketing

1. Better understanding of consumer feelings about usage of their personal data for marketing purposes
2. Better understanding of consumer motivations for information disclosure
3. Conceptualization of the importance of ethical issues for promotional program implementation

E. Research sites

   1. Six retail chains using club cards

   2. Southern California locations of Lucky, Ralph's, and Vons Supermarkets

IV. Methods of Data Collection

  A. Observations of supermarket culture, including

    1. Shopping behaviors

    2. Item selection process

    3. Card use during check-out

    4. Checker's interaction with consumer

  B. Interviews with members of the culture, including

    1. Shoppers about their shopping habits

    2. Checkers about card requests, card usage, and expressed customer fears

    3. Management about card usage policies

  C. Survey

    1. Random sampling of exiting shoppers

    2. Minimum of 200 shoppers for each venue

V. Methods of Analysis

  A. Observational field notes will be analyzed

    1. For behavioral commonalities, using Ethnograph software

    2. For contradictions and surprises as revealed by researchers

  B. Interview transcripts will be analyzed

    1. By clusters of thematic statements using Nud*ist software

    2. By researchers who will meet and identify common meaning statements

    3. By meaning statements that will be coded and analyzed for their significance to answering the research question

  C. Surveys will be analyzed

    1. To develop descriptive statistics with SPSS software

VI. Validity Issues

  A. Observations during 3 day-parts will provide a variety of shopping patterns and user demographics to eliminate a single focus.

  B. Multiple researchers will provide cross-checks and contribute to consistency.

  C. Triangulation of three data collection methods will provide multiple perspectives to remove the limitations of a single method.

  D. Multiple coders will reduce researcher bias by requiring consensus.

VII. Ethical Issues

  A. Consent forms will be issued to interviewees that guarantee anonymity.

  B. Interview transcripts will be destroyed 1 month after study completion.

  C. Identity of interviewees will be hidden by referring to them by gender and age.

VIII. Expected Outcomes

A. Consumers will report varying levels of comfort with card usage.

B. Shopping behaviors will reveal comfort level of card usage.

C. Attitudes will influence the outcome of current legislation regarding privacy issues.

IX. References

A. Text citations—Chicago style

B. In-person attributions—legislator's plea for more research

X. Time Table

A. Interviews will be conducted over a 4-month period, from September to December.

B. Six 3-hour visits will be made in each of three time blocks, early morning (9:00 to noon), evening commute hours (4:00 to 7:00 PM), and late night (9:00 PM to midnight), for a total of 44 hours.

C. Surveys will be distributed during each time block on the final day of field research.

XI. Appendices

A. Interview questions

B. Survey instrument

Notes

1. From Booth, W., Colomb, G., & Williams, J. (1995). *The craft of research.* Chicago: University of Chicago Press.

2. See Denzin, N. (1988). *The research act.* New York: McGraw-Hill.

3. From Turner, J. (1985). In defense of positivism. *Sociological Theory, 3,* 24-31.

4. Denzin (1988, p. 49). See Note 2.

5. Booth et al. (1995, p. 144). See Note 1.

6. See Maxwell, J. (1996). *Qualitative research design: An interpretive approach.* Thousand Oaks, CA: Sage.

7. Based on a study by S. Sayre and D. Horne presented to the annual meeting of the Association of Consumer Research, Columbus, Ohio, October 1999.

■ Part III

CHOOSING
A RESEARCH
MODEL

W hether you're studying one life or one organization, multiple lives or an entire culture, *models* function to help researchers understand the meanings consumers attribute to products and consumption experiences. Research models are guides. They draw from disciplines that study humans, such as anthropology, education, psychology, and sociology. Once we acknowledged the value of humans in the purchase process, marketplace researchers began borrowing humanistic research methods. Instead of simply counting or compartmentalizing consumers, we now consider consumers important for the meanings they bring to the exchange process.

In this section, four chapters present five research models that are most commonly invoked for studying the marketplace. Living biography (Chapter 6), case study (Chapter 7), phenomenology and grounded theory (Chapter 8), and ethnography (Chapter 9) are reviewed for their application to meaningful marketplace research. Further information for each model can be obtained by consulting the texts recommended at the end of each chapter.

6 History, Living Biography, and Self-Narrative

History is not what was but what is.
　　　　　—William Faulkner

W e approach the past in a variety of ways. This chapter offers three ways of understanding products and consumers from a historical vantagepoint. The notion that a problem is only understood within its historical context is illustrated here in a personal anecdote concerning demarketing. While developing a campaign for saving natural resources, I chastised a friend for taking long showers and leaving the lights on during his visit to my home. He replied that he'd been raised by the state [orphanage] where there were no controls on or concerns about water and electricity usage. Reflections of his experiences brought to light some relevant consumption issues.

First, my campaign had assumed that everyone was raised to respect energy sources, and that conservation would come naturally when people were reminded of its scarcity during hot summer months. After listening to my friend, I realized that education about energy usage was necessary for marketing targeted to a general audience. By considering the history of one consumer, I identified the context for grounding the campaign.

Understanding who consumers are means knowing "where they were when"— in other words, knowing the historical influences on their lives. The same principle applies to products. My grandmother's dislike of homogenized peanut butter stems from the fact that she made her own and enjoyed stirring the oil into the peanut meat before eating it. History provides a glimpse of her temporal relationship to peanut butter, and her biography brings depth and details to an understanding of that relationship. If I were marketing peanut butter to granny and her peers, I should bring a "homemade" quality into copy and visual advertising elements.

This chapter highlights the importance of history and life stories for understanding consumers and their relationships to products over time. The role of these methods in marketplace research is important as audiences diversify and mature. Historical methods play a vital role for understanding consumer life stories and self-narratives.

The Historical View

History is inherently political. There is no single standard by which we can identify 'true' historical knowledge. . . . Rather there are contests about the substance, uses and meanings of the knowledge that we call history.[1]

—Joan Scott, 1989

Historical research demands a point of view that includes an interpretive framework to deliver the author's notion of "meaning."[2] This notion is explained by an advertising analogy. From a feminist perspective, male art directors creating early advertising characterized women as objects to be gazed on. In a historical context, we see that portrayals of women reflected the times, not because of men's notions of meaning but because women assumed role-based duties of homemaker and mother. Feminists considered such duties to be subordinating and demeaning; thus, 1970s advertising was accused of subordinating women.

Today, women are once again embracing their more domestic roles and are less offended by advertising portrayals of them as mothers and wives. By bringing a historical context to the problem of how to present women in television commercials, we approach today's consumers with sensitivity and insight. History is more than a passing of time with dates to memorize; it has continuing relevance for the present.

Some interesting histories are product centered. Coke, for instance, has a fascinating history of television commercials. Beginning in 1956, Coke was carried into cowboy drama where actors talked to the audience about the product. "Things go better with Coke," sang the Andrews Sisters in their poodle skirts from the 1950s. An international chorus characterized Coke as "The Real Thing" during a 1970s commercial filmed in a meadow with panoramic views. Why do we care about the history of Coke? Because Coke's story dramatizes the role of products in our lives and the role of advertising in reflecting our lives.

The goal of historical research is to *illuminate*. Historical demographies study family life to illuminate product usage in the home. Case studies look at companies to illuminate an organizational culture's meanings. History characterizes the past and provides richness to unique or particular events.

Writing a Product History

If you're going to produce a product history, you begin by *reading secondary sources* of the period under study, using Homer, the most common computerized library index to a library. Books and magazines and newspaper articles describing your era of interest are a good beginning. Pay attention to footnotes and reference citations for clues to other materials. Next, locate *primary sources,* which are documents from the period you are trying to explain. Here's where detective work comes in. Coke's history appears in video archives that contain original versions of the commercials.

The Directory of Archives and Manuscript Repositories in the U.S. is a good place to learn what is available and where it's located. Many universities provide grants or funding for "travel to collections," where you may study original documents first hand. For her history of perfume advertising, one researcher spent a year at the Smithsonian Institute combing advertising archives, her main source of primary data.

In a study of women's underwear and the rise of women's sports,[3] two researchers took a historical approach to understand the relationship between garments and athletic performance over time. They began in 1988, when sprinter Florence Griffith-Joyner's record time in the 100-meter race proved she could outrun any man in the world. The incident makes the most sense when placed in a historical context. Had anyone suggested the possibility of this happening a century before, they would have been laughed out of town. One hundred years ago, all men and women were convinced that active sport was not for women, who were thought to be physically and biologically unsuited for it.

The study traces women's competition over the years with respect to dress, particularly underwear. Relegated to wearing dresses instead of knickers for hygienic reasons, women could not compete in active sports until electricity allowed the heating of wash water, and detergent was invented to remove fungus-causing microbes from woolen undergarments. Elastic changed underwear by replacing tapes or strings in drawers. Golf matches were won in ankle-length dresses until tennis permitted a shorter costume in 1926. Cotton replaced wool, corsets were discarded, and bras allowed women to compete more comfortably. History documents the changes in underwear and technology that significantly assisted the rise of women's sports.

The client, an elastic manufacturer, hailed these discoveries. The product hero—elastic—was neatly woven into the company's history. The company portrayed itself as a true advocate of women's sports, embracing sponsorships to improve its image and capitalize on the discovery of this relationship by market-place researchers.

Evaluating Documentary Evidence

Historical research is essentially a document search. But locating documents is only the beginning. The primary role of historian as detective is evaluating the evidence of a document's authenticity. Journals, letters, and diaries are common sources of evidence for marketplace and communications researchers. If the writing is from the period from which it claims to originate, it will reflect a writing style and vocabulary indicative of the times. Forgeries of documents are not uncommon; artwork and wartime journals are especially vulnerable targets for forgers.

A good researcher will distinguish between "genuine" and "authentic." *Genuineness* is whether or not the document is *forged* or an action is false. A consumer reporter who reviews a Mercedes Benz without test driving it provides a genuine review because it is not forged, but it is not authentic because he or she did not drive the car. *Authenticity* is offering an ostensibly *truthful* document. An authentic recording may be copied and sold in another country as an original; the recording is authentic because the star did the original, but it is not genuine because it is a copy of the original.

Internal and external techniques, called criticisms, are useful for verifying document authenticity. *External criticisms* are comparisons made between two texts and author verification. *Internal criticisms* verify (a) the historical accuracy of an account, (b) the linguistic and stylistic accuracy of the writing, and (c) the bias of the author. *Author credibility* appraises the writer's proximity to the event and how important the event was to the writer (by determining or eliminating the presence of bias).

Consumer Journal Evidence

Some researchers collect consumer product usage journals as evidence when writing product histories. Once in possession of journals, researchers must ask what the journal reveals about its author. What is the level of revelation—is this the person's private or public voice? Is the author conscious of a potential reader? Other questions to answer are the following:

1. What does the journal tell you about the social-cultural context of the consumer's life?

What does the journal tell you about the author's age, sex, ethnic or racial heritage?

Is the author a native citizen or an immigrant?

2. What is the consumer's personal or relational world like?

Who are the consumer's significant others?

3. What social values are important to the consumer?

4. How does the consumer's reality and values relate to the social context in which he or she lives?

Is the journal revealing or concealing?

5. Where would you go to answer the questions left from reading the consumer journal?

What other sources and evidence exist?

Here are a few examples of how historical research fits within a marketplace framework. Pin-up advertising calendars are the documents of evidence for a historical study conducted for Snap-On tool company.[4] The study surveys the history of the pin-up calendar, discusses its promotional role, and presents an interpretive analysis of images of women featured on calendars from 19th-century origins to the present. Calendars from company archives were content analyzed for suggestive poses and scanty attire. The results were compared with legal cases of workplace harassment of women at corresponding intervals. Results found that the pin-up advertising calendar's century-long status as a sanctioned promotional medium is being challenged by recent court rulings and general social climate relating to sexual harassment. Based on this research, the company has pulled its promotional calendars featuring women.

In another historical study, two researchers argued that the mania-depression continuum (highs and lows) describes relationships that can be found among several consumption phenomena previously thought to be unrelated. Such phenomena include risk taking, sensation seeking, product involvement, innovativeness, and hedonic consumption.[5] They examined a specific population through historical sources to access the tradition of association between manic depression and consumption behavior. Their sources were clinical and genetic literature and biographical studies of prominent persons now considered to have been manic-depressive (e.g., Beethoven and Van Gogh) as well as current autobiographical texts by persons diagnosed as manic-depressive. The study identified manic and depressive consumption practices among this population. The results allowed marketers to comprehend and predict consumption phenomena for consumers whose lives are marked by cycling into and out of mania and depression.

Last, a historical method having applications for marketing was used in a study to understand alien residents and offspring of immigrants who live in ethnic communities.[6] Researchers presented the historical contexts that have shaped immigration and assimilation in America and society's understanding of those phenomena. They suggest that history, which may not give a clear answer to formulating appropriate marketing strategies for the second generation of immigrants, does indicate important issues for future investigation.

Product and company histories, which borrow from anthropology to investigate what people thought as well as what they did in the past, are useful for addressing questions of policy, ethics, and appropriate business practices. They play a significant role in developing marketing strategy to reflect changing consumer needs and wants.

Using the Consumer as Researcher

The symbolizing self centers on its own narrative, a life story that is itself created and constantly recreated.

—Robert Jay Lifton

Stories describe turning points in people's lives and help us understand how products figure into their social and personal lives. They feature one person and his or her experiences as told to a researcher. Stories are given many different names, most falling under the rubric of *biographical studies,* which includes individual biography, autobiography, life history, and oral history.

Marketplace researchers select a type of biographical study according to the purpose of the research. *Individual biographies* are written about another person, living or dead, using archival documents and records. Bell's biography of author Virginia Woolf is one example. With *autobiographies,* people write about themselves; *Ogilvy on Advertising* is the autobiography of a famous creative director.

Life histories are reports of an individual's life gathered during interviews and conversations with the person. They are conducted to determine how a life reflects society's cultural themes. Life histories of travelers, filmgoers, amusement park junkies, and so forth are gathered so we might better understand how these forms of consumption fit into the lives of our target audience. Collected over time, these projects are often ongoing and involve several different researchers. In a collaborative approach to life histories, multiple researchers gather information about a person and come together to compare notes. The result is timely and beneficial for understanding the consumption experience of a single target audience member.

Oral histories are collections of historical materials that bring to light a variety of people's lives, from common folks talking about their jobs, such as Studs Terkel's *Working,* to historical recollections of famous people. Ballads and folksongs, archived in libraries and private collections, give marketers incredible insight about the role of products in the lives of consumers.

An author may tell the stories of others by incorporating much of his or her own perspective in the written document; this method is called *interpretive biography.*[7]

Interpretive biographies are recommended for marketplace research because they "blur the lines between fact and fiction,"[8] providing readable accounts of consumer lives that are more easily assimilated by clients and corporations than the more classical approach to biographical writing. Writers' lives are most reflected in interpretive biographies that present a chronology in life-course stages and experiences. The focus is on gathering consumption stories and organizing them around themes in the person's life. The researcher searches for meaning in these stories, looking also for larger structures to explain these meanings within a historical context.

Stories as Purchase Experiences

The basis for all consumer histories is the *stories* they tell as fictional accounts of real consumption events. People tell stories about their personal marketplace experiences to researchers as narrative discourse. Self-stories are often told to focus groups. Stories of addictive consumption are told to members of 12-step programs or shared during motivational seminars. Stories, sometimes motivated by group reactions and response, are often entertaining. Consumer research on compulsive consumption appears as a self-narrative or a story written for a specific audience.[9] During a study of antisocial behavior conducted for a video surveillance company, two men recall stories from their pasts:

I think appearance makes a lot of difference to how people react to you. Like, one time I went in a 7-11 store to rob it. . . . I was smiling and looked pretty good. When I asked the guy for the money, he shook his head no. So I pulled up my collar, messed my hair, frowned, and robbed a store down the way. No problem this time . . . when I yelled and acted crazy, he gave up the cash.

This girl and me, we went into a music store 'cause I needed some guitar strings. She pretended to slip on the floor, and like, yelled loud so the guy came over and tried to help. That's when I grabbed the pack of strings and we walk out. Then I see a rerun of this movie, "Alice Doesn't Live Here" or something, and they do the same trick, and I think, did I copy them . . . or what?

Personal experience narratives are also useful for marketplace research. They differ from stories in that personal narratives are more likely to be based on commonplace anecdotes or mundane experiences told to an individual, whereas stories involve pivotal life experiences. Here is an example of a woman talking about her recent personal experience of shopping at Home Depot:

> When I got there . . . it was a huge store . . . I started looking around for some tile. Big banners hung down, so I read where it said "tile" and headed in that direction. I found lots of tile . . . all kinds . . . . and I was confused about what kind I needed for my bathroom. The contractor just said to pick out some tile . . . he didn't say what kind. So I stood there for a while, and finally a young man came up to me. . . . He asked if I needed help. So I told him my problem, and he spent a half hour with me. He seemed to know what he was talking about . . . certainly more than I knew . . . so I took some samples to show the contractor. It was a nice experience. I will go back there again.

Group storytelling sessions are useful for investigators who can work with participants over time using specific writing assignments. Topics such as shopping for a friend, watching a soap opera, taking a trip to Disneyland, and so forth are assigned, and participants return with their stories written for sharing with the other group members. Such story sharing is different than a focus group because topics are preassigned, and members are free to include whatever information they deem pertinent to the topic. Stories and discussions of those stories give researchers an inside glimpse of a phenomenon under study.

During a group discussion of Disneyland, consumers nodded in agreement about the dismal task of waiting in line for each ride or attraction. The waiting process was mentioned in all of their stories and anecdotes. Some waiting experiences were comical, others tragic. Disney used the information collected during this group storytelling session to reevaluate their queuing procedures. A policy to limit park entrance minimized the time visitors spent waiting in line. Group sessions conducted after the new policy went into effect revealed fewer "waiting" stories, indicating the policy's success.

Marketplace Biographies

Biographies produce narrative texts to be interpreted as documentary evidence of real experiences. To be useful for marketing, biographical texts must be organized and analyzed using an *interpretive* framework of analysis. This framework—a process of reading lives—has several steps, which are discussed briefly here.

During interviewing, researchers gather contextual biographical materials. Interviewers then prompt consumers to expand on various sections of their stories. The researcher or research team interprets the narratives, isolates segments, and identifies patterns of meaning. Researchers compare the texts of several respondents for similarities and differences, to form theoretical generalizations that produce a model of their consumption world. The research is triangulated for multiple perspectives on the same consumption experience.

Two interpretive formats are used for marketplace research using biographical text: The first is written from the subject's perspective for interpretation, and the other occurs when the subjects help the researcher interpret their point of view. Researchers using the first format can collect the data, excuse consumers, and proceed with interpretation on their own. In the second instance, consumers must remain in the study throughout the entire analytical stage.

Consequences of consumer stories about their shoplifting or robbing experiences provide a pattern useful to a video surveillance company for positioning cameras and briefing clients on offender behavior. Self-narratives collected about shopping experiences in large home supply outlets reveal that consumers who were helped with their purchase decisions are more apt to return to that particular outlet than to a competitor.

Product and company histories are collected to situate them within a *historical* framework. Consumer story anecdotes and lived experiences provide primary data of consumption narratives within a *cultural and materialistic* framework. In both cases, the researcher plays an active, not passive, interpretive role in data analysis. Immersion in research data is a necessary condition for successful marketplace researchers.

Researcher as Consumer

Occasionally, marketers use their own personal experiences as a research method. The process can occur individually or as a group and is another way of telling a consumption story. Each story has a plot that begins with past experience, describes a current experience, and ends with how the experience will affect future experiences. To act as a research instrument, you focus experiences in four directions simultaneously: inward, outward, backward, and forward. Inward focus captures your internal feelings, hopes, reactions, and so forth; the outward focus is your environment, your reality. Backward and forward are the past-present-future aspects of the experience. The data for your research are collected in journal entries, field notes, photographs, letters, artifacts, and so on, and should be thought of as field texts. Collected artifacts are used to trigger your memory so that you can recall the story to write up at a later time.

Using all the collected data, you then organize your materials so they make sense and construct a story. The story is written from your point of view and should combine all the elements of the experience, including conversations with others and your personal thoughts. While writing, imagine you are in conversation with an audience. Think of all the questions they might ask you about your experience and answer them. Include photographs and depth descriptions in your story so readers can feel what you felt.

Biographical research groups doing research can share their experiences from the story narratives to identify patterns and themes. A final report summarizes the collective approach to the phenomenon, including what things you had in common and what things were different.

The advantage of using yourself as collection instrument is that you are able to bring more insight to a consumption experience than you can achieve by interviewing others. As a traveler, your trip becomes a journey of discovery that, when recalled, provides valuable clues for understanding the difficulties and joys associated with tourism and travel. Once scoffed at by traditionalists, the self-narrative is now considered a legitimate method for conducting consumer and marketplace research.

Whether gathered from historical, biographical, or personal narratives, the past informs consumption experiences better than surveys or scaling techniques can inform them. The personalized perspective brings dimension and depth to consumer research and is readily available to students of all marketplace phenomena.

Summary

1. Historical research is conducted to illuminate product consumption and usage in everyday life.

2. Document searching and verification are essential for authenticating historical data.

3. Consumers tell their stories to researchers who understand their experiences with products in their daily lives. Biographies, autobiographies, life histories, and oral histories are all modes of consumer storytelling.

4. Story text is interpreted by researchers either from the consumer's perspective or from the researcher's perspective with the help of the consumer.

5. Marketers occasionally tell their own experiences as consumption stories and analyze story text in the same manner as if they were not the source of the text.

Stretching Exercises

1. You and a friend keep journals of your consumption experiences for 2 weeks, including anecdotes and stories. Swap journals and analyze the narrative to answer these questions:

   a. Is the journal written as a personal exposition, or does it assume that you will be reading it?

   b. What can you tell about the gender and age of the writer from the text?

   c. Can you see a theme in the anecdotes presented?

   d. If brands are named, what do they tell you about the writer?

   e. How would you use narrative from this journal to help a client who manages a regional shopping center decide where to advertise?

2. Using the Internet, prepare a short history of your favorite brand. What information that you learned about the brand will help you to identify an event, sport, or cultural activity for a sponsorship opportunity?

Recommended Readings About History-Based Research Methods

Angrosino, M. V. (1994). *Documents of interaction: Biography, autobiography, and life history in social science perspective.* Gainesville: University of Florida Press.

Denzin, N. (1989). *Interpretive biography.* Newbury Park, CA: Sage.

Morgan, G. (1983). *Beyond method.* Beverly Hills, CA: Sage.

Himmelfarb, G. (1987). *The new history and the old.* Cambridge, MA: Harvard University Press.

Mukerji, C., & Schudson, M. (Eds.). *Rethinking popular culture: Contemporary perspectives in cultural studies.* Berkeley: University of California Press.

Plummer, K. (1983). *Documents of life: An introduction to the problems and literature of a humanistic method.* London: George Allen & Unwin.

Case in Point: Biographical Life History as Consumer Research[10]

Client: Newport Beach Surgery Center

Problem: How to market cosmetic surgery to women over 40

RQ: *What is the consumption experience of aesthetic cosmetic surgery?*

Data Collection:

1. Self-disclosure through a variety of elicitation devices, such as

   - High school yearbooks

   - Family and personal photo albums

   - Personal diaries

   - Media from the 1950s and 1960s, including audio recordings, magazines, comic books, and films

   - Collection of 40 pairs of eyeglasses worn during the consumer-researcher's life

2. Documents of information on face lift procedures

3. Interviews with plastic surgeons

4. Informal discussions with women who had successfully completed the operation and with family and friends about these decisions

5. Postoperative photographs

6. Audio tapes of preoperative and postoperative narrative

The researcher, once deciding on plastic surgery, agreed to compile thoughts and feelings before and during the operation by the funding center. Following surgery, the researcher decided on a retrospective examination as to her motives for the surgery. Memorabilia, momentos, media, and visual records (listed earlier) were collected for analysis to help the author recall her life as it related to making a decision to undergo surgery.

Elicitation devices were used to initiate the writing process, which began several months after the operation during an overseas assignment in Brussels and continued for 4 months.

Data Analysis: The author immersed herself in a process of analysis to understand what past and present elements led to the decision to elect surgery. Emotional and physical changes occurred during the analysis period.

Notes were sorted, edited, and arranged in chronological order. Four areas of influence emerged from the notes: Presurgery account of significant events, categories of influencers in the decision process, details of the surgery and recovery period, and reflections on the purchase.

Results: The author identified six factors that were primary contributors to the decision to have cosmetic surgery:

1. Place of residence and its accompanying lifestyle and expectations of residents

2. Peer group and their social values

3. Popular media during childhood and current Hollywood influence

4. Family, including two grown children, sister, mother, and grandmother

5. Timing of operation coinciding with personal and professional milestones

6. Adequate financial resources

Several factors were incorporated into a report for the surgery center, such as physician selection, satisfaction with the care and medical service received, and an analysis of print advertising for plastic surgery services in the immediate area.

A 40-page article was accepted for publication in a consumer research journal.

Discussion: This project is a unique approach to exploring cosmetic surgery. Other research reported on respondent testimony about why they had surgery, how they felt after, and reactions from their friends and family. Valuable information was gleaned from a series of in-depth interviews, and the researcher analyzed testimonies for similarities and differences.

What was not contained in past research was the perspective of a consumer before, during, and after the consumption of a face-lift. The resulting narrative provides a window of understanding for women considering surgery and for the medical professionals who market such services.

The client was able to use the narrative as a launching point for developing informational tools and a sensitive marketing campaign. Rather than featuring bathing-suit-clad, large-breasted coeds, ads contained the faces of mature women discussing their options for continuing and vibrant lives. Hotlines and Web pages were developed to link potential users with women who had undergone surgery. The surgery center provided these links and a physician referral service free of charge, using criteria provided from the research to match consumer needs with provider services.

Conclusion: Life history method enabled the author to elaborate on a consumption experience more completely than previously achieved with other research methods and techniques. The study revealed that, for one woman, consumption choices were made for reasons that revolved around her place in the physical and psychological universe that defined her. By understanding that place, marketers can more appropriately target their audience.

Notes

1. From Scotte, J. W. (1989). History in crisis? The other's side of the story. *American Historical Review, 94,* 680-692.

2. For a complete treatment of the subject, see Tuchman, G. (1994). Historical social science: Methodologies, methods and meanings. In N. Denzin & Y. Lincoln (Eds.), *Handbook of qualitative research* (pp. 306-323). Thousand Oaks, CA: Sage.

3. From Phillips, J. (1993). History from below: Women's underwear and the rise of women's sports. *Journal of Popular Culture, 27*(2), 129-146.

4. Based on a study by Frederick-Collins, J. (1993, April). *The workingman's constant companion: The pin-up advertising calendar and sexual harassment in*

the workplace. A paper presented to the annual conference of the American Academy of Advertising, Montreal, Canada.

5. See Hirschman, E., & Stern, B. (1998). Consumer behavior and the wayward mind: The influence of mania and depression on consumption. *Advances in Consumer Research, 25,* 421-427.

6. See Lavin, M., & Archdeacon, T. (1989). The relevance of historical method for marketing research. In E. Hirschman (Ed.), *Interpretive consumer research.* Provo, UT: Association for Consumer Research.

7. See Denzin, N. (1989). *Interpretive biography.* Newbury Park, CA: Sage.

8. From Creswell, J. (1998). *Qualitative inquiry and research design: Choosing among five traditions* (pp. 50-51). Thousand Oaks, CA: Sage.

9. See Hirschman, E. (1992). The consciousness of addiction: Toward a general theory of compulsive consumption. *Journal of Consumer Research, 19,* 155-179.

10. From Sayre, S. (1999). Using introspective self-narrative to analyze consumption: Experiencing plastic surgery. *Consumption Markets & Culture, 3*(2), 99-128.

7 Using the Case Method

Most of us who study marketing or communications have been introduced to case studies, probably prepared by the Harvard Business School, as a way to learn about the world of business. A written description of a company's situation at a specific point in time, case studies are written most often to provide an opportunity for applying a concept or theory to a particular business situation. Cases are a popular form of learning because they illuminate the analytical anomalies of business problems.

Case Writing as Research Technique

Case studies can be qualitative or quantitative. We are most interested in those employing naturalistic, culture-based data collection methods. The case is a closed and integrated system of patterned behaviors. We use three types of cases for research purposes:[1] An *intrinsic case study* is undertaken for a better understanding of a particular topic of interest rather than of theory building or understanding of a phenomenon. An *instrumental case study* is examined to provide insight into an issue or to refine a theory; the case is secondary as it facilitates our understanding of something else. *Collective case studies,* several instrumental studies conducted independently, are chosen because they may lead to better understanding of larger issues.

Case studies are one of the most underused tools in marketplace scholarship. Included among the benefits,

Case studies provide descriptions of a situation faced by a company or consumer. Cases bring the corporate environment to practitioners and students who cannot personally investigate issues.

Case studies enhance the application, testing, or generation of a theory. Researchers enter the case environment with a question in mind, which may or may not change during the course of preparing the case analysis.

Case studies incorporate a variety of data collection and analysis activities. Single or multiple researchers, qualitative and quantitative data, and archival information provide effective triangulation.

Television documentaries and legal cases are also examples of the case study approach to understanding something unique. Uniqueness is extended to the nature of the case, its historical background, its physical setting, and its informants, through whom the case is known. Holistic case study[2] calls for the examination of complexities—such as subsections, groups, occasions, and domains—to dramatize the coincidence of events. After identifying topical concerns, researchers pose problems that may occur. By concentrating on issue-related observations, we see patterns of data emerge that re-form the issues. This process of issue development is illustrated in the following example using Rainbow Technology, a computer software company with an e-commerce problem.

Topical issue: The impact of the Internet on purchasing and customer service

Anticipated problems: Online consumers perceive e-commerce as a "faceless" salesperson that minimizes positive contact between buyer and seller.

Issue under development: How can purchasing over the Internet be structured most effectively to keep sales and distribution costs minimized while increasing customer service?

Assertion: Order fulfillment can be structured to enhance customer service and sales efficiency.

Preparing to Research

The Rainbow Technology case is based on research conducted on site in Southern California at a company that manufactures Internet security products for end users. Once the issues were developed, the researcher took the following steps **to prepare the story** of Rainbow Technologies:

1. Contact the company. The public relations officer was called to explain the study objectives and needs, such as number of meetings, records, and interviews. The researcher requested 3 weeks on site, two group meetings, access to customer ordering data, and interviews with the vice-chairman, chief technical officer, public relations specialist, director of sales, and six members of the e-commerce marketing department.

2. Collect background information. The normal procedure is to check out Internet sites and articles written on the company prior to a visit to speed up the process of understanding the company and identifying what type of information will need to be gathered. In this case, a Rainbow employee who was a friend of the researcher provided much of the company's background information before the first meeting.

3. Collect data on site. The researcher interviewed company officers and employees and read company publications (newsletters, annual report, advertising, customer feedback e-mails, etc). Data were collected from customers, sales representatives, online sales reports, and the researcher, who had firsthand experience with on-line ordering systems.

4. Analyze the data. The researcher reviewed notes and transcripts with careful scrutiny until patterns emerged and options for solutions appeared.

5. Write up the case story. Using the standard elements of a case to present the story, the researcher's narrative flowed from the general to the specific.

Collecting Case Data[3]

Case research relies on five key sources to provide information:

1. Company archives: Most organizations have records of their financial, human resource, marketing, legal, and corporate philosophy information. They may also have files on competitors' advertising campaigns, market share data, effectiveness studies, and so forth. Data come in both electronic and paper formats and are essential for learning about the company under study.

2. Literature: Previous research helps the case developer generate research questions and hypotheses; it can help identify consistencies and conflicts of data generated through the case development process.

3. Questionnaire: Written questions are appropriate when interviews are not possible or a large number of responses are necessary. Usually containing unstructured and open-ended questions, these questions require some analytic skills to decode.

4. Interviews: Key personnel provide in-depth understanding of perspectives and may uncover organizational conflict. Well-prepared interview protocols yield the best information; results depend on insightful interpretation.

5. Observations: When the researcher acts as a participant in the phenomena studied, observations are a powerful tool for understanding process and levels of conflict within organizations.

Table 7.1 Analysis Alternatives Within Case Studies[1]

Variables	Alternatives	Example
Number of observations	Single or multiple cases	Most cases focus on a single company; however, most case studies contain an analysis of the competitive environment or commentary on other cases.
Issue level	Strategic or tactical	Strategic: brand positioning Tactical: evaluation of advertising media vehicles
Structural level	Industry or firm	Most cases analyze the behavior of a single firm. Cases can focus on an industry, such as the role of advertising in the coffee industry.
Audiences	Internal	Top and middle management
	External	Customers, regulatory agencies

Case Analysis Methods

Researchers have a variety of analytic approaches to case studies. Table 7.1 presents an overview of the case variables and alternatives and examples.

Writing the Case: Rainbow Technologies[4]

Case writing has no standard format, but certain elements are found in most case studies prepared as research projects. Excerpts that begin each section of the case follow to better acquaint you with the writing process.

Introduction: Set up your audience and interest them in the situation.

We've been told that we're part of a technology generation and that soon we'll be doing everything from scheduling vacations to ordering groceries on-line. Those of us who order through the Internet may not be as convinced that technology are [sic] the best solution to purchasing. One company that uses the Internet to sell its products found that its customers were among the doubters and decided to enhance the interactive experience to erase those doubts.

The Internet and the World Wide Web have brought many changes to the business landscape and will bring many more. The omnipresent nature of the Internet and the Web defines the "New World" of electronic commerce. The impact of e-commerce—buying and selling over the Internet—spans international boundaries and crosses sector differences.

The popularity of e-commerce is of increasing importance for the marketing communicator in today's commercial environment. There is a mounting concern, however, that e-commerce is a "faceless" salesperson and that it severely minimizes the contact between the consumer and the marketer. Companies are attempting to use the Internet as a means by which to actually improve customer service and capture more information by direct consumer-sales representative interaction. This is the story of one such company's efforts at efficient order fulfillment through exceptional customer service.

The setting: Present information about the company and the situation.

Founded in 1984 by a team of seven technology specialists, Rainbow Technology begins by producing software protection devices (hardware dangle) to prevent software from being copied or illegally distributed. Three years later, it is publicly listed on NASDAQ. In 1994 they launch Internet Security Group (ISG) to produce *CryptoSwift,* a product that enables Rainbow to take advantage of the rapid adaptation of the Internet for e-mailing, file transfer, and messaging. Now its leading revenue earner, *CrypotSwift* positions ISG to take advantage of the increasing demand for secure information transfer across the Internet. They focus on banking and finance, health, student records, insurance, tax, travel, and other e-commerce environments. Today, Rainbow's revenues are over $110 million and it has 350 employees with headquarters in Irvine, California, and offices in Canada, France, Germany, China, The Netherlands, India, Russia, Belarus, and the UK. The company has distributors in fifty countries and a customer base of 30,000 worldwide.

The industry: Describe events and trends occurring in the company's industry.

The onset of personal computer use causes an explosion of software, which in turn inspires a technological revolution. In March and April of 1998, Yahoo! and MCI announce branded Internet access, Yahoo! launches an Internet telephone service with IDT, and Netscape announces its formation of a new unit focused on its Web site business. Yahoo!'s stock passes the $100 per share mark, and the Internet Advertising Bureau announces that Internet ad spending reached $906 million in 1997, up 240% from the year before. Investments in Internet-related companies double to $1.8 billion, and the U.S. Commerce Department announces that information technology is growing twice as fast as the overall economy. Internet commerce among businesses is expected to surpass $300 billion by 2002! A very productive two months indeed. Rainbow responds to this explosion with e-commerce.

The problem: Set up the issues that will drive the case story.

In response to customer demand for an electronic means to place orders for hardware products, Rainbow establishes its e-commerce system in 1998. Customers locate the site via industry advertising and trade shows. Industry events are geared toward secure information transfer and e-commerce audiences who have explicit needs for secure Web server performance acceleration.

Orders are placed using the company web site (http://isg.rainbow.com) to view photographs of CryptoSwift's three product types. A price-information box lists three pricing levels with product specifications and performance data for selecting the most appropriate product for customer speed and throughput requirements. After making their selection, customers click on the "order now" icon and are taken to the Product Secure On-Line Ordering page. This page includes a disclaimer for export restriction requirements, requests billing information, and presents payment options. A "comments" box is included for special instructions, questions, and requests. Upon completion, the customer clicks on the "submit" icon and then sees an acknowledgment of receipt. This form is electronically sent through to the gatekeeper in the marketing department for e-commerce orders, who ensures that a sales person responds immediately by fax or email to confirm the order.

At this point, a sales person asks important questions so they can provide customers with further information, "moments of truth," or opportunities to connect with the customer in a positive manner. As part of an ongoing analysis of the on-line ordering model, a review of the service is conducted during January, February, and March of 1999 to measure the level of customer satisfaction with the current system and to identify the need for improvements.

Transcripts of customer and sales personnel interviews are analyzed for themes and categories and reveal five issues of concern about the ordering process: 1) ease of access, 2) accuracy, 3) contact through a post-order message, 4) comparisons for performance evaluation, and 5) product files and white papers. The area of most concern is identified as *a lack of human contact* after the order is placed to answer questions and recognize the customer.

Study transcripts confirm the importance of human contact in the ordering process. Management has two options to correct the problem identified by the interviews: hire more sales representatives to personally confirm customer orders or add an 800 line to the current system for customers to call sales representatives with specific questions. Direct access to sales representatives is more costly, and an 800 number is more efficient. The marketing manager is responsible for deciding which option to implement.

The outcome: The researcher examines the results of company action to resolve the problem. (In cases prepared for teaching, this section is omitted and students are asked to select a decision action and provide a rationale for their choice.) Here is an abbreviation of the Rainbow problem solution:

Preference for immediate personal contact with customers prompts the marketing manager to institute a policy of personal phone calling to confirm orders. Telephone dialogue will help build rapport, gain trust, address specific concerns, and understand what new features are needed for product development. Both customers and sales representatives feel that the on-line ordering system cannot fully replace the traditional sales/customer relationship, especially in the area of personal dialogue. After the calling policy is enforced, the study is replicated, and results, which reveal high levels of customer satisfaction with the new policy, validate the notion that human interactions improve customer service.

Troubleshooting Problems[5]

Case writing enables a researcher to learn how to approach a problem or situation, to gain familiarity with different businesses and industries, and to realize the importance of situation analysis for problem solving. Of the problems encountered by case writers, the following three are the most common:

1. *The case contains too little information.* The idea is not to report every detail but to provide enough information for making intelligent decisions. In the case of Rainbow, the reader receives the results of a study of customer satisfaction to highlight the problem.

2. *The case focuses on a single issue.* It's difficult to write a case about a broad range of issues. Decide what you want to investigate and focus on it. Rainbow also has problems with competition for its security software, but this researcher only addressed the customer service-related problem for this case.

3. *The writer must think about the reader.* Clear, accurate, and interesting writing is a must. Use subheads to guide the reader, include tables and exhibits, and write in an informal style for ease of reading. Survey results of the Rainbow study are presented in tables in the original case and include anecdotes and interesting quotes from interviews.

Last

The Internet is fast becoming a communications infrastructure with the advantages of speed, availability, and a "different time, different place" mode. It is now possible to conduct case studies and surveys electronically via e-mail without the necessity of face-to-face meetings, and interviewees can respond in their own timeframes. File transfer protocol is a cheaper alternative to recording and transcribing interviews, and intercontinental case studies are possible when interviewer and interviewee are in electronic mail contact. Internet case studies have three phases: (a) preparation phase, to build knowledge, questionnaires, and a list of respondents; (b) correspondence phase, to establish virtual relationships, complete questionnaires, and do supplementary reading; and (c) documentation phase, for analysis, drafting, and feedback.[6] This method for carrying out case studies via the Internet may be a useful template for future researcher.

Summary

1. A case is an in-depth description of a marketing situation faced by an industry or organization that involves strategy and decision-making actions.

2. The case information is collected by the author/researcher, organized to meet one or more learning objectives, and produced in a paper or electronic format.

3. Company collateral materials, published articles, archival materials, interviews, and observations are data collection techniques used to prepare a case study.

4. Case data analysis variables include the number of observations, issue level, structural level, and intended audiences for the case.

5. Case writing formats typically include an introduction, company history, industry trends, problem, and solution sections.

Stretching Exercises

1. Prepare an issue development outline for a case study using Internet resources to select and research a small company. Define the topical issue, foreshadow a problem, state the issue under development, and provide an assertion.

2. Identify a marketing problem (e.g., brand image) and locate five companies that would be appropriate for a multiple-case approach to the problem. Provide a rationale for your choices.

Recommended Readings
About the Case Study Model

Lincoln, Y. S., & Guba, E. G. (1985). *Naturalistic inquiry.* Beverly Hills, CA: Sage.

Stake, R. E. (1995). *The art of case study research.* Thousand Oaks, CA: Sage.

Yin, R.K. (1989). *Case study research: Design and method.* Newbury Park, CA: Sage.

Case in Point: Wyland's Whales[7]

Client: ArtWalk Gallery Association

Problem: Understanding the role of local art star for generating tourism revenues

RQ: *How do local artists market themselves to tourists?*

Background: Wyland is a renowned painter of whale murals throughout the U.S., Canada, and Japan. He also produces life-sized public art featuring marine animals, especially whales and porpoises, and advocates natural habitat protection for sea creatures. Wyland's 200-person organization is family run out of Laguna Beach, California, home of three galleries and a cafe. Producer of over 300 works each year, much of his art results from mass production and relies on anonymous craftspeople to meet tourist demands for new pieces. At 43, Wyland has 48 galleries worldwide that carry his name and 86 whaling walls, painted for free, to publicize his art. The study, which is a profile of this artist and his business strategy, is made to identify marketing strategies and techniques that have proven successful for this artist to apply to other artists seeking to achieve similar success.

Data Collection: During a 2-month period during the summer tourist season in a seaside resort, the researcher investigated the $100 million business. The researcher made observations of gallery visitors and conducted interviews with tourists, art consultants, gallery owners, art critics, and the artist himself. She gathered promotional documents; studied gallery visuals and artifacts, articles written about the artist, and critical reviews; viewed promotional videos; and visited the artist's Web site.

Data Analysis: Interviews were transcribed and thematic sorting was used to analyze the narratives. Collateral materials were analyzed for quality, style, readability, and visual appeal. Gallery space and Web site were analyzed for user-friendliness and visual appeal. Sales transactions were evaluated for buyer-seller interactivity and outcome. Newspaper and magazine articles, video footage, and art reviews were categorized according to content and impact. Two informants who were gallery employees reviewed the conclusions for accuracy and authenticity.

Results: The case yielded a profile of an artist as art star that identified seven components used by the artist to achieve success:

1. Maintenance of identification with and residence in a tourist destination from which visitors may purchase artifacts

2. Establishment of a unique artistic style that is easily adaptable to multiple media

3. Development of that style into a recognizable brand

4. Association with a societal or environmental message that evokes emotion from the tourist destination audience demographic

5. Production of brand extensions, licensing, and distribution rights

6. Alliance with religious, social, and political advocates of the adopted message

7. Careful integration of advertising, press coverage, marketing, and community relations programs

Discussion: The success of this artist and his company is a result of shrewd business practices, dedicated family participants, and a tourist space with an identity that complements his environmental concerns and conceptual subject matter. Tourists like his brand of art, buy it, take it home, and through it, relive their trip. Wyland's art serves the purpose of a memory jogger for tourists who spend time in Laguna Beach. Art stars such as Wyland enable destination visitors to experience a *materialistic embolism:* Their purchase combines shopping, bargaining, acquisition, aesthetics, possession, and exhibition into a single engagement activity. The experience is the culmination of their journey—a purchased commodity fulfills their quest for the authentic and becomes their entertainment within a comfortable and familiar geographic context.

Conclusion: Mutual dependence between seller and buyer is the business of tourism. Tourists are as instrumental in creating art stars as they are in creating tourist art. Like his art star counterparts throughout the globe, Wyland provides tourists with the consumption service without which their trips could not be consummated. This study provides a glimpse into marketing art and art stars to tourists. Although this is just one case, it is indicative of similar art in similar tourist situations and can serve as a model to study the phenomenon.

Notes

1. See Stake, R. E. (1989). Case studies. In N. Denzin & Y. Lincoln (Eds.), *Handbook of qualitative research* (pp. 236-247). Newbury Park, CA: Sage.

2. See Guba, E., & Lincoln, Y. (1989). Competing paradigms in qualitative research. In N. Denzin & Y. Lincoln (Eds.), *Handbook of qualitative research* (pp. 105-117). Newbury Park, CA: Sage.

3. Adapted from a presentation made by C. Patti to the annual conference of the American Academy of Advertising, August 1993, Montreal, Canada.

4. Based on research written by Haysom, I. (1988). *A case study of effects of e-commerce on customer service.* Unpublished master's thesis, California State University, Fullerton.

5. From advertising case notes by C. Patti, Professor of Marketing, Queensland University of Technology, Brisbane, Australia.

6. See Chadwick, D. W. (1996). A method for collecting case study information via the Internet. *IEEE Network, 10*(2), 36-39.

7. Sayre, S. (2000, October). *Tourism, art stars and consumption: Wyland's whales.* Paper presented to the annual meeting of the Association of Consumer Research, Salt Lake City, UT.

8 Phenomenology and Grounded Theory

These two models are presented together because one is an extension of the other, and they use very similar data collection methods. The difference is that phenomenology begins with a research question, and grounded theory is conducted to discover a research question for testing. Phenomenologies describe the meanings of *lived experiences* for multiple consumers about a concept or phenomenon, whereas the intent of grounded theory study is to generate or discover a theory. Text from both methods can be interpreted by a philosophical approach called *hermeneutics*. This approach is briefly explained for its relevance to both conceptual models presented in this chapter.

Phenomenological Learning

There may always be another reality to make fiction of the truth we think we've arrived at.

—Christopher Fry, 1970

With beginnings in psychology and philosophy, phenomenology was first used in a study of high school students that asked them to describe situations when they felt understood by someone. An analysis of 356 descriptions yielded rich characterizations of feeling understood and identified persons who were most likely to be trusted by those students. This approach involves gathering personal experiences to obtain descriptions that portray the essence of that experience.

In the marketplace, a phenomenological approach seeks to learn about and elaborate on a behavioral or consumption phenomenon as it manifests itself for consumers. This can be accomplished in two ways:[1] (a) gathering data of consumers' *native descriptions,* as obtained through open-ended questions and dialogue, and (b) describing the experience based on reflective analysis and interpretation of consumers' accounts or stories. In both cases, the aim of the research is to determine what consumption experiences mean for the people who have had them and who are able to provide comprehensive descriptions.

The four main points are as follows:

A researcher searches for the essential or underlying meaning of an experience.

A phenomenology emphasizes the experiences containing both outward appearance and inward consciousness, based on memory, image, and meaning.

Specific statements and *themes* are analyzed for all possible meanings.

The researcher sets aside all prejudgments to rely on intuition and imagination to obtain a picture of the experience.

This model requires researchers to understand the philosophical concept of *epoche,* the suspension of judgments about what is real, to understand the phenomenon through consumer voices. By assuming a natural attitude, the research allows discovery to provide a more certain basis of understanding.

Asking for Information

Phenomenology also requires the researcher to seek meaning by asking consumers to describe their everyday *lived experiences.* Information is collected from between 5 and 25 consumers during long interviews. The phenomenological interview involves an informal, interactive process and uses open-ended comments and questions. The interviewer is responsible for creating a climate in which the consumer will feel comfortable and will respond honestly and comprehensively.

Interviewing[2] always begins with a broad statement. During a study conducted to understand how women buy their first car, the interviewer began like this: "Try and remember your first thoughts and feelings about buying a new car." From that point on, the interviewer has no a priori questions concerning the topic. The dialogue tends to be circular rather than linear; the descriptive questions flow from the course of the dialogue and not from a predetermined script. The interview is intended to yield a conversation, not be a question-and-answer session. Consumer dialogues are called "native descriptions" because they result from a free-flowing narration of a consumer's thoughts. Here is an example of a woman's thoughts about buying a car on her own for the first time:

> I was really kind of nervous, you know, about going into a showroom. I felt like a minnow in shark-infested waters with all those salesmen and all. So I put on my "look tough" outfit, threw my shoulders back, and marched into the dealership. I hate it when they look at you like you don't know what's up. Sure enough, the eyes

of at least four greedy-looking men stare at me as I walked in. At first, I avoid their eyes and just look at the cars. The ones inside. But I don't see the model I wanted. I knew I have to ask one of them to help. Purposefully, I look in the direction of the youngest man I see and smile. Young ones don't think you're as stupid as the older ones. Right away, he comes over. I try to act nonchalant, but I started to stumble over my words. Damn, I thought, he'll think I'm a fool. Turns out, he was the fool. I was ready to buy and all he did was run back and forth to his manager, making me crazy. I decide to take a test drive and order on the Internet. So much for bravery . . . I flunked the test. Wish there were women car sellers . . . I'd feel much better about trying again.

Interviewers are urged to avoid "why" questions because they shift the focus of the dialogue away from describing the experience to a more abstract discussion. "Can you tell me about" questions work well for probing further into the person's experiences. An extensive discussion of depth interviews is presented in Chapter 12. The main point to remember about this model is that a phenomenology consists of multiple descriptions of experiences, not explanations or analyses. Notice how the description retains the original texture of the experience and keeps it alive to accentuate underlying meanings.

Deciphering Meanings

To make sense of a series of narratives, consumers' transcript protocols are divided into statements, transforming them into *clusters of meaning* or *themes*. Then the researcher prepares a textual description of *what* was experienced (entering a showroom) and a structural description of *how* it was experienced (suspiciously, fearfully). The final report provides clients with an understanding of how these consumers feel when they experience their first automobile purchase.

Analysis of 14 interviews with women about their first car purchasing experiences revealed several clusters of meaning. These clusters are thoughts about the topic from numerous transcripts. For instance, descriptions of the first encounter with a salesmen indicated that women feel intimidated by male salespeople. They think men perceive them to be dumb or naive about car shopping. So the presence of males in the showroom means discomfort to many women buying their first cars. A report on buying a car was prepared for the Ford Motor Company, which is aggressively recruiting female salespeople to avoid the negative encounters described by women experiencing the first-purchase phenomenon.

Anticipating Problems

Conducting a phenomenology is extremely difficult for some researchers because it requires a solid grounding in the philosophical precepts of the model.

Researchers must select study participants carefully to make certain that they have experienced the phenomenon under study and are willing to discuss it at length. Four participating dealerships identified potential candidates for our study during their initial visits to a showroom. Achieving epoche may be difficult for novice researchers. The interviewer of these 14 women had to suspend his views about female purchasing experiences to learn about and understand their reality.

Grounded Theory

Strive not to laugh at human actions, nor to weep at them, nor to hate them, but to understand them.

—B. Spinzoa, 1664

Inductively derived from the study of the phenomenon it represents, grounded theory is discovered, developed, and verified through systematic data collection and analysis. Grounded theory is used to explore phenomena within their own terms of reference; it is not intended to yield ultimate solutions for world problems but rather as a means to contribute to a continuing body of work in a field.

Concerns of grounded theory methodology include:

Importance of theory, grounded in reality

Need for field study

Nature of experience as continually evolving

Active role of consumers in shaping the world they live in

Emphasis on process and change

Interrelationships among conditions, meaning, and action

Grounded theory methods are particularly appropriate when the purpose of the research is to discover consumer-based constructs and theories. Here, researchers look for key patterns or relationships in the data, engaging in grounded readings that allow patterns to emerge from the data to direct researchers toward literature that may help them to interpret those patterns. The analysis continues as the researcher moves between observed empirical evidence and established concepts to construct a novel perspective of the phenomenon being studied.

Grounded theory must meet four central criteria for judging the applicability of theory to a phenomenon: *fit* (the area where it will be used), *understandability* (by lay people), *generality* (for multiple applications), and *control* (over the situation as it changes).[3] The difference between theory and description is that theory uses *concepts*. Similar data are grouped and labeled by the researcher who interprets the data. Concepts are related by *statements of relationship*. In descriptions, data are organized according to *themes*. Themes are summaries of words taken from the data but not interpreted. Themes are used to organize data that are analyzed for relationship to form concepts at a later time. The difference resides in the level of analysis and stage in the research process.

Data transcription should be selective. Analysis for grounded theory research follows a logical procedure that begins with transcribing and analyzing the first interviews and field notes before going on to the next set. Early coding gives guidance for interviews that follow. In later stages, you listen to interview tapes for specific portions that relate to your theory development.

Building Questions Through Research

A research question in a grounded theory study is a statement that identifies the phenomenon to be studied. Questions are oriented toward action and process. Suppose you are interested in studying how families organize their lives following a natural disaster. Your question might read: How do families replace (repurchase) possessions after losing them to natural disaster? The question tells us the study will investigate families and that they have suffered loss. The study will also look at purchase process to identify decision makers and influencers.

We look at purchasing from the family's perspective, not the retailers' or manufacturers' who are selling product. It is also important to investigate what merchants do for families because these actions may influence how families manage their purchasing. Understanding how and to what extent family actions are influenced by others is only part of what we want to find out. The study focus is on families, and keeping that in mind prevents researchers from getting sidetracked.

We might also want to probe other areas for a better understanding of the repurchasing process. Three types of questions can be used for this purpose:

1. *Interactive questions* can be used to ask, "What communications take place between your family and retailers? Between family members? With the media?" and so forth.

2. *Organizational questions* focus on the broader issues, such as "What procedures are required by your insurance company for repurchasing household items?"

3. "How have you coped emotionally with the trauma?" is a *biological question* to illuminate the mental state of survivors as they consider purchases.

Researchers come to a situation with varying degrees of sensitivity and knowledge of the phenomenon under study, depending on their background and relevant experience. One researcher was himself a survivor and had empathy; another had experience with relatives and friends who were victims of natural disaster. These sensitivities gave them an advantage for question development.

Creativity is essential in this type of research to maintain a sense of distance and perspective. Researchers break through assumptions and create new order. You develop skills in naming categories rather than making lists, you let your mind wander and make free associations, you generate stimulating questions and come up with interesting comparisons. You can increase creativity by stepping back and asking, "What's going on here?" How are these people recreating their lives—are they duplicating the brands they had, or are they making different brand choices? You must also maintain an attitude of skepticism and validate your questions about categories and assumptions about the data you collect.

We projected that durable goods purchases were not duplications but upgrades. We made certain we had evidence to support this supposition. By following the research procedure closely, we alternated between data collection and analysis to allow concepts to emerge as relevant. Revision and change drive the collection and analysis process. Coding procedures ensure that your conclusions are founded on evidence, not conjecture.

Layers of Understanding

Open coding, a process of breaking down, examining, comparing, conceptualizing, and categorizing data is discussed in detail in Chapter 15. Suffice it to say that we use four coding procedures: labeling phenomena, discovering and naming categories, developing those categories in terms of their properties and dimensions, and writing code notes. The basic procedures are asking questions about the data and making comparisons for similarities and differences between each incident and event in the phenomenon.

Axial coding, where the investigator assembles the data in new ways after open coding, is the next step. In *selective coding,* the researcher identifies a "story line" and writes a story that integrates the categories in the axial coding model. The process concludes with a conditional matrix to visually portray the social or economic conditions influencing the phenomenon.

Studying disaster victims using grounded theory allows researchers to explore the same group in different ways. Use testimonial comparisons to probe deeper and deeper until the process is understood.

Using a Hermeneutic Approach

Consumer research now acknowledges the profound role culture plays in shaping behavior. Gender roles, mass media images, rituals, and traditions are a few of the cultural factors that influence consumer experiences. One approach to the study of consumer meaning is a hermeneutic perspective.[4] This perspective argues that a person's understanding of his or her life experiences reflects broad cultural viewpoints as they are expressed through language or retained as self-interpretations. Hermeneutics seeks to highlight an often unspoken background of socially shared meanings to reveal how cultural viewpoints are adapted to the consumer's unique life situation. Access to the person-culture dialogue provides researchers with a useful framework for interpreting the text of depth interviews. The approach also demonstrates important linkages between consumption activities and the construction of one's self-image.

Circles of Meaning

The hermeneutic view differs from more traditional ones because it suggests that preconceptions serve a positive rather than a negative function and that they provide a necessary frame of reference rather than act as biases that hinder understanding. Hermeneutic research assumes that a shared context of meanings exists between the researcher and the consumer. This "fusion of horizons" is conceptualized in Figure 8.1.

Similar to the techniques used in grounded theory to collect interview data, a hermeneutic dialogue agenda is set by the consumer. After an initial general question, the interviewer uses probes and follow-up questions to get clarification and elaboration of the experience being described by the consumer. Interpretations proceed by means of the continuous part-to-whole and whole-to-part movement, as well as back and forth movement that is characteristic of grounded theory discovery methods.

A key aspect of the interpretive logic is the identification of a symbolic metaphor in each interview text. The metaphor is an exemplary image or event that conveys assumptions, concerns, values, and meanings that regularly occur in the dialogue. The *symbolic metaphor* plays the same role in hermeneutic analysis as *themes* play in phenomenological and grounded theory analysis, as described earlier. Themes stand for themselves, where as metaphors stand for something else, thus the interjection of meaning into transcript dialogue interpretations.

Researchers study consumption chart transcripts for metaphors. We can see how the charting process works by using the dialogues of three women as they describe a consumption experience; they show three metaphoric perspectives:[5]

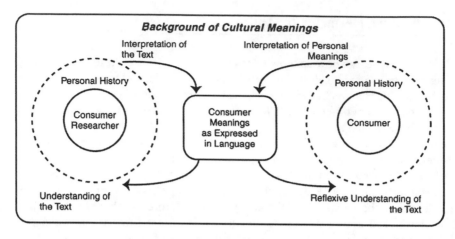

Figure 8.1. Fusion of Horizons

SOURCE: From Thompson, C., Pollio, H., & Locander, W. (1994, p. 434). Reprinted with permission.

skeptical, nostalgic, and pragmatic. The skeptical woman interprets commercialized products as presenting attractive images that do not always correspond to actual benefits. Her symbolic metaphor is a television commercial:

> For 9 months, I have used all these cleaning products that said the same thing in their TV commercials. But they really only do surface cleaning. My floor looked like it had not been mopped for 6 months.

The nostalgic perspective of the second woman manifests itself as an "antique" metaphor. Antiques exemplify the meaning of lasting value and symbolize an era when people cared about making things that would last:

> When I buy things, I buy antiques because I don't find the quality in things today. Not like the things that were your mother's or your grandmother's or something. I went to the store to buy a blow dryer and they said, "Well, you're lucky if it lasts a year." That's what I was told.

Pragmatism, the third woman's perspective, yields a "game" metaphor:

> What I like to do is, if a store has Fab on sale for $1.29, I'll buy six of them this week and then the next week I don't buy it. It's the kind of game I play with myself. It usually averages out to be pretty much the same weekly tab, about $140.00.

As we interpret symbolic metaphors, we become aware that the self-interpretations expressed by consumers reflect unique perspectives of the meaning of shopping, brand names, promotional information, and the relation of consumption activities to their own self-identities. The logic of *intertextual analysis*—which offers insights into the sociocultural meanings that underlie consumer orientations—is explained further in Chapter 15.

Hermeneutics is appropriate for analyzing narrative text that is collected during interviews as part of the five models discussed in this text. It is one of many philosophical and methodological approaches to understanding meanings, both stated and implied, that are contained in consumer dialogue.

Summary

1. The aim of phenomenology is to determine what consumption experiences mean to the people who have them and who can provide a comprehensive description of them.

2. Phenomenology requires the researcher to explore the meaning of a consumer's experience through descriptions of their everyday lived experiences.

3. Grounded theory methods are particularly appropriate when the purpose of the research is to discover consumer-based constructs and theories.

4. Grounded theory must meet four central criteria for judging the applicability of theory to a phenomenon: fit, understandability, generality, and control.

5. Both phenomenology and grounded theory use depth interviews to collect dialogue-texts that are analyzed for themes and clusters of meaning.

6. Hermeneutics seeks to highlight an often unspoken background of socially shared meanings to reveal how cultural viewpoints are adapted to the consumer's unique life situation.

7. The symbolic metaphor plays the same role in hermeneutic analysis as themes play in phenomenological and grounded theory analysis, as described.

Stretching Exercises

1. Develop two ideas that are appropriate for study using phenomenology and two for grounded theory. Explain what differences exist in each approach.

2. Trace the origins of hermeneutics for recent application to consumer research. What practical value does hermeneutics have for marketing managers?

Recommended Readings About Phenomenology and Grounded Theory

Glaser, B. G. (1992). *Basics of grounded theory analysis.* Mill Valley, CA: Sociology Press.

Moustakas, C. (1994). *Phenomenological research methods.* Thousand Oaks, CA: Sage.

Ricoeur, P. (1981). *Hermeneutics and the social sciences.* Cambridge, UK: Cambridge University Press.

Strauss, A. (1987). *Qualitative analysis for social scientists.* New York: Cambridge University Press.

Strauss, A., & Corbin, J. (1990). *Basics of qualitative research: Grounded theory procedures and techniques.* Newbury Park, CA: Sage.

Case in Point: Moviegoers' Interpretations of Brands in Films— A Grounded Theory Investigation[6]

Client: International consumer goods manufacturer

Problem: Determining how effective brand placement is for advertising dollars

RQ: *How are brand props interpreted in everyday lived experiences of movie audiences?*

Data Collection: Collection involved listening, observing, occasional note taking, and audiotaping.

- Eight focus groups were formed for informant reaction within social interactive situations; focus groups were unstructured and primarily self-managed.

- Thirty depth interviews were held to gather accounts of audience-based experiences with movie brand props, including how those experiences are interpreted in relation to movies, movie viewing, other media content, and other viewing situations. Interviews took the form of informal conversations with friends in which empathy, trust, and understanding were shared.

The sample included 20 younger (18-21) frequent moviegoers and 30 younger infrequent moviegoers, 23 older (35-48) frequent moviegoers, and 26 older infrequent moviegoers.

Data Analysis: Interviews were transcribed and coded at the open, axial, and selective levels used in grounded theory research.

Emerging themes and concepts were checked by respondent verifications for the accuracy of their testimony as it was transcribed.

Results: Themes of movie centrality and consumption-specific themes were uncovered during transcript analysis. Greater distinctions in experience and interpretations emerged between older frequent and infrequent moviegoers than between younger frequent and infrequent moviegoers.

Discussion: Three interrelated themes of *movie centrality* emerged from the data of moviegoers: (a) appreciating realism, (b) noticing the familiar, and (c) relating to characters.

1. Brand props are significant because they add realism to the stylistic aspect of movie scenery. They are especially effective to note a specific time period. However, moviegoers dislike inappropriate brand props that clash with their expectations of movie scenery.

2. Moviegoers were particularly attuned to familiar branded products and services that they had previously purchased and consumed in their everyday lives. Younger audiences felt a sense of reassurance from familiar brands that fostered a relaxed viewing experience.

3. Both groups stated that brand placement is significant because it provides relevant information about the character's personality, lifestyle, and role in the movie plot. These placements also enable informants to empathize with and relate to characters and further involved them in the movie. Character associations also contribute to viewers' own self-perceptions. Character usage of a particular brand also influences brand purchase for younger audiences ("I like Baby Ruth because it was in *The Groonies*").

Four themes emerged from *consumption-specific* relevance: (a) tools for purchasing decisions, (b) tools for identity and aspirations, (c) change and discomfort, and (d) belonging and security.

1. Brand props reinforced consumer confidence, reduced cognitive dissonance, and acted as symbols of distrust. They assisted in providing useful purchase-related choice, like product identification, and name recognition. Older moviegoers expressed distrust of brands placed in films and interpreted them in relation to their own consumption experiences apart from viewing interpretations.

2. Moviegoers compare their consumption worlds with those depicted in films. Brands enable further understanding and appreciation of viewers' social worlds. Exposure to previously purchased brands reinforces their identities.

3. To older viewers, brands represented signs of cultural change and feelings of concern. They also equated brand props with negative consequences for the viewing public, especially children.

4. Younger moviegoers who grew up with brands in movies think brand props are an invitation to belong and evoke feelings of emotional security. Brands foster sharing of experiences between viewers and characters, providing a common bond for self and group identification.

The study reinforces the notion that audience members are not passive consumers of media persuasion but are active producers of perceived meaning. What audience members do with brand props is what is important here. Brand placements are interpreted as part of the audience's ongoing everyday experience that come to life as a reflection of moviegoers' past, present, and anticipated experiences.

Six working hypotheses came from the research that can be used to direct future research.

Conclusion: The study has specific implications for marketers, especially advertising agencies, who place brands in films. Practitioners should acknowledge the potential long-term nature of brand placement on memory. They should closely examine brand placement and its synergistic relationships with other types of brand exposures that occur in the consumer environment. Practitioners also need to monitor the treatment of brands carefully within the context of particular films and to study audience experiences and interpretations of those conditions. Brand props do not uniformly influence moviegoers; it is wise to consider individual and international differences when planning placements. Brand placement operates within a dynamic, changing environment where the overuse of props may heighten moviegoers' resistance to persuasion.

Notes

1. From Moustakas, C. (1994). *Phenomenological research methods.* Thousand Oaks, CA: Sage.

2. For an in-depth presentation of phenomenology, see Thompson, C., Locander, W., & Pollio, H. (1989, September). Putting consumer experience back into consumer research: The philosophy and method of existential-phenomenology. *Journal of Consumer Research, 16,* 133-146.

3. For an explanation, see Glaser, B., & Strauss, A. (1967). *The discovery of grounded theory: Strategies for qualitative research.* Chicago: Aldine.

4. See Thompson, C., Pollio, H., & Locander, W. (1994, December). The spoken and the unspoken: A hermeneutic approach to understanding the cultural viewpoints that underlie consumers' expressed meanings. *Journal of Consumer Research, 21,* 432-452.

5. Thompson et al. (1994). See Note 4.

6. Based on a study conducted by DeLorme, D., & Reid, L. (1999). Moviegoers' experiences and interpretations of brands in films revisited. *Journal of Advertising, 28*(2), 71-95.

9 Using an Ethnographic Approach

Ethnography: A Primer

Marketplace ethnography is the art and science of describing a company, target audience, or consumer culture. Ethnographers draw on skills from investigative reporting or criminal detection; but unlike reporters and detectives who seek out the sensational, ethnographers seek out the routine. Predictable patterns of thoughts and behaviors are the focus of our inquiry. Intense anthropological ethnographers have invaded academia in recent years as professors study average, hard working, middle-class Americans. "We're interested in the extraordinariness of everyday life," says a professor from San Jose State University in California.[1]

Because most people like to talk about themselves, urban anthropologists use ethnographic anecdotal material to make policy and propose legislation based on the issues and problems discovered "in the field" of American cities. The same willingness to disclose is also prevalent among consumers, who offer hours of "consumer palaver," which is my term for product stories.

Before venturing into consumer territory, market ethnographers establish a problem to solve or question to answer. Then, they select a theory and develop a research design. Specifying data collection techniques, tools for analysis, and a writing style completes the planning process.[2] This chapter takes you through the basics for getting started and focusing your research to investigate a marketplace issue ethnographically.

Problems and Theories

Your study problem or question may come from a professor, a client, or a personal interest you have (see Chapter 5 on developing a research question). Theories can come from a variety of sources, but ethnographic researchers usually prefer either ideation or materialistic theory.

Ideationists believe that fundamental change is the result of mental activity: thoughts and ideas. *Cognitive theory*—an assumption that we can describe what people think by listening to what they say—is the most popular ideational theory in anthropology. This linguistic approach reveals how people think from the metaphors they use to describe their world. Ethnomethodology takes its basis from cognitive theory. *Materialists,* on the other hand, see the world according to observable behavior patterns. *Marxist theory* and *cultural ecology* are two materialistic views.[3]

Research Design: Fieldwork

In practical terms, ethnography is effective for marketing and media research when participant observation—watching people do what they do where they do it—is a necessary component. Ethnographic research, which is conducted in the "field" or location of the culture under investigation, has these characteristics:

Explores the nature of a particular social or marketing phenomenon

Works with an unstructured approach to data gathering

Gathers data from a range of sources, with observation and informal conversations the main sources

Collects data in settings where they take place

Focuses on one company, audience, or culture

Analyzes data that involve the interpretation of the meanings and functions of consumer actions

Uses emic and etic perspectives, with an emphasis on emic

Relies on symbols and ritual for cultural insight

Works with informants (native speakers) to answer questions in the language of the culture

During fieldwork, researchers become immersed in the culture under study. That means they become participants in the activities of those they study. The investigative process has four stages:

1. *Naturalistic observation:* The researcher learns the native language, uses the symbols and symbolic patterns as data, and studies human meanings.

2. *Contextualization:* The environment under study is crucial for its understanding. Meanings are determined by the context in which they are studied, and learning

takes place from outside inward. All present events are seen as flowing from past events.

3. *Maximized comparisons:* Personal experience of the researcher can be used as one set of data. Situational and historical comparisons of natural and social groups are made.

4. *Sensitized concepts:* These form categories that are meaningful to people, and schemes are discovered within the data. Meaning is captured at different levels and labeled.

Locating and Questioning Informants

One of the most important and often the most difficult task in undertaking a market ethnography is selecting reliable informants. Successful interviews depend on the quality of the person being interviewed. Interactions between informants and ethnographer have profound influences on interview outcomes. A good informant helps the researcher learn about the informant's culture. To do that, she or he must be a native who is currently involved in the culture, has enough time to spend with the researcher, and is nonanalytic.[4] Informants are translators, not interpreters.

Unlike randomized subjects used in most quantitative studies, informants are specially selected for their insight into a particular consumer culture. A comparison of the differences between marketplace research with subjects and research with informants is shown in Table 9.1, using questions posed in each case.

Without thorough enculturation, informants cannot provide the insight necessary to interpret idiomatic language and behavioral nuances. A first-time shopper at Bloomingdales would not serve the researcher's purpose to understand a Bloomie's shopping culture, nor would a salesperson recently transferred from another retail location. Taking time off from work or family may be a hardship for store employees and customers, and only willing participants should be included in the study. The worst kind of informant is one who tries to speculate on the motivations of other people. Restrict the informant to providing descriptions, confirmations, anecdotes, stories, or elaboration and from providing an objective assessment of the situation. Their perceptions must be those of an insider to have any value for the research. These few criteria are essential for selecting informants; using several informants is always advisable. Interviewing techniques appropriate for questioning an informant are presented in Chapter 11.

Going Native

Getting into a field study is a little like going to Club Med. The first thing you do is dress like the locals. Then, you try to learn the customs, such as when meals

Table 9.1 Differentiating Research With Subjects and Informants

Research With Subjects	*Research With Informants*
1. What do I know about a problem that will allow me to formulate and test a hypothesis?	1. What do my informants know about their culture that I can discover?
2. What concepts can I use to test this hypothesis?	2. What concepts do my informants use to classify their experience?
3. How can I operationally define these concepts?	3. How do my informants define these concepts?
4. What scientific theory explains the data?	4. What folk theory do informants use to explain their experience?
5. How can I interpret the results and report them in the language of my colleagues?	5. How can I *translate* the cultural knowledge of my informants into a cultural description my colleagues will understand?

are served, how to use "bead" currency, and how to get on the water volleyball team. An example of a naturalistic field study follows to elaborate on how the process works. Such a study is described as an ethnomethodology or an "empirical investigation of the methods people use to make sense of and accomplish communication, decision making, and action in everyday life."[5]

Field Research and Naturalistic Study in a Fast-Food Culture

In this ethnomethodological study, researchers analyzed the social conventions of a Taco Bell restaurant in southern California.[6] They learned from examining the locally produced social order. Although this study is not generalizable to other Taco Bells or fast-food franchises, it is transferable to other foci of inquiry.

Gathering Field Text

Researchers recorded observations at Taco Bell during four weekday lunch peaks, five weekday dinner peaks, and three off-peak periods (naturalistic observation). Customer behavior during arrival, queuing, ordering, waiting, seat selection, eating, and exiting were plotted; employee behavior in order taking, order filling, food preparation, and orchestrating of functions was recorded.

Seven informants were interviewed, a management trainee meeting was observed, and audiotaped focus group sessions were reviewed to gain insights into the service philosophy of Taco Bell. A videotaped interview with the CEO was accessed to contextualize the culture. Cultural participants in the employee domain consisted of order takers, order fillers, food preparers, a local manager, and a management trainee. Customer domain participants included white-collar employees, adults and children, workers, and students. Interaction occurred with consumers in queues or groups and with order takers.

Text Analysis

Four themes emerged from the observations and transcriptions gathered in the culture: a visible hierarchy, routinization, queue formation, and boundary construction. Researchers noted a *visible hierarchy* of clothing and name tags among employees, with management wearing business suits and other employees donning uniforms with job titles. Employees appeared to accept the hierarchy as part of the fast-food service delivery, despite the contradiction to a stated emphasis on team effort.

Routinization is the process put in place to ensure that the service encounter does not deviate across time or space. Taco Bell prizes its high degree of conformity for customers across locations. Quality is the sum of the comfort of the encounter and the accuracy of the order. One employee commented that "people get pissed off sometimes when the order doesn't look like the picture." A scripted dialog is given to employees to "leave nothing to chance." Customers are expected to use the menu titles of meals; departing from this norm causes anxiety for the order taker. An ideal encounter is one that is tightly scripted and highly routinized and that results in an accurate end product.

Queue formations have specific properties, and in this Taco Bell, all queues form from right to left facing the counter. A beverage bar functions as a visual cue to consumers lining up. Customers seem to understand the queuing phenomenon and the socially accepted sequence that must be adhered to: "order, pay, get food." The restaurant has two entrances, one opening directly into the dining area and a side entrance rarely used because food traffic from the street is minimal.

Boundary construction and the practical order the boundaries create are important for cultural participants. In this instance, the counter functioned as such a symbolic border. It served as a buffer between the realms and was an artifact of the cultural divide between the employee in-groups and the customer out-groups. Customers are visitors in this culture. Cleanliness is maintained on the employee side, and the customers lurk in "unclean" areas. Despite careful attention to the border, all employees take breaks in the consumer domain, during which all rules seem to be suspended.

In this analysis of the locally produced social order in a specific Taco Bell restaurant, we see that members know the local conventions across roles. The main aspects of practical action in the society are apparent to all culture participants. Employee nuances are of no importance to consumers who are most interested in the service outcome. The differences in priorities are physically signified by the counter, an important boundary region physically separating the employee and consumer domains.

Focus in Ethnographic Research

As evidenced in the Taco Bell study, ethnography begins with a wide focus that closes down, much like an inverted triangle. Researchers began by conducting secondary research on the fast-food industry and the Taco Bell Corporation. When on site, they surveyed the space and located informants. Once located, informants were interviewed and observations were recorded in field notes. Researchers asked descriptive questions, analyzed the interviews, and made a domain analysis (employee and customer domains were identified). Structural and contrast questions (see Chapter 11) were asked and analyzed to discover cultural themes. The focus was narrowed to discover cultural nuances, and symbols became meaningful. Lastly, the report was written as an ethnography.

In market ethnographies, researchers are encouraged to bring their own previous experience to the interpretation and analysis of what is going on in a specific culture. The interpretive framework of a market-oriented ethnography addresses the fundamental reciprocity between individual-level perceptions and shared social meanings of consumers. The ethnographic focus is on the behavior of people constituting a market for a product to explicate patterns of cultural or social action. Interview narratives are analyzed to reveal the operation of a general system of cultural beliefs.

Marketplace ethnographic interpretations differ from hermeneutics in the level of meaning gleaned from interviews. Rather than being socially construed, patterns of action are cognitively based in hermeneutic interpretations. With hermeneutics, personalized cultural meanings of consumption experiences are found in the consumer's narrative of self-identity. Hermeneutic frameworks focus on the ways in which people use cultural meanings and consumption practices to manage issues of identity.[7]

Analyzing Field Text

In ethnographic work, analysis is concurrent with and drives data collection. And, although fieldwork ends when you leave the site, the analysis process must exhaust the data. Attending to data analysis includes a reflective activity that results in a set of analytical notes. During this stage, notes are organized, interviews are transcribed, documents are read, and photographs are developed. These data become the text for analysis.

Text is reviewed, verified, reviewed again, and verified again. Then, it's scoured for patterns of thoughts and behavior. Beginning with a mass of undifferentiated ideas and behavior, we collect pieces of information to compare, contrast, and sort into gross categories until a discernible thought or behavior is identified. Data are segmented into relevant and meaningful units with a connection to the whole. These data systems are categorized according to an organizing system that is derived from the data themselves; the process is *inductive*.

The primary intellectual tool is *comparison*. Categories for sorting segments are tentative and preliminary at first and remain flexible. Manipulating qualitative data during analysis is an eclectic activity; there is no right or wrong way. By comparing your observations with a model or theory, exceptions emerge, and you can detect variations on a theme. Once themes are further sorted, a ritualistic activity of observed reality becomes obvious. The "aha" part of marketing ethnography occurs when all your work begins to make sense.

Key events provide a lens through which we view a culture—like using Sunday morning breakfast ritual to understand newspaper readers. We often use key events as characterized in videos or photographs to analyze an entire group activity. This key event becomes a metaphor for the culture under observation. For instance, the metaphor for sports products manufacturer Patagonia is function, based on the founder's approach to developing new products: "I build it for myself and sell it to whoever wants the best thing available."[8] His philosophy emanates from the key event—the building and selling of his first climbing piton—which is told and retold as a mythical story in the folklore of the organization.

Data analysis is a sorting procedure: "the quantitative side of qualitative research."[9] Charts, semantic tables, and taxonomies[10] can be used to present patterned regularities. Comparisons to other cultural groups, evaluating the group in terms of standards, and drawing connections between your study culture and larger theoretical frameworks can be made during the analytical stage. Patagonia's culture, when compared with other more traditional companies evidenced its unique approach to innovation development, consensus management, and face-to-face communication.

Verbatim quotations are useful for presenting evidence of your findings in your report. Consumer thoughts are expressed best in their own language. A user of Patagonia's kayaking anorak remarks, "It's like it was designed for me especially. I love their stuff." These words add authenticity and meaning to reports and television commercials produced about the company or its products. Last, data may be transformed by answering the question, "What does all this mean?" as the researcher draws inferences from the data or uses theory for interpretive structure. When analysis is completed, the final task of writing the report begins.

The Ethnographic Field Narrative

Our first consideration is the audience—the person who will read this report. We direct the focus accordingly. The most central task in presenting an ethnographic study is to identify its main findings and the evidence presented in support of them. Using the Taco Bell study, I'll discuss three categories of arguments typically found in ethnographic accounts:[11] definitions, factual claims, and value claims. A thorough report contains *definitions* of the terms used in it. In the Taco Bell report, employees and customers are defined and their jobs specified by the fast-food researcher so that their roles are clear to the reader.

Factual claims document features of the case and their causes or consequences. They take three forms: descriptions, explanations, and predictions. A good starting point for writing the report is to describe the group and the setting you study. *Descriptions,* verbal representations of some feature of a scene, are the basis for all arguments made in ethnographies. Begin chronologically to describe the "day in the life" of your culture. The traffic patterns, entrances, and structural configurations of the Taco Bell restaurant are such descriptions.

Explanations are concerned with why a feature occurred in a description. In the restaurant culture, queues are described and then explained in terms of customer behavior on entering and how they avoid the drink counter while ordering. *Predictions* are claims that suggest cause and effect: If that happens, this will probably also happen. Taco Bell researchers note that when a customer receives food that does not resemble the meal pictured on the menu board, that customer often complains to a server.

In addition to all the claims mentioned earlier, *value claims* also express a view in terms of one or more values. *Evaluations* involve a description of and explanation for a set of phenomena plus some indication that the thing described is good or bad. Dress codes for Taco Bell employees differentiated them from management and customers—good for the desired routinization but perhaps confounding for some employees. Occasionally, market ethnographers make some *recommendations* about what changes ought to be made in the phenomena they study. Although researchers made no recommendations as part of the Taco Bell ethnography, some discussion of the role of the beverage bar location might be warranted for clients who are interested in making improvements to benefit their customers.

Creative reports may include poetry, drawings, or photographs to enhance the reader's ability to grasp the essence of the culture under study. Well written ethnographic reports often read like fiction, possessing a storylike quality that both informs and delights the client, professor, or journal reader audience. After all, there is no law that research reports must be boring and stodgy. Qualitative presentations, to the contrary, are often rewarding journeys to the core of a previously unknown world of consumption culture.

Studying Corporate Cultures

Based on the belief that culture is socially embedded, socially constructed, and socially reproduced over time, we approach the study of corporate culture by examining the influences of organizational members on the enculturation process. Marketers often study a company's culture in order to develop marketing and collateral materials that reflect the company's values. Young, entrepreneurial companies, especially Internet-related ventures, expect logo and corporate image recommendations to communicate their company's unique culture.

To understand what makes a company unique, we use ethnographic studies to investigate organizational founders', leaders', and members' contributions to the culture creation process. For instance, Patagonia was started by founder Ivon Chinouard who began by selling climbing gear from the trunk of his car. The myths associated with his success, the role of a female CEO's gender influence on the company's leadership style, and member involvement with policy development on child care all factor into the organization's culture.

Similar to market place data collection, materials for corporate studies are gathered from field notes, organizational documents and artifacts, and interviews. Aspects of the culture are identified through thematic analysis of textual data. Results explain how a corporation's culture is created as founders and their followers engage in the process of making sense of their shared, organizational experience.

Shared values and stories extracted from the study can then be applied to logo design and the development of catalogs, annual reports, and internal newsletters. Whether you research a marketplace or a place of business, ethnographic techniques capture the essence of the culture under study. No other investigative approach is as demanding for the researcher or as thorough for understanding a phenomenon.

Last

The study of social worlds built by people on computer networks challenges the classical dimensions of ethnographic research. Scholars are now exploiting the possibilities offered by new, powerful, and flexible analytic tools for inexpensively collecting, organizing, and exploring digital data. Computer-mediated communication research on virtual communities is becoming similar to research on traditional communities in so-called real life. And although ethnographic studies have so far been of text-based virtual realities, studying cultural cyberartifacts, such as audiovisual experiences, is now possible through multimediated technologies, such as CU-SeeMe or Internet Phone.

Perhaps, such advanced concepts will find application in marketplace research, partially repaying the debt of computer-mediated communication research to older and more eminent disciplines.[12]

Summary

1. Marketplace ethnographers study everyday routines of consumers in a particular exchange culture.

2. Ideationist and materialist theories usually ground ethnographies.

3. Researchers are encouraged to incorporate their own previous experience of the phenomenon into the study; they serve as instruments in the data collection process.

4. Fieldwork is the primary component of ethnographic data collection and consists of naturalistic observation, contextualization, maximized comparisons, and sanitized concepts.

5. Informants are crucial for helping researchers learn about the culture under study and must be selected for their involvement in the culture and their availability.

6. Informants differ from subjects in the roles they play. Subjects provide results; informants help translate knowledge for the researcher.

7. Ethnography begins with a wide focus and progresses toward a metafocus on meanings and myths.

8. Data analysis helps researchers locate thematic clusters and results in answering the question, "What does all this mean?"

9. The narrative report includes a description of the group and setting, explanations of behavior, and predictions of what might be expected in the future. Evaluation and recommendations are sometimes included.

10. Studying corporate cultures requires analyzing secondary sources, participant observation, and field interviewing.

Stretching Exercises

1. This activity is designed to develop skill in field observation. Visit a coffee cafe or bookstore to study as an observer. Draw the setting and take notes on what you see

and hear in one hour's time. Then, analyze your field notes to answer the following questions:

a. What activities are you interested in studying in this culture?

b. What did you learn about the people you saw and heard?

c. What did you learn about what the place means to the people inside?

d. How can you study "how and why" about this setting rather than "what or who" is the group?

e. What patterns can you identify from your observations?

2. In each of the situations described, tell who you would select as informants to help you understand the marketplace culture. Use chapter criteria to explain your choices.

a. Commuter train travel between New York City and Connecticut

b. Blackjack playing in Las Vegas

c. Lexis car dealership in Beverly Hills

d. Morton's Steak House

Recommended Readings About Ethnographic Research

Coulton, A. (1995). *Ethnomethodology.* Thousand Oaks, CA: Sage.

Denzin, N. (1997). *Interpretive ethnography.* Thousand Oaks, CA: Sage.

Fetterman, D. (1989). *Ethnography step by step.* Newbury Park, CA: Sage.

Schwartzman, H. (1992). *Ethnography in organizations.* Newbury Park, CA: Sage.

Stewart, A. (1998). *The ethnographer's method.* Thousand Oaks, CA: Sage.

Thomas, J. (1992). *Doing critical ethnography.* Newbury Park, CA: Sage.

Wolcott, H. F. (1994). *Transforming qualitative data: Description, analysis, and interpretation.* Thousand Oaks, CA: Sage.

Case in Point: Harley-Davidson as Consumption Subculture[13]

Client: Harley-Davidson, Inc.

Problem: Understanding how innovators and opinion leaders have imbued motorcycles with meaning that is shared and consumed by a large market. To expand product rollout, opinion leaders must be reached.

RQ: *What are the characteristics of a consumption subculture?*

Method: Ethnography

Data Collection: Field notes are based on observation, brief interviews, and photographs taken along the road from Ames, Iowa, during the week of the motorcycle rally in Sturgis, South Dakota. An expected 300,000 motorcyclists, the majority riding Harley-Davidsons, pass through the small town of Sturgis. The first author makes retail observations while the second author conducts participant observations with key informants during two motorcycle rallies in June and July. Both authors participate in the Western Regional Rally of the Harley Owners Group (HOG) in Santa Maria, California. They ride with Los Angeles-based chapter members who embrace the authors as fellow chapter members.

Interview and observational data are also collected at other venues in naturalistic sites, such as informants' homes, motorcycle swap meets, club meetings, rallies, rides, bars, and restaurants, with field notes recorded afterward via microcassette recorder and subsequent transcription.

Immersion in the culture enables a familiarity with magazines such as *Biker, Easyriders, American Iron, Supercycle, Enthusiast,* and *Hog Tales,* as well as rally publications and newsletters that help with interpretation of interviews and other data.

Interviews are also conducted with key members of the organization at Harley-Davidson corporate offices in Milwaukee, including the president of the motorcycle division, vice-president of motorcycle styling, public relations manager, and director of business planning. Interviews with four Harley-Davidson dealers in Iowa and Oregon and with dozens of vendors of biker accessories, clothing, and paraphernalia at swap meets and rallies help the researchers gain a marketer's perspective of Harley ownership.

Informants are selected to represent different types of Harley owners identified in the course of ethnographic inquiry. These types included "Ma & Pa" bikers, "RUBs" (rich urban bikers), clubbies (such as Hells Angels), and yuppies who ride with enthusiasts of European cycles. Data were triangulated with multiple primary and secondary sources.

Data Analysis: Observational and photographic data analysis and symbolic interpretation of dress, grooming, and motorcycle customization yield revelations of the underlying subculture ethos (of values among subgroups) and the ability to track the movement of embodied meanings through the subculture. Interpreted meanings are validated through interviews and member checks and close readings of biker literature.

Data from interviews and observation field notes are coded, compared, collapsed into categories, and abstracted to yield interpretive themes. A back-and-forth process of data analysis and literature review reveals four themes that form the basis of this paper.

Results: The text shows four characteristics of relationships between marketers and consumption-oriented subcultures:

1. Consumer-initiated new product development

  2. Mass-marketed mystique

  3. Extraordinary brand identification

  4. Transcendence of national and cultural boundaries

Discussion: "Grass roots R & D" was one of the most interesting phenomena reported by
  researchers. Innovation originating at the core of the biker subculture is responsible for much of the bike, accessory, and clothing styles now manufactured by
  Harley for sale to the general public.

  Certain cultural innovations appear to emanate from the core of the subculture, ultimately to be adopted more broadly in some form. Some designs are "sanitized"
  and promoted for mass consumption, like the rap music and competitive body-
  building. A tension between the resonance and dissonance with social norms gives
  this subculture its mystique—the lure of the outlaw culture prevails in the American marketplace as a motorclub.

  Researchers report a strong sense of brand identification among Harley owners
  that translates to extraordinary brand loyalty. They find two distinct types of
  Harley riders: those who will not ride if Harleys are not available and those who
  like motorcycles first and Harleys second. Signs of loyalty include tattoos, bumper
  stickers on their other vehicles, and frequent wearing of Harley-licensed apparel.
  Owners are predominantly blue-collar workers who begin with used bikes, which
  are customized with aftermarket parts. RUBs spend lavishly on accessories and
  play at the role of biker on weekends, after which they return to their suits and imported cars. Ma & Pa bikers are motivated by travel and comfort, choosing fully
  dressed bikes with radios, intercoms, heated hand grips, floorboards, and protective fairings. Loyalty stems from the love of Harley's heritage and unique sound.

  Consumer subculture members transcend racial, ethnic, and national differences.
  Russian enthusiasts ride WWII-military-imported Harleys; a "Motorbike Con-
  certo" by a Swedish composer evidences implications for marketing Harley-
  Davidson internationally.

Conclusion: Harley owns 49% of the cycle market, and clothing sales have doubled since
  1993. Parts and accessories sales are increasing by 20% annually. Harley continues to promote the brand's mystique and the love that riders feel for the brand.
  This ethnographic study has important marketing implications associated with
  consumption-oriented subcultures. It is, however, just a beginning for understanding the longevity and degree of commitment to the subculture on the part of new,
  upscale bikers. Regional and international differences need further exploration.

Notes

  1. From an article by Stephanie S. (1999, October 14). A life more ordinary,
  all the better for these anthropologists. *Los Angeles Times,* p. A6.

2. See Fetterman, D. M. (1989). *Ethnography step by step*. Newbury Park, CA: Sage.

3. For a discussion of theories in ethnographic research, see Fetterman, D., & Pitman, M. (Eds.). (1986). *Educational evaluation: Ethnography in theory, practice, and politics*. Beverly Hills, CA: Sage.

4. For more details on informant selection, see Spradley, J. P. (1979). *The ethnographic interview*. London: Harcourt Brace Jovanovich.

5. Rogers, M. (1983). *Sociology, ethnomethodology and experience*. Cambridge, UK: Cambridge University Press.

6. From a study conducted by H. Schau and M. Gilly presented to the annual meeting of the Association of Consumer Research, 1997.

7. Thompson, C. (1997). Interpreting consumers: A hermeneutical framework for deriving marketing insights from the texts of consumers' consumption stories. *Journal of Marketing Research, 24,* 438-455.

8. Based on field notes collected for Sayre, S. (1986). *Leader communication and organizational culture: A field study*. Doctoral dissertation, University of San Diego, CA.

9. From Wolcott, H. (1994). *Transforming qualitative data: Description, analysis, and interpretation*. Thousand Oaks, CA: Sage.

10. Spradley (1979). See Note 4.

11. See Hammersley, M. (1990). *Reading ethnographic research: A critical guide*. London: Longman.

12. From an article by Paccagnelli, L. (1997). Getting the seats of your pants dirty: Strategies for ethnographic research on virtual communities. *Journal of Computer Mediated Communication, 3*(1), 347-356.

13. From a study conducted by Schouten, J., & Alexander, J. H. (1993). Market impact of consumption subcultures: The Harley-Davidson mystique. *European Advances in Consumer Research, 1,* 389-393.

■ Part IV

DATA COLLECTION: TECHNIQUES AND TOOLS

W hether you plan to conduct research in the field or probe problem solutions in the confines of an organization, you should be familiar with ways in which information is extracted from marketplace consumers. Qualitative data collection involves skill building in techniques of observation and interviewing. To help you decide on the best method to achieve your study objectives, this section is dedicated to previewing the skills necessary to conduct field and off-site research.

Chapter 10 presents four levels of participation for field observations and the role field notes play for data collection. In Chapter 11, you will learn how and when to conduct informal, unstructured field interviews with members and informants alone and in groups. Cyberethnography is also included for its role in text collection. Chapter 12 presents techniques on formal interviewing in both single-respondent and focus groups situations. Conducting structured interviews and focus groups on the Web is also included. Because we often need additional tools for eliciting information, Chapter 13 shows you how to use projective techniques for creative and effective data collection.

10 Observation and Fieldwork

To a researcher, observation is a "field of adventure." Rather than assume seeing is believing, we assume that believing is seeing.

—Alfred Schultz, 1944

If you've always wanted to be a voyeur, this technique is for you. Observation is a key element in most research models, especially case study and ethnography. Through participative fieldwork, researchers are able to assimilate themselves into the lives of consumers in the marketplace or audiences engaging in a variety of mediated activities. Cultural immersion, somewhat haphazard and erratic in the beginning, is mostly a discovery process on the researcher's part. Carried out through loosely structured rules, observation invokes framing that permits us to enter and join the world of those who we want to study.

With great attention to detail, researchers begin the assimilation process into a strange culture with caution. Called *systematic observation,*[1] this process has seven characteristics:

1. *Sustaining:* It remains in the consumption activity environment for a long period of time.

2. *Explicit:* Take logical and copious notes on how you are observing the consumption phenomenon.

3. *Methodical:* Be ready to improvise, but stay on course.

4. *Observing:* Direct your attention to all aspects of the activity with a keen eye and astute awareness.

5. *Paraphrasing:* Put what you see into your own words.

6. *In social situations:* Note the interaction of and interdependencies of the place, the consumers, and their activities.

7. *In naturally occurring contexts:* View the consumption activities within the context of their social environment.

The advantages of observation are several: It helps you understand what's going on in the place you are studying, it helps you determine what questions to ask informants, and it is an unobtrusive way of getting information about groups and their behavior.

Participation Is Key

The success of any observation depends on how much you can learn from the encounter. The systematic process is referred to by marketplace researchers as *participant observation.* Participant observers watch people to see how they confront ordinary consumption situations and how they behave in them. We engage consumers in conversation to discover their interpretations of what we see. In other words, we try to fit into consumptive situations through social engagement with its members. We communicate, but we don't formally interview, remaining focused at all times on the purpose of the observation—being there.

As participant observers, we don't just notice, we collect evidence. Then, we organize the evidence to accumulate the best possible explanation of what's going on. With multiple activities occurring, it's the researcher's job to decide what's important and attend to those details. And we do it in a "good guy" fashion that allows blending in, not standing out in the situation.

Standing out in a situation may result from sex, ethnicity, age, or some aspect of the researcher's person that sets him or her apart. Personal traits should not be a problem if you are on common experiential grounding with those you are trying to understand. In other words, if you're a shopper, what you look like shouldn't be cause for notice in a shopping mall. Neither do you want to be invisible. Interaction requires participation and communication within the construct of the activity you are observing.

Categorizing Observational Roles

Strive not to laugh at human actions, nor to weep at them, nor to hate them, but to understand them.

—B. Spinzoa, 1664

Your participation role may differ from situation to situation. Four so-called master roles have been developed for a more refined typology: complete participant, participant as observer, observer as participant, and complete observer.[2] The differences are not insignificant, and you must select your role prior to entering the field.

Complete Participant: Here, researchers are covert, hiding their identity and infiltrating completely into the scene. For instance, studying the culture of a weight-loss program, a researcher will weight in, adhere to the diet, and go through the program the same as all other participants, without disclosing the research agenda. Participants who might otherwise be reluctant to share their feelings will openly disclose if the exchange is mutual—your secrets for their secrets. One problem with this complete immersion is a loss of objectivity that results from being so closely aligned to the situation, and some situations are more problematic than others. As discussed in Chapter 4, ethical issues determine the appropriateness of assuming the role of complete participant.

Participant as Observer: Most consumption situations enable researchers to join into activities and still openly acknowledge the purpose of their membership. Observing parents of small children at Disneyland is accomplished as you stand in line or take rides as a visitor. Asking other visitors to clarify your assumptions as a fellow amusement park attendee, if not invasive, casts you in the role of interested person. Disclosing the purpose of your verbal exchange should not compromise that exchange. Riding along gives you the first-hand experience of the activity and provides common topics for discussion with other riders. This is the most desirable role for marketplace researchers to assume.

Observer as Participant: Observing with detachment is useful for situations in which movement rather than communication is necessary for achieving the objective. Watching how consumers enter a shopping mall, how long they take to select parking places, and counting their purchases when they return are some shopping activities where observation does not have to be supplemented with discourse. Gatekeepers are more likely to grant access to researchers whose purpose is to look at rather than to engage in the situation. This observation level allows a researcher to draw conclusions about actions over time. The risk here is one of reading too much of our own conceptions into what we see.

Complete Observer: This is the "fly on the wall" role that disengages researchers from activity and keeps them virtually invisible. In contrast to the complete participant who engages in the action, the complete observer withdraws from it. Both roles are hidden. This role is often preliminary to later integration into a situation, allowing researchers to scope out the place before beginning participative involvement. Video, photography, audio, and computers enable remote sensing to be done with a low probability of detection. By using a camcorder to tape the ritual activities of a celebrity wedding, a researcher can gather data without any face-to-face contact with the wedding party. This is a "hide and watch" approach to data gathering.

Membership and Functional Roles

We think of audience and group roles as *membership roles*—as a complete member, active member, or peripheral member, according to our involvement in the activity. Each role entails different obligations, liabilities, and responsibilities. These roles correspond closely to the roles described earlier, with an additional element of belonging.

During an observation, researchers have *functional roles* that correspond to a specific field site. Acting as a department store shopper, a researcher may act as a controlled skeptic who voices doubts about products being purchased or as an ardent consumer who uncovers the best deal for the lowest price. A researcher who assumes the skeptic's role is able to solicit points of view in a naive, curious, yet skeptical manner. Beliefs about value and quality are better revealed during conversations of intense comparison that may result from taking the role of an ardent consumer. Role assumption gives us a purpose by normalizing relations and removing the more tenuous surveillance approach to research.

Scenes and Fields

As researchers, we enter a field location and begin observing the activities of people to understand the setting. A field is the physical setting and social activity arena of a research problem. We think of our study as a field study and look from outside inward at the participants. People we watch, however, think of themselves as part of a consumption scene, as insiders.

Information gathering begins with *unfocused observation* where we remain open to the unexpected. We look at the general features of the landscape. What kind of space is it? How is the space organized? What kinds of things are in the space? We note the people and the events taking place. How many people are there? What do they look like? What are they doing?

As we transcend to *focused observation,* our attention shifts to matters of specific interest. For starters, we treat units of activity as self-contained events, and we look for patterns across these units of activity. As patterns emerge, we begin to understand what is going on. First, we develop our own perspective of the field, making careful observations of the full range of behaviors and objects. Next, we begin to adopt a member's perspective. Our goal is to produce descriptive observations; our process goes from general to specific.

The following example features a young woman acting as complete observer during her first time in a retail outlet selling golf equipment.[3] She stands near a sock display and watches unobtrusively as if she were a customer. To explain "What's going on here?" she orients her activity by addressing this series of questions:[4]

Who are the actors in the scene?

How do they fulfill their roles? What understandings are implied in these roles (how are people supposed to act in these roles)? These questions are answered within the context of the consumption culture under observation.

Except for the cashier, the salespeople are men; one in his 50s, the other in his mid 60s. They are expected to be experts, or pros, at golf and help customers with club selection. Most of the customers are male, although many are accompanied by female companions who either share the male's enthusiasm, yawn of boredom, or talk with the cashier.

How is the scene set up?

Artifacts found at the scene signify what is important to the group or individual identity of members. Objects of the material culture are studied for their importance to the activity.

The store layout is appropriate to the merchandise and clientele: golf attire, clubs, and accessories. Aisles are neat, well organized, and wide. Merchandise is displayed aesthetically. The cashier's desk is near the entrance to the left. A television at the store's rear plays a golf match. Clothing worn by salesmen is casual but fresh. Customers shop in golf-like clothing, also casual. Point-of-purchase displays feature golf balls and tees. All actors seem to know how to use the equipment and refer to it in golf jargon.

How do initial interactions occur?

The ways consumers interact with each other and clerks for the first time reveals much about protocol, communication, and sociability of the actors involved.

Two customers enter the store from a single door and drift to the right. The older salesman greets them with a smile, but does not approach them. After several minutes of browsing, a male customer asks for assistance with a three iron. Both are social and polite; they look directly at each other when they speak. They share anecdotes as the customer takes a few practice swings with a three iron. The pro explains the process used to make the club and shows him another club for comparison. As other shoppers enter, the second pro makes himself available. About half the customers know what they want, the others are "lookers."

When and how do actors claim attention?

Most activities take place in routines where members' roles are ordinary and unchallenged. Acculturated members understand the scheme of things within the group or activity. By paying attention to actions or communications that are confusing, researchers may be briefed on meaning to clarify and illuminate what is going on. Vocabulary, terminology, jargon, nonverbal behavior, and procedures are clarified with informal dialogue. Learning informal nuances allows researchers to understand when and how actors request and get attention.

> Salesmen acknowledge customer presence by being visible but not intrusive. If a customer looks back, he smiles. If, as one woman does, the customer seems confused, the pro approaches politely. Names of clubs and their manufacturers, golf stars, clothing brand names, and terms like "birdie," "bogie," and "eagle" are bantered about casually; everyone seems to understand the jargon. Customers who enter as couples often exchange comments intended to be overheard by pros, who accommodate them by moving closer and addressing their comments politely.

Where and how do actors congregate?

Informal interactions give us clues to human traffic patterns, spatial relationships, and body juxtapositions. Two concepts in public behavioral interactions are *markers* and *tie signs*.[5] Markers are nonverbal behaviors and actions that distinguish a relationship. Markers between the pros/salesmen and customers are nods, handshakes, spatial distance, polite smiles, and so forth. *Tie signs* are symbols or social artifacts that indicate a type of relationship. Pro nametags that distinguish them from customers and their branded visors are tie signs.

> Women in the company of men often drift back to the television, or over to the women's wear section. Men seem to prefer being near the rack of clubs and do most of their conversing there. They practice swinging on a patch of synthetic turf situated near the clubs. The cashier remains seated at her post, addressing direct-mail sale announcements. Sales pros keep distance between themselves and customers, and move away as soon as questions are answered or problems resolved.

What communication events are significant?

Verbal interactions provide insight into how information is obtained and shared.

Pros reply to customer queries with a "sir" or "ma'am". Women who are buying gifts for male golfers are the most verbal, posing questions to thin air and hoping for expertise from both other customers and the two salesmen who may or may not be within earshot. Pros often ask one another for a specific size garment or answer to a technical question. Occasionally a shopping couple will come together to discuss what they have found, then each will go separate ways until verbal or physical contact is stimulated by a new discovery. Some customers begin familiarized conversations with the pros and are later identified as store "regulars". Clothing communicates a golf affiliation: matching pants or shorts and knit shirts with collars and a few buttons. Everyone is well manicured and polite.

During this preliminary observation, the researcher makes note about what she sees that served as the basis for questioning an informant: the cashier. Data from this observation are analyzed for patterns she looks for during a second visit.

Tips for Beginning Field Observation

Fieldwork is defined as systematic gathering of data on specific aspects of consumption by means other than surveys, demographic techniques, and experimentation that includes an ongoing relationship with those studied. Although no standardized procedure exists for fieldwork, I present 10 guidelines for approaching field observations:

1. Be as descriptive as possible in field notes.

2. Gather a variety of information from different perspectives.

3. Cross-validate and triangulate by gathering different kinds of data and using multiple methods.

4. Use quotations to capture consumers' views of their experiences in their own words.

5. Select key informants wisely and use them carefully. Remember that each informant has his or her own point of view.

6. Be aware of the different stages of fieldwork:
   a. Build trust and rapport on entering the field.
   b. Stay alert and disciplined as you progress.
   c. Focus on pulling together a useful synthesis near the conclusion.
   d. Be conscientious in note taking at all stages of the observation.

7. Be as involved as possible in experiencing the program while maintaining an analytical perspective grounded in the research objectives.

8. Clearly separate description from interpretation and judgment.

9. Provide formative feedback as part of the verification process of fieldwork.

10. Include in your field notes and evaluation report your own experiences, thoughts, and feelings. These are also field data.

Whether written, audiotaped, or videotaped, field notes must be recorded and analyzed on a continuing basis. How we create and analyze text in the field is our next topic of discussion.

Creating and Analyzing Field Texts

The *creation of texts*—field notes, documents, transcripts, and visual media—is a process of converting field notes into a narrative. During the field narration process, data are coded and analyzed for later interpretation and rewriting. Remember, data are all types of texts we use to gain meaningful understanding of the consumption activity. Field notes come in a variety of forms: scratch notes, head notes, and field notes.

Scratch notes are quick scribbles taken down on entering the field. Bits of dialogue, objections, statements, reminders, and diagrams are cues to the researcher about what was observed. *Head notes,* compiled all during the research, are recorded memories and impressions or evaluations of the project as a whole.

Field notes are written about social and physical contexts, including analytic reflection, and are considered by some to be "gnomic shorthand reconstruction of events, observations and conversations"[6] observed in the field. These notes are written and organized chronologically. They are a literal record of everything: mundane facts, descriptions of people, problems, questions, feelings, and impressions. Videotapes, maps, and photographs help to illuminate your notes, and you are encouraged to include as much visual media in your field notes as possible.

Text analysis is covered in more depth in Chapter 15. However, some of the more salient analytical concerns are presented here as process, reduction, explanation, and theory. The *process* of analyzing qualitative data continues throughout the entire study. From the onset, we put our data into categories to help discern meaning.

In qualitative research, numerical coding helps us *reduce* the data at the physical and conceptual levels. Physically reducing text means to sort, categorize, prioritize, and interrelate data according to emerging schemes of interpretation. Coding and configuring data reduce amounts to manageable clusters of meanings and themes. A conceptual structure is necessary to make sense of and communicate the field experience.

Analysis is a way of *explaining* the how and why of the research. The analyst makes sense of the way consumers make sense of their own actions, goals, and motives. *Theories* are ever-evolving constructions that depend on the comparison of cases. Single observational cases can test how and where a theory can be applied, although field-specific research does not always permit cross-comparisons that modify theory.

Analytic coding is a method of categorizing and sorting data to enable interpretation of marketplace phenomena. At this stage, you must decide what is worth saving, how to divide up the data, and how an incident of talk or behavior relates to another coded item. The coding process begins with a preliminary reading of data. Codes range from simple and topical to more general abstract conceptual categories. The simple codes sort out people, behaviors, time periods, events, and so forth. More complex codes categorize concepts, beliefs, themes, cultural practices, or relationships.

One method for generating categories from field observations of any culture is with semantic relationships:[7]

Strict inclusion: X is a kind of Y—*Brookstone is a kind of store.*

Spatial: X is a place in Y, X is part of Y—*A store is a place in a mall.*

Cause/effect: X is a result of Y—*Purchase is a result of need.*

Rationale: X is a reason for doing Y—*Fun is a reason for shopping.*

Location for action: X is a place for doing Y—*A mall is a place to shop.*

Function: X is used for Y—*Credit cards are used to purchase goods.*

Means/end: X is a way to do Y—*Internet is a way to shop.*

Sequence: X is a step in Y—*Payment is a step in the purchase process.*

Attribute: X is a characteristic of Y—*Mirrors are a characteristic of cosmetic counters.*

A *constant comparative method* of coding[8] specifies the means by which theory, grounded in the relationships among data, emerges through the management of coding. This and other coding and filing strategies allow researchers to identify and label a phenomenon in terms of basic components or elements. Coding allows us to look for patterns and relationships among facts and to compare and construct similarities and differences. Data sorting and reconstruction facilitate a disassembling of data into elements and components that enables us to examine the data for patterns and relationships.

Member checks, which come near the end of the field study, constitute critiques from both insiders and outsiders of the study culture. Willingness to provide member checks depends on the relationships built between researcher and consumers during the study process. Because these checks provide important situations of interpretative validation, researchers are encouraged to develop positive interactions with study participants.

Semiotics and Fieldwork[9]

Semiotics, the science of signs and symbols, is used as a data analysis tool by researchers who seek to understand how signs perform or convey meaning in context. The usefulness of semiotics for field study is presented here, but a thorough understanding can only be achieved with further study and practice. It is included here to familiarize future managers with the techniques and their value.

Following fieldwork, semiotics serves as a *mode of problem identification.* Using the golf retail observation as an example, communication problems can be identified by looking at how actors are oriented to messages and at channels of communication present in the store.

Semiotics is also a *mode of pursuing relevant units of analysis* within a context. Social codes for exchanging anecdotes exist in the store. Anecdotes may be coded as experiences that (a) happened to the teller, (b) happened to a friend, (c) were seen on television, or (d) were witnessed by the teller. From these units in context, one can move to connections between these anecdotes and other types of telling about golf, such as stories or myths.

Semiotics *requires comparisons* based on the notion that oppositions in context are a source of meaning. By comparing this golf store to, say, a store selling diamond watches, one would find oppositions in language (formal vs. informal), attire (business suit vs. golf casual), store layout (counters containing merchandise vs. open displays), the role of salespeople (professional knowledge vs. experiential advice), and so forth.

Semiotic analysis requires us to *penetrate surface meanings* or mere description and extract underlying modes of understanding. Replying to a customer inquiry about a certain brand of golf club, the salesman might respond that the store "does not carry that brand." Taken on the surface, it means what it says. But by listening to voice inflections and watching facial expressions, we learn that the brand is not in the store because it is deemed "inferior" to the brands carried there. Immediately, the inquiring customer is categorized as unworthy of serious attention by employees of a store that only carries "finer" brands.

Semiotics also *assumes different perspectives on social life.* The essence of this concept is recognition of change in meaning and interpretation over time.

Researchers look for metaphors of social life and how they work in context. The "hole in one" metaphor connotes excellence and is relayed through myths and stories passed down among generations of golfers. Thinking about one thing in terms of another allows us to gain deeper understanding of consumer narrative.

Last

Observation is one of the most interesting research techniques, but it also one of the most difficult. It is difficult because consumers, as all humans, are complex and because interpersonal and group communication and relationships are so complicated. However, observation is unique because it is one of the few ways we can obtain information about what consumers do in contrast to what they say they do. And we get the information in the place where they do what they do. Whether you go unannounced or with a formal introduction, your responsibility as an observer is to make sense of what you see taking place for those of us who cannot be there to understand what's happening.

Summary

1. Participant observation is a process of researcher assimilation into the lives of consumers and immersion into the marketplace culture.

2. Observation has four levels of participation: complete participant, participant as observer, observer as participant, and complete observer. Levels are chosen for their appropriateness to the situation and for their ethical application.

3. Researchers assume roles of membership and function in field studies.

4. Observation progresses from a general, unfocused description to a focused attention on matters of special interest.

5. Fieldwork builds an ongoing relationship between researcher and consumers under study; field notes gather information on those consumers and their consumption setting.

6. Field notes become texts that are analyzed by reducing the amount of data to explain the study and construct theory about what has taken place.

7. Texts are coded to allow patterns and themes to emerge from the textual data.

8. Semiotic fieldwork is data analysis at a deeper level that invokes a system of signs and symbols to bring meaning to consumer narratives.

Stretching Exercises

1. From the vantage point of where you are sitting, record what you observe in the next 5 minutes using field note format. When time is up, go to another vantage point and record your observations. Did you see anything differently in the second observation after you changed seating? What was most difficult for you in this observation?

2. Make a floor plan of a record store near you. What does its physical configuration say about the kinds of social and consumption activities that take place in this store? Can you redesign the store to improve the interactions between customers and merchandise? Between customers and other customers?

Recommended Readings About Observation Techniques

Jorgensen, D. (1989). *Participant observation: A methodology for human studies.* Newbury Park, CA: Sage.

Lindlof, T. R. (1995). *Qualitative communication research methods* (Chapters 5 & 7). Thousand Oaks, CA: Sage.

Patton, M. Q. (1990). *Qualitative evaluation and research methods* (Chapter 6). Newbury Park, CA: Sage.

Reason, P. (Ed.). (1988). *Human inquiry in action: Developments in new paradigm research.* Thousand Oaks, CA: Sage.

Spradley, J. (1997). *Participant observation.* New York: Holt, Reinhart & Winston.

Case in Point: Discount Records[10]

Client: Discount Records

RQ: *How do customers use and relate to the store?*

Background: Discount Records is an alternative music store with an attitude problem, located in a strip mall near a community college. Similar to the situation presented in the film "High Fidelity," this store has the reputation of being particular about the demographics of its patrons—clerks only service people perceived to be true music aficionados. Unwittingly, the owners believe that other factors, such as store layout, are the main contributors to declining revenues. This research was conducted to assess the store's operational nuances, identify problems, and make recommendations for correcting them.

Data Collection: Participant observation in the store over one week's duration. Because this researcher is a regular customer, employees did not think it odd for him to be in the store for several hours at a time. He made four 3-hour observations.

Store setting: With 300 sq. ft. of space, the store is organized to minimize theft. Valuable items are kept in the front display case or are hanging on walls. Two employees from behind the front counter can easily see most areas of the store. LPs and CDs are stacked in shelves and boxes around the store. In some places, stacks reach from floor to ceiling. No signs or banners mark music choices; only regular customers know where everything is. The small space prohibits maintaining any distance of personal space, and it is difficult to avoid interacting in some way with the other customers. Hardcore punk and heavy metal posters depicting various scenes of mutilation, sex acts, and left-wing political propaganda hang on all the walls.

Actors: Two employees in their 20s, one male and one female. Numbers of customers range from a low of 9 to a high of 21 at one time. About 60 customers come in and out during any 3-hour visit. Four basic types of customers enter the store:

1. *Punks/Skateheads*—usually have short, dyed hair and multiple body piercings or tattoos (or both). They prefer music by The Clash, Black Flag, and so on. Subgroups within this category include Mall Punks, Surf Punks, East Coast Punks, and so forth.

2. *Metalheads*—usually have long hair; wear jeans, T-shirts, and boots; and have tattoos, earrings, or both. They prefer listening to Pantera, AC/DC, Metallica, and so forth. Within Metalheads are subgroups called Long Hairs, Short Hairs, Glam, Thrash, Death, and so on.

3. *Goths/Vamps*—usually dress in black; hair is dyed black. Musical preferences include Sisters of Mercy, Christian Death, and Nine Inch Nails.

4. *Yuppies*—usually dress in khakis and pressed shirts and have neat, stylish haircuts. They like Bruce Springsteen and Prince.

Action: Yuppie encounters. The main activity takes place between the protagonist regular consumer or employees and an outcast consumer antagonist, the Yuppie. Whenever Yuppies come into the store, employees and most of the customers ignore them. Unaccustomed to such posters and memorabilia hanging on the walls, Yuppies are initially amused. It quickly turns to disgust or repulsion. If they still don't get the message, employees turn up the stereo system to a near-deafening volume and play hardcore punk rock. Yuppies usually leave after a few minutes. Here are some typical encounters:

Three female yuppies enter the store, pausing to look around. A group of 10 Punks and Skateheads are near the front counter talking and looking at magazines. The girls begin pointing and "ooohing" and "aahhing" at the stuff on the walls. They notice a poster featuring a close-up of Type O Negative's lead singer's naked butt. It is titled "Origin of the Feces." One says "gross," and they file out of the store. Total time: 72 seconds.

Four Yuppies (2 males, 2 females) come in and talk loudly, heading toward the CD section. Sixteen people are in the store. Five Punks occupy the space at the front counter and the employees are talking to each other about a concert. The male employee stops and turns up the volume on a CD by the Circle Jerks. The Yuppie yells at him to "turn the damn noise down." He turns the volume up higher; they leave. Total time in store: 3 minutes.

Action: Punks, Metalheads, and Goths/Vamps.

Two female Vamps come in and go directly to the poster section, select a couple of posters, and head in the direction of the counter. Instead of buying, they run out of the door without paying. The male employee jumps over the front counter, but it's too late. Screeching tires indicate a getaway car. Total time in the store: 2½ minutes.

(Fifteen such incidents included in the field notes are not duplicated here.)

Data Analysis: Conversations are transcribed and sorted by group for common themes and patterns.

Conversations between Punks and employees reflect mutual admiration.

Typical exchange:

> Employee: "Hi, shithead."
>
> Punk: "Hi, Jen. You like my shoes? Got 'em on sale."
>
> Employee: "Hate 'em."
>
> Punk: "Cool."

Metalheads stick to dialogue about various artists and new posters.

Typical exchange:

> Employee: "Greetings, rivetheads. Don't steal anything. Some chicks already stole some posters from me tonight."
>
> Metalhead: "Which ones?"
>
> Employee: "Robert Smith shit."
>
> Metalhead: "Bad taste."

Employees insult everyone who enters, but most customers are used to it and provide equally insulting retorts. One of the most entertaining employee conversations concerned the authenticity of Hillary Clinton's breasts.

Activities are identified as either "hanging out" or "music hunting." Two types of shoppers, "loners" and "groupies," populate the store. Discount Records functions as a gathering place and information center for music junkies, providing music that is no longer available through mainstream outlets. The store is an information clearing house on all things concerning punk, metal, and goth/vamp subcultures.

Results: After comparing Discount Records with mainstream music stores in other locations, as well as alternative record stores named Moby Disc and Beggar's Banquet, the researcher identified problems related to sales and formulated the following theories to be tested with future research:

T1: Alternative record stores exist because members of a given subculture keep them alive and are highly protective of them.

T2: Customers who are not members of a subculture will not have a pleasant consumption experience in alternative record stores.

Conclusion: Participant observation techniques enabled this researcher to determine that the problem of sagging sales was not due to the disorganization of the store merchandise but to the diminishing subculture population at that location. Recommendation: To increase revenues, the client was advised to relocate the store to an area that enjoyed heavier subculture traffic.

Notes

1. From Weick, K. (1985). Systematic observation methods. In G. Lindzdey & E. Aronson (Eds.), *Handbook of social psychology: Vol 1. Theory and method.* New York: Random House.

2. From Gold, R. L. (1958). Roles in sociological field observations. *Social Forces, 36,* 217-223.

3. From an observation made by K. Teenor (1994). *Field observations.* Unpublished paper, California State University, Fullerton. The quoted passages that follow are from pages 2, 5, 6, and 7.

4. See Chapter 5 in Lindlof, T. R. (1995). *Qualitative communication research methods.* Thousand Oaks, CA: Sage.

5. See Petronio, S., & Bourhis, J. (1987). Identifying family collectives in public places: An instructional exercise. *Communication Education, 36,* 46-51.

6. See Van Maanen, J. (1988). *Tales of the field: On writing ethnography.* Chicago: University of Chicago Press.

7. From Spradley, J. P. (1980). *Participant observation.* New York: Holt, Rinehart & Winston.

8. Glaser, B. G., & Strauss, A. L. (1967). *The discovery of grounded theory: Strategies for qualitative research.* Chicago: Aldine.

9. From Manning, P. K. (1987). *Semiotics and fieldwork.* Newbury Park, CA: Sage.

10. Manasay, A. (1997). *Ethnography of Discount Records.* Unpublished paper, California State University, Fullerton.

11 Ways of Knowing

Field Interviews

Everyone has probably listened to or seen at least one interview. Whether they're conducted by David Letterman late at night, moderated by Chris Matheson on HardBall, or sponsored by the grand jury, interviews facilitate our understanding of a subject by probing people who know about it. Because they allow us inside the minds of others, interviews are tools to help marketplace researchers understand consumer behaviors and attitudes about what they know best—consumption.

Interviews allow researchers to find out about people's ideas, their thoughts, their opinions, their attitudes, and what motivates them. Interviews complement observations. Observations give us a sense of context but not an understanding of how people think and feel. Following are four basic differences between observation and interviews:[1]

Observation	Interviews
Present	Past and present
Actions	Attitudes
Context	Motivations
Seeing	Hearing and probing

The biggest advantage of interviews is the ability to record them for later analysis.

As you've undoubtedly seen on television, interviewing techniques range from humorously casual to embarrassingly serious. The more formal the setting, the more structured the questions. Our overview of interview situations begins with the most casual and works its way through increasingly structured situations. Although the purpose is always the same—to learn—the techniques vary with the degree of discovery needed to solve the research problem. Whether we

134

require general insight from a consumer or need something clarified from an informant, interviews are structured to facilitate elicitation in particular consumption cultures.

This chapter presents an introduction to the interview genre for use in marketplace research. Field interviews take three forms: those with single members, those with informants, and those with groups. Structured interviews (discussed in Chapter 12) are conducted in off-site venues with respondents and focus groups.

Field Interviewing Techniques

It takes two people to speak the truth—one to speak, and another to listen.
—Henry David Thoreau, 1849

Conducted during the process of understanding a consumption culture, interviewing in the field requires a researcher to develop rapport with members or informants and gather information from them. Field researchers are often apprehensive about engaging strangers in conversation; however, once an initial discomfort has passed, discourse usually flows smoothly. The objective is to keep the consumer talking. By exploring a mutually satisfactory relationship through purposeful conversation, interviewers gain the confidence of members.

Rapport is built by explaining what you want to know, repeating key phrases used by members, and restating what they say in your own words. What differentiates field interviews from more structured situations is the absence of questions that ask for meanings or motives. "What do you mean" or "Why would you" questions contain hidden judgmental components; members may think they haven't clearly answered your questions and begin to feel pressured.

An alternative approach is to employ *use questions*. By asking them how they use the phrase or gesture, we allow cultural meanings to emerge. For instance, suppose you're observing an audience during a musical performance. After each song, you see people raising their thumbs during the applause. Rather than ask, "What does it mean to raise your thumb?" ask, "In what other situation would you raise your thumb?" The response of an equivalent use of the gesture provides you with insight into how thumbs are used to express response to performance.

On entering the field, researchers look to members of the consumption culture or audience to explain what is going on. After members have familiarized us with the *scene* (location of the activity), we look to informants to help us clarify what we have learned. Members inform, informants clarify.

Interviewing Members[2]

Once you establish rapport between yourself and members of the culture under study, the process begins to be more participative. Unlike talk shows where questions are asked, then answered, participative interviewing begins with the assumption that the question-answer sequence is a single element in consumer thinking. In other words, we assume that both questions and answers must be discovered from members.

When we're attempting to learn about a specific consumption culture, we must develop ways to discover questions. One way is listening to the questions posed in conversations between consumers or audiences, such as "When are they playing?" or "How much does that cost?" Another way is asking consumers directly: "What is an interesting question about going to the theater?" or "If I heard shoppers talking among themselves during a sale, what questions would I hear them ask each other?"

A more subtle but thorough approach is to ask consumers to talk about a particular consumption scene. Here, generally, the use of *descriptive questions* allows consumers to paint word pictures of what's taking place. One example of a descriptive question is, "Can you tell me about shopping at a Macy's Day sale?"

Asking Descriptive Questions

Descriptive questions that encourage consumers to talk about a particular consumption activity are ideal for eliciting large amounts of information. To expand on the Macy's question, we might say: "I've never been to a Macy's Day sale, and I don't know what to expect. Can you take me through a typical sale day and tell me what it's like?" Five types of descriptive questions are used for eliciting information. They are briefly presented here.

1. Grand tour questions (GTQ): Similar to the foregoing expanded question, GTQs are asked to extract a verbal description of a consumption scene through space, time, events, people, activities, or objects. Four varieties are suggested for adaptation to specific marketplace needs:

   a. Typical GTQ—asks for a description of how things usually are: "Can you describe a typical Macy's Day sale?"

   b. Specific GTQ—specifies a time, day, or location of an event: "Can you describe what yesterday's sale was like at their downtown location?"

   c. Guided GTQ—requests a personal tour of a location or activity: "Can you show me around the housewares department and tell me how you decide what to buy?"

   d. Task-related GTQ—requires a specific task for a consumer to perform to expand their descriptions: "Could you draw me a map of the store's first floor and tell me what shopping there is like?" You may ask questions along the way, such as "What is this?"

2. Minitour questions: These questions deal with much smaller amounts of information and are usually derived from information gathered in GTQs. For instance, five women describing a typical Macy's Day sale may all use the term "bargain basement." This prompts a minitour question, such as: "Can you tell me about other types of bargain basements?" All four types of GTQs are applicable here as well.

3. Example questions: These narrow down a single activity or incident by asking for an example. If a consumer says she was cheated out of a good deal, you might ask, "Can you give me an example of how people are cheated at this sale?"

4. Experience questions: These focus responses on a particular setting or activity. "Can you tell me about other experiences you've had with department store sales?"

5. Native-language questions: Because consumers tend to use language that is consumption specific, these questions provide an opportunity to hear the terms and phrases most commonly used in that consumption scene. If you've heard terms such as "bargain basement" and "free-for-all" during GTQs, you might want to ask consumers, "How do you refer to Macy's Day sales to your friends?" Answers will give you insight into their shopping "lingo." Three types of native-language queries are available:

    a. Direct-language questions—simply asking: "How do you refer to the Macy's Day sale?" Or in response to a consumer remark about "dumb sales clerks," you might ask, "How do you refer to sales clerks?" To which the reply might be, "I'd probably call them 'dumbos.'"

    b. Hypothetical-interaction questions—posing a hypothetical situation: Elicitation may come easier for some consumers if you give them a hypothetical situation. "If a friend of yours was to refer to a sales clerk at Macy's, what would she call her?"

    c. Typical-sentence question—asking for specific typical sentences: Usage is often important to understanding language. You can ask, "What are some sentences I would hear at the sale that contain the term *bargain basement*?"

Open-ended, descriptive questions enable field researchers to gather information naturally in the setting where the activity occurs. Information flows freely in a conversational fashion in the absence of directive probes. Ethnographic interviewing techniques are valuable for gaining a thorough understanding of the way consumers talk about and understand their consumption experiences.

Member interviews are intended to establish meanings (e.g., bargain basement) and opinions ("clerks are stupid"), to distinguish elements of those opinions ("they never know where anything is"), to determine influences ("my daughter told me to shop there"), and to classify attitude patterns ("we feel good when we shop on Saturdays").

Interviewing Informants[3]

Informants, as defined in Chapter 9, play a key role in enabling researchers to understand consumption cultures. Unlike members, who explain a phenomenon, informants *clarify meanings* for researchers, acting as cultural interpreters. Particular characteristics of informant interviews help distinguish them from those conducted with other members.

When a researcher meets with an informant, the interaction is *directed and purposeful,* not conversational. Researchers must offer *explanations* about the study so informants can teach them about the culture. Researchers use *ethnographic questions* to gather information, including descriptive questions, structural questions, and contrast questions.

Descriptive questions provide researchers with a sample of the informant's language. One example is, "Can you describe a department store sale you have been to recently?" The easiest to ask, descriptive questions are used for all field interviews.

Structural questions enable the researcher to discover information about how informants have organized their knowledge, such as "What are the different types of sales clerks you have encountered while shopping?"

Contrast questions help us with meanings. Language and terms used by consumers are interpreted by informants who make distinctions among the objects and events of a consumption scene. A typical question might be, "What's the difference between a bargain basement and a free-for-all?"

During interviews with informants, researchers attend to these four steps:

1. *Ask the questions;* informants talk about their experiences.

2. *Repeat what the informant says,* restating responses using the informant's terms, *and* repeating the questions. This last component expands on the less intense repetition used to interview members.

3. *Express interest* in the subject and claim ignorance about the language. This stance provides informants with confidence and a sense of being important to the study results.

4. *Encourage informants* to expand by repeating and rephrasing questions; discourage abbreviation of responses.

Interviewing informants requires a variety of interpersonal skills, especially those of listening instead of talking, taking a passive rather than an assertive role, expressing verbal interest in the other person, and showing that interest with eye contact and other nonverbal means. Researchers often identify a *key informant,* who acts as the primary source for validation and confirmation during member interviews.

Cultural understanding is not always the focus of interviewing. Researchers seeking attitudinal information, evaluations, or answers to specific questions conduct structured interviews at locations away from the field site. Methods for structured interviews differ from those used in field situations in ways that will become obvious in the next chapter.

Interviewing Groups[4]

Group interviews involve a researcher and more than one consumer. Conducted in the field, focus groups are informal and open-ended. Groups are advisable when you need to gain a lot of information in a short period of time. Interviewing in groups allows field researchers to gather information in the idiomatic language and communication patterns of consumer or audience discourse.

Group interviews are ideal for obtaining the history of a situation or event. No question protocol is used, and conversations evolve and continue through participant interactions rather than from directed questions. Timing is spontaneous and not previously determined. Self-selected participants choose the setting; the group size is subject to natural conditions in the field. Members are volunteers who agree to continue their relationship with the interviewer in an information-sharing spirit.

During a field study of a devastating firestorm that raged around a college campus, I found myself talking with students who were forced to evacuate their dorms. This study focused on the possessions people chose to take with them as they evacuated their living spaces. By coincidence, some of the students who shared my table during a lunch break were discussing that very topic. After disclosing my purpose, I asked them to share their evacuation experiences on audiotape. A group of 11 students pulled chairs around a table and talked for about an hour. My role was one of listener; I posed an occasional query for clarification purposes.

The group session provided an opportunity to gather a range of opinions and a variety of actions taken in response to the evacuation notice. One student remembered her roommate taking a sheet and throwing every possession she had into it, dragging the menagerie to her car, and driving off without a word. Another spoke of specific selections she made, such as an answering machine tape, computer discs, class notes, and a CD collection.

Incident recollections were disclosed in a chain reaction fashion. As one student remembered something to share, another's memory was triggered. Exchanges were rapid fire and humorous at first; after a while, conversations reverted to situations of parents and friends who were not lucky enough to return home because their dwellings were consumed by the fire. At the session's conclusion, I collected names and numbers of students willing to act as informants, if needed, to clarify parts of the recorded discourse.

Informal field interviews are valuable adjuncts to more formalized data collection. Opportunities to talk informally with groups of people occur in unpredictable ways and at unpredictable times. By being constantly vigilant, researchers can take advantage of such opportunities to enhance their understanding of a theme, situation, or event.

Customer Visits[5]

Most of the investigation discussed here involves interviews with consumers—single entities and their behavior. In certain instances, research involves companies rather than individuals; we refer to them as *customers*. Customer interviews can take the form of specially designed customer visits conducted by individuals or teams on site at a particular company.

Customer visit programs, designed especially for business-to-business research, are conducted in the context of either *new product development* or *new market development* or initiatives to improve *customer satisfaction*. Some programs are part of larger market research efforts, but often, customer visit programs stand alone as the primary research tool. Here are examples of objectives that are fulfilled through customer visits:

Identifying emerging customer needs not met by current versions of a particular product

Describing customers' purchase decision models and procedures for qualifying and selecting vendors

Testing which of several possible product configurations will be preferred by customers

Forecasting potential sales from segments identified as candidates for market expansion

A planning program for customer visits has seven stages: (a) setting objectives; (b) selecting a sample; (c) composing the visit team; (d) developing the discussion guide; (e) conducting interviews; (f) debriefing after each interview;

and (g) analyzing, reporting, and storing visit data. The use of team visits brings depth and texture to study results.

Customer visits replace survey research and usability tests and differ from each in several ways. When the situation for identifying appropriate survey questions is uncertain, customer visits can identify them. Both focus groups and customer visits enhance interviewing through multiple opinions and perspectives. But customer visits are best for business-to-business situations because of their ability to pursue highly technical issues at length. Examining interaction between user and product, usability research is conducted in a laboratory context. When usability is more relevant to strategic planning, customer visits provide a broader approach, including nonusers, decision makers, and opinion leaders in the research process.

Customer visit programs have the most value in high-uncertainty situations where the issues are complex and when perspectives rather than facts are necessary outcomes. Because interviews are a key component of customer visits, the method is included here for its application to business-to-business situations.

Active Listening[6]

Listening is a skill many of us take for granted. Someone speaks, we listen. To understand better, we ask questions. But questions give us answers, and often, these answers do not help us understand the issue. A useful way to get information is to use "tell me about" statements. Using tell-me-abouts, we receive consumer thoughts, including feelings, frustrations, problems, successes, and so forth. Probing topics of conversation allows us to follow a person's train of thought on a subject. We find out their ideas, not just their answers. Tell-me-abouts can take the researcher into a consumer's mind.

Active listening is a technique of interviewing that uses subtle probing to get a full picture of what is going on in the minds of members and informants, to find out what is motivating and what is not, as it relates to a topic, concept, or stimulus. Active listeners must identify four obstacles to gathering information: (a) generalization, (b) deletion, (c) distortion, and (d) contradiction. Once identified, these problems can be overcome with subtle probes.

A *generalization* is a vague word or phrase that has no meaning in and of itself. People often speak in generalizations, and they occur frequently during interviews. An example is, "This is a good pen." To an active listener, "good" is meaningless. So we ask the person, "What do you mean by *good*?" You hear in response, "It costs a lot of money." The response lets you know that *good* means *expensive* for this consumer.

Probing a generalization has limits in that the meaning of an idea is defined within the context of the statement made. Probing generalizations is the base-level skill of active listening.

A *deletion* is something left out of a conversation that could be key to understanding the person's attitudes or decision making. An active listener probes a deletion by using an open-ended question to determine what has been left out: "What else?" After you get the response about the pen costing a lot, you ask, "What else do you like about the pen?" A response might be, "I like the shape, the way it fits my hand." By probing a deletion, the active listener will get a fuller picture of the complexity of a member's thinking, what different ideas are operating. Although probing deletions yields a list of items that are part of the process of choosing a pen, it does not tell each item's meaning or its relative importance.

A *distortion* is a situation in which the listener doesn't fully understand the role of a consumer's idea in the overall decision-making process of that person. If we learn all about what the member likes about the pen, we still don't know what he or she dislikes about the pen. So we ask, "You've told me what you like; what do you dislike about the pen?" Response: "The refills are hard to find." Active listening helps us to avoid misconstruing the meaning of what the person is saying by asking for additional details.

A *contradiction* is at least two statements that imply opposite or conflicting ideas. This is the most difficult problem to detect. Because it may be socially impolite to point out contradiction, the interviewer must be tactful and take the blame for not hearing them. We put the consumer at ease by placing him or her in the position of "helping" us. Suppose, while listing the items disliked about the pen, the person once again mentions it's high price. Price at once becomes what they both like and dislike about the pen.

So we say, "I'm sorry, I think I missed something. Earlier, you said that the pen was good because it was expensive, but then you said that one of the things you did not like was its high price. How do they fit? Can you help me?" Hopefully, they will clarify with something like, "Well, it costs $89, which is a lot, but it's worth it because it will last a long time and because people will know how much I paid—even though I don't like paying it." By probing the contradiction, a third idea emerged about the subject that we might not have gotten otherwise. Here, we know that the user is most interested in the pen's image and what it contributes to the concept of self.

By listening for meaning, we get meaningful communication. Listening is understanding what people mean by the words they use. Finding out what they mean requires knowing these four problems and how to overcome them during the interview process.

Cyberresearch

In cyberspace, the relationship between suppliers and users increasingly resembles the kinds of relationships that the culture industries have forged with audiences over the years. We are entering a more cerebral period of capitalism whose product is access to time and mind.

—Jeremy Rifkin, 2000

Because of the growing importance of technology to research, this section is dedicated to information about the Internet as an appropriate tool for studying consumption and marketplace cultures. An overview of Web-based resources and an overview of Internet research using qualitative techniques both follow.

Cyberspace has been likened to a "consensual hallucination."[7] Some say it's like Oz: We get there but there's no "there" there. Others say virtual reality allows us to play God. For these and other reasons, researchers who study consumption reality face some dilemmas regarding the role of the Internet for collecting and analyzing text.[8] One such dilemma is the consideration of identity in a technoreality as a matter of freedom and choice. In virtual reality, we can choose to represent ourselves as anything we wish. New identities, mobile identities, exploratory identities—a world of let's pretend—create havoc for consumer research results. Internet environments are particularly receptive to the projection and acting out of unconscious fantasies.

Given the potential for disaster, we wonder about the future of the Internet for studying so-called reality and ask some of these questions: If cyberspace is imagined as a zone of unlimited freedom without barriers or restrictions, how can truth prevail? Without directly meeting others physically, will our ethics languish?[9] And, can an area of existence that is neither inside the person nor outside in the world of shared reality act as a space for cultural experience? What about the virtual communities of cyberspace that live in the borderlands of both physical and virtual culture? Although we can't address all of these issues here, the questions are posed for your reflection.

Cyberethnography

Computer-mediated communication (CMC) is studied ethnographically using the Internet as field of study.[10] As we've discussed, ethnography presumes a marketplace culture from which consumers derive interpretive strategies and a sense of identity. CMC can be conceptualized as a virtual community.

Virtual communities produce a variety of collective goods. They allow people of like interests to come together with little cost to exchange ideas and provide the kind of identification and feeling of membership found in face-to-face interaction. The novelty of the medium means that the rules and practices that lead to successful virtual community are not yet well known or set fast in a codified formal system.[11]

As one study of an electronic cafe shows,[12] a virtual community describes how users engage in networked relationships and account for the moral order of their activity. A computer bulletin board system (BBS) serves users by using a "bar fantasy" where patrons move about in the bar's physical features (fireplace, hot tub, chair, etc.) ordering beverages, making new friends, and so forth. Regulars are able to recognize inappropriate behavior of "newbies" (newcomers to the cafe) and impose collective sanctions. "Bashers" who disrupt the cafe's atmosphere are met with defensive strategies by the patrons. This cafe is an example of a virtual community founded intentionally by people who share a set of similar interests. These communities provide virtual fields of interaction for study by cyberethnographers.

Of particular relevance for marketplace research is the technical utility of data generation for accomplishing research tasks. Asynchronous communication interaction (where users do not communicate in real time) can be studied by saving individual messages or archiving all postings for later perusal. Most important for our use are electronic mail, news groups over Usenet, and list servers.

Electronic mail is quick in terms of transmission and reply, text based, and configured for multiple connections (one-on-one, one-to-many, or many-to-many).[13] E-mail can be stored in external memory for future retrieval, searching, editing, and forwarding to others. Meanings can be changed by editing, and the historical records can be used for surveillance of personal or group interactions. E-mail is particularly suitable for ethnographic research because of its personal contact and archival functions.

In a yearlong participant observation study of a computer system firm, a researcher used E-mail in the following ways:[14]

Being placed on the company's distribution lists to receive internal documents, meeting minutes and agendas, and announcements

Scheduling interviews

Accessing hundreds of BBSs, including company correspondence going back several years

Communicating with informants

E-mail as a medium for conducting interviews is less informative than personal interviews because it does not promote the same qualities of rapport or spontaneity, nor does it permit thoughtful interpretation of questions or replies.

In another study,[15] special software automatically saved headers of all departmental E-mail to a designated file. This narrative archive provided a nonreactive means of learning who communicates with whom, when, and about what. Information can be augmented with interviews, but using the data without users' permission poses potential ethical abuse.

Usenet is a protocol that describes how groups of messages can be stored on and sent between computers, even outside the Internet. Usenet creates a virtual forum for the electronic community that is divided into a plethora of news groups dedicated to varied areas of interest.[16] In a participant observation of a news group of soap opera fans, news group articles are read and written through newsreader programs that keep track of articles read and allow editing and replies to previously posted messages.[17] The researcher was able to develop "thick descriptions" of the personalities of this community based on features of their postings: signature files, humor in the messages, self-disclosure, and comments made about personal lives. Usenet news groups facilitate variations of focus group interviewing. One computer-mediated focus group was set up to determine what motivated frequent and active BBS use.[18]

Listserv groups are similar to news groups in that they are both discussion groups, but listserv groups use the Internet E-mail system to exchange messages. Listserv subscribers' names are added to mailing lists that receive postings from all subscribers to the list.[19] Users may search and retrieve archive files, allowing anyone from a remote site to access archived messages for study from the host computer. Ownership of the archived materials is a matter still under debate.

Some of the more recent real-time technologies are (a) Internet Relay Chat systems (IRC); (b) multiple-user, object-oriented, and MUSHes (multiple-user-shared hallucination) technologies; (c) groupware, and (d) desktop video-conferencing. These technologies provide many more personal communication options for researchers.

IRC is available worldwide, providing multithreaded conversational chat lines sometimes called *electronic cocktail parties.*[20] Party attendees are able to use false identities and communicate with others from all over the globe. Multiuser programs are designed to offer a pseudophysical dimension via object orientation for entertainment and amusement. Groupware, on the other hand, is used mainly for business and professional communication, such as conferencing. Ethnographers have access to common threads running through the programs, similar to what is called "shared memory."[21] Groupware allows the researcher to observe the virtual office and record interactions for study.

Technologically driven research is dictated by the characteristics of the medium. Synchronous media enable types of research equivalent to naturalistic observation, whereas asynchronous media yields only written narrative. Interpretive analysts are interested in the common cultures moving through the Internet. The difference between embodied and virtual ethnography is participation. Virtual ethnography allows a researcher to explain and engage in experience while being physically absent, even without informed consent.

Cyberspeak

As "geek chic" takes hold of our technology-obsessed culture, cyberslang seeps into everyday language. Earlier technology left its marks on our language in much the same way. Railroad metaphors once prevailed in terms such as *getting sidetracked* and *full steam ahead.* Today, a sort of social Darwinism prevails in the form of phrases drawn from comic books, sci-fi films, and kids' stories.[22] Popular culture has survived as fittest for our communication in the 21st century.

An unforgiving place ruled by the merciless dynamics of the marketplace, the high-tech world mirrors our casino society. According to tech informants, cyberland politics are libertarian, and its presiding muse is Ayn Rand, author of *Atlas Shrugged* and *Fountainhead.*[23] This is a world with an acronym for "fear, uncertainty, and doubt" (FUD) and another for "waste of money, brains, and time" (WOMBAT).

Flush with disparaging references to the real world, geek speak refers to the nonvirtual as "carbon community" or "meatspace," and scoffs at "wetware" (humans). Cyberethnographers have a wonderful opportunity to study virtual culture and its language. Here are a few phrases translated from a Silicon Valley cyberculture:

Domainist: Someone who judges people by the domain of their E-mail address

Kavork (after Dr. Jack Kavorkian): to kill something—"Kavork that project, and let's go out for a beer."

Kubris: An extreme form of arrogance found in multimedia auteurs who think they're Stanley Kubric

PANS: Pretty amazing new stuff[24]

The implications of computer networks and cyberlanguage for the construction of text are of great importance to marketplace researchers. Virtual space is the place for the field studies of today.

Summary

1. Interviews enable researchers to get inside consumers' minds to learn about their ideas, thoughts, opinions, and attitudes.

2. Field interviews are conducted with individuals or groups, have an informal structure, and take place where the study is being conducted.

3. Active listening identifies four problem areas and uses subtle probes to derive meanings from members and informants in single or group situations.

4. Member interviews take place in the field using description questions.

5. Informants provide researchers with explanations, validations, confirmations, and interpretations of information collected from members.

6. Researchers doing cyberethnography make use of E-mail, Usenet, and Listserv to gather text from the Internet.

7. Tools of real-time technology include Internet Relay Chat systems, multiuser group technologies, groupware, and desktop video conferencing.

Stretching Exercises

1. Conduct and record a 5-minute informal interview with a friend to find out how he or she shops for sneakers (or another product). Use as many active listening techniques as you can. Then, play back the tape to count and identify the types of your probes. How might you improve on your technique?

2. As the basis for a group interview, write out a list of descriptive questions, beginning with a GTQ, that are appropriate to investigate the experience of being at a Grateful Dead concert. Send the questions to 10 people online, and summarize their responses.

Recommended Readings About Interviewing

Atkinson, R. (1998). *The life story interview.* Thousand Oaks, CA: Sage.

Kvale, S. (1996). *Interviews: An introduction to qualitative research interviews.* Thousand Oaks, CA: Sage.

McCracken, G. (1988). *The long interview.* Thousand Oaks, CA: Sage.

Rheingold, H. (1993). *The virtual community.* Don Mills, Ontario, Canada: Wesley.

Stewart, C. J., & Cash, W. B., Jr. (1988). *Interviewing principles and practices.* Dubuque, IA: William C. Brown.

Case in Point: The Sacred
and Profane in Consumption[25]

Client: Association for Consumer Research

Problem: Describing the processes of consumption at work in contemporary society

RQ: *What are the properties and manifestations of the "sacred" inherent in consumer behavior?*

Data Collection: Depth interviews were used requiring unstructured responsiveness to consumers and intimacy between researcher and informant. Interviews were collected at swap meets, antique flea markets, farmers' markets, yard sales, community fairs, festivals, and private homes. Interviews were audiotaped or videotaped.

Data Analysis: Interview transcripts were transcribed and computerized for use in systematic data analysis using ZyiIndex, a program for qualitative data management and analysis.

Results: Data indicate that there are seven ways through which an object can become sacralized in contemporary consumer culture: ritual, pilgrimage, quintessence, gift giving, collecting, inheritance, and external sanction. Samples of transcript data are included here to illustrate the testimony used to understand the concept of sacralization.

Ritual: Home renovation—a ritual symbol of a transformation that made the home sacred

> The first day that we were able to be here, we ran in. My husband's stepfather came and photographed inside and outside; and then we also took pictures of states of change as we remodeled last summer. It's just fun to get those out and remember how, oh, it was awful.

Pilgrimage: A journey away from home to a consumption site

> We sold our house, truck and other stuff . . . we gave up our jobs. And we took the kids out of school. To see the West, the real country. That is our idea. In this covered wagon, just like the pioneers did. We're going west.

Quintessence: Objects that possess a rare and mysterious capacity to be just exactly what they ought to be . . . unequivocally right; tourists regard places they have visited that are exceptionally natural and unspoiled as quintessentially sacred.

> We hadn't planned on going to Prince Edward Island, but we heard so many people in Nova Scotia say good things about it that we decided to go. One stretch of beach was the most beautiful place I've ever seen. It looked like God had reached down his hand and touched it.

Gift giving: Something bought for someone else, as in the case of a 14-year-old boy who bought a gift for his uncle who didn't come on the trip, using money he earned mowing lawns

> Interviewer: How does it make you feel to be in a place like this; kind of fun? Old?
>
> Boy: Yeah, it makes me feel old; it makes me feel like going back into history. It makes you feel old, like you are in that time.
>
> Interviewer: What will it feel like when you wear your belt buckle?
>
> Boy: I don't know. I guess it will feel (pause) make me feel like I'm a soldier or somethin' like that. Or it could give you some sort of, I can't explain. You know how you feel sort of proud? The Civil War makes you feel like you're a general or something like that; like you are in the army.
>
> Interviewer: So you will wear your belt buckle and that will kind of bring back what this place was like?
>
> Boy: Well, the buckle's not for me.
>
> Interviewer: It's not?
>
> Boy: It's for my uncle. So he gets the buckle. If I had it, I'd feel proud.

Collections: Regarded by their owners as special, unique, and separate from the everyday items they have and use; each piece is a part of the whole unit

> Interviewer: Would you take the elephant piece out of your collection and sell it to me?
>
> Man: No, never. It wouldn't be as important if I was able to just put this elephant out in the store and sell it. If I liked it that well and I bought it, then it must be important to the collection. So I'm going to keep it there.
>
> Interviewer: So once a piece joins the collection, then it stays with the collection?
>
> Man: It becomes the collection. It's part of it. It's going to stay there, period.

Inheritance: Heirlooms and other items unique because of their sentimental associations with the owner's past history

> Dad gave me his ring. Don't think it's worth much . . . maybe. But I like it 'cause it reminds me of Dad. He died 4 years ago. My Dad.

External sanction: Here, external authority designates something sacred (e.g., cathedrals).

> I saw this like, mansion, and we went on a tour through it. Like, it was a museum. All their furniture was still there and all.

Discussion: Consumers accord sacred status to a variety of objects, places, and times that are value expressive. By expressing these values through their consumption, they participate in a celebration of their connection to the society as a whole and to particular individuals. For society, defining as sacred certain artifacts that are value expressive provides social cohesion and societal integration. For the individual, participating in these expressions provides meaning in life and a mechanism for experiencing stability, joy, and occasionally ecstasy through connection.

Conclusion: The process used by marketers to attempt to singularize and occasionally sacralize a commodity so it becomes a differentiated, branded product has been described. Often, quite apart from marketers' efforts and considerations of brand, consumers themselves sacralize consumption objects and thereby create transcendent meaning in their lives. By laying the foundation for an understanding of the sacred in consumption, the researchers have demonstrated how rich a naturalistic approach to interviewing consumers can be.

Notes

1. From Berger, A. A. (2000). *Media and communication research methods* (p.113). Thousand Oaks, CA: Sage.

2. From Spradley, J. P. (1979). *The ethnographic interview.* London: Harcourt Brace Jovanovich.

3. Spradley, J. P. (1979), pp. 78-91. See Note 2.

4. See Schensul, J. J., LeCompte, M., Nastasi, B. K., & Borgatti, S. (1999). *Advanced ethnographic methods* (Chapter 2). Walnut Creek, CA: AltaMira.

5. From McQuarrie, E. F. (1998). *Customer visits: Building a better market focus.* Thousand Oaks, CA: Sage.

6. Adapted from materials prepared by Communication Development Company, West Des Moines, Iowa.

7. Gourgey, H., & Smith, E. B. (1996). Consensual hallucination: Cyberspace and the creation of an interpretive community. *Text and Performance Quarterly, 16,* 233-247.

8. See Robbins, K. (1996). *Into the image: Culture and politics in the field of vision* (Chapter 4). New York: Routledge.

9. The Forum on the Ethics of Fair Practices for Collecting Social Science Data in Cyberspace, with a special section of the scholarly journal *The Information Society,* illustrates the variety of positions about ethical guidelines in online social research.

10. From Lindlof, T. R., & Shatzer, M. (1998). Media ethnography in virtual space: Strategies, limits and possibilities. *Journal of Broadcasting and Electronic Media, 42*(2), 170-190.

11. Smith, M. (1993). Voices from the WELL: The logic of the virtual commons. Text available from Smithm@nicco.sscnet.ucla.edu.

12. Correll, S. (1995). The ethnography of an electronic bar: The Lesbian Café. *Journal of Contemporary Ethnography, 24,* 270-298.

13. Garton, L., & Wellman, B. (1995). Social impacts of electronic mail in organizations: A review of the research literature. In B. R. Burleson (Ed.), *Communication Yearbook 18* (pp. 434-453). Thousand Oaks, CA: Sage.

14. Workman, J. P. (1992). Use of electronic mail in a participant observation study. *Qualitative Sociology, 15,* 419-425.

15. Huff, C. W., & Rosenberg, J. (1989). The on-line voyeur: Promises and pitfalls of observing electronic interaction. *Behavior, Research Methods, Instruments & Computers, 21*(2), 166-172.

16. Edings, J. (1994). *How the Internet works.* Emeryville, CA: Ziff-Davis.

17. Bym, N. K. (1995). From practice to culture on Usenet. In S. L. Star (Ed.), *Cultures of computing* (pp. 29-52). Cambridge, MA: Blackwell.

18. Myers, D. (1987). Anonymity is part of the magic: Individual manipulation of computer-mediated communication contexts. *Qualitative Sociology, 10,* 251-266.

19. Kent, P. (1994). *Ten minute guide to the Internet.* Indianapolis, IN: Alpha.

20. Wellman, B., Salaff, J., Dimitrova, D., Garton, L., Guilia, M., & Haythornthwaite, C. (1996). Computer networks as social networks: Collaborative work, telework, and virtual community. *Annual Review of Psychology, 22,* 213-229.

21. Snyder, J. (1997). *Groupware: Colonizing new ground for industrious networks.* Available: www.Techweb.com /se/directlink.cgi?NWC19960315.

22. From an article by Kakutani, M. (2000, June 27). When the geeks get snide. *New York Times,* p. B1.

23. Borsook, P. (2000). *Cyberselfish.* New York: Putnam.

24. For more cyberterms, see the Ultimate Silicon Valley Slang Page at www.sabram.com/site/slang/html.

25. Based on a study conducted by Belk, R., Wallendorf, M., & Sherry, J. (1991). The sacred and the profane in consumer behavior: Theodicy on the odyssey. In Belk, R. (Ed.), *Highways and buyways: Naturalistic research from the consumer odyssey* (pp. 59-101). Provo, UT: Association for Consumer Research.

Structured Interviews

W hen field studies are not feasible because of time constraints or other criteria, interviews can be scheduled and structured to address the specific needs of a client or student. Media, entertainment, and advertising researchers who are interested in effects and attitudinal studies that do not require naturalistic settings choose a more formal approach to information gathering. Here, the focus of the research is not to answer the question, "What's going on here?" but rather to ask questions such as, "How do you feel?" about something and "Why do you feel that way?" These questions are addressed to individual respondents or to groups.

Venues for respondent and group interviews are dedicated settings or research sites technologically designed to record or view (or both) the interaction that takes place between interviewer and respondents. Although similar in purpose, single-respondent and multiple-respondent interviews differ in probing techniques and interviewer skill levels. Structured situations presented here are respondent interviews, focus group interviews, and nominal grouping sessions.

Respondent Interviews

The first contact between researcher and respondent often takes place at the time of the interview rather than in the field, limiting information gathering to verbal exchange. Interviews are more formal than those conducted in the field. Interviewers use a predetermined set of directive, open-ended questions in the form of *interview protocols.*

The objectives of respondent interviews:[1]

Clarify the meanings of common concepts and opinions

Distinguish elements of an expressed opinion

Determine what influences an attitude or behavior

Classify complex attitude patterns

Understand the motivations consumers attribute to their actions

Interviews begin with questions similar to GTQs. "What do you remember about television commercials for SUVs?" is typical of what one might say to study consumer attitudes toward a new advertising campaign for Jeep. A typical response may be, "They show lots of rough terrain."

Probing Techniques

In cases where responses are short or off base, *probing techniques*[2] are invoked. When systematic information gathering is a primary concern, one or all of these four probing types are available:

Informational probes ask for more explanation. "What do you mean by 'rough riding'?"

Nudging probes prod the respondent to continue giving information. A few words will do, such as these:

I see.

Go on.

And?

What else?

Clearinghouse probes make sure that respondents have said all they can about a subject before going on to the next question. "Is there anything else you remember about the commercial?"

Reflective probes and *mirror questions* verify and clarify answers, to check accuracy of understanding and interpretation. "You think SUV commercials should include statistics, gas mileage, and price?" (reflective probe) "OK then, you don't think any one SUV campaign is better than any other, is that right?" (mirror question)

Here's another example of how probing works with research on media audiences.

> GTQ: With over 140 available channels to choose from, tell me how you make decisions regarding what television program you'll watch?
>
> Response: I use my remote mostly.
>
> Informational probe: And just how do you use the remote?
>
> Response: I click on a show for a few minutes, and if I don't like what I see, I change channels.
>
> Nudging probe: Go on.
>
> Response: Well, sometimes I stay on a program until the commercials, then start switching again.
>
> Nudging probe: I see.
>
> Response: Yeah, I rarely use the TV guide because the channel numbers are different than the ones I get on my satellite. But if I see a show advertised on another channel, then I'll go right to it without flipping around.
>
> Clearinghouse: Have you told me all the ways that you choose a program to watch?
>
> Response: Let me see. Sometimes, a friend will call and say, "Turn on Channel 5. There's a good movie on." But I'd rather just look for myself.
>
> Reflective probe: So you think that program guides are useless and that remotes do a better job of letting you preview what's on TV?
>
> Response: Pretty much. If my dish company would send me a free guide, I'd probably use it. They charge to send one out, and I don't want to pay.
>
> Mirror question: So the reason you don't make choices on what to watch in advance is because you don't have any way of knowing what's on, is that right?
>
> Response: That's right.

Probing Problems

Similar to sand traps in a golf course, hidden pitfalls lurk among question protocols and interview dialogue. Sometimes, interviewers fall into the yes/no trap where the question falls flat with a monosyllabic response. To avoid the trap, don't ask: "Can you tell me the name of the channels that carry movies?" Ask instead, "What are the movie channels you watch?"

Also, avoid leading questions. Stay away from asking, "Do you think it's the satellite's responsibility to send you program information?" Ask instead, "Whose responsibility is it to provide program information?"

Table 12.1 Group Versus Respondent Interviews[2]

Element	Group	Individual
Group interaction	Elicits ideas from others	No interaction; ideas from interviewer
Peer pressure	Challenges to thinking	Planned challenges from interviewer
Respondent	Competition for talk time	No competition; much detail
Influence	Halo effect	No influence
Detail gathered	Little detail	Much detail
Subject sensitivity	Hesitation to talk	More likely to talk
Interviewer fatigue	Multiple group potential	Boredom after a few interviews
Information amount	Large in short time period	Large in long time period
Scheduling	Difficult to assemble up to 10 people	Easy to arrange with one person

SOURCE: Adapted from a comparison prepared by the Qualitative Research Council of the Advertising Research Foundation, New York City, 1985.

Lastly, don't guess. Avoid asking, "Why do you think the satellite company charges for program information?" Ask instead, "Do you think that the cost of the program guide's distribution is the reason they charge for it?" Effective rephrasing techniques come with experience, but the best way to stay on track is to carefully plan your questions in advance. By anticipating answers to those questions, you can eliminate problematic replies. Resource A contains a protocol for a structured interview.

Respondent interviews are limiting to the extent that there is only one avenue for memory jogging—through the interviewer's questions. By adding other people to the mix, respondents are able to piggyback onto other answers and comments to expand their own. Table 12.1 compares group and respondent interviews.

Focus Group Interviews

A focus group is a formal method for interviewing multiple respondents. Like their field counterparts, researchers use groups to gather large amounts of information in a short period of time. One or many groups can be employed, depending on the size of the study and the size of your budget.

Interviewing in groups has its advantages. Among them is your ability to record and analyze members' reactions to ideas and to each other. Focus groups can be structured formally or informally. We conduct informal focus group interviews to learn about ways consumers are thinking and making decisions about a topic. They are also helpful for developing advertising concepts or obtaining reactions to performance. The interviewer requires minimal training, as no question protocol is used. Conversation evolves and continues through participant interactions rather than from directed questions.

Formal focus group interviews rely on a previously determined set of questions and are directed by a trained facilitator. Participants usually receive an incentive to compensate them for their time and travel expenses. Differences between focus group and field group interviews include the necessary planning and scheduling, the contrived setting, the controlled group size, and preselection of respondents. The focus group interviewer usually has no previous relationship with group members.

Since the mid-1940s, advertising agencies have used focus groups to pretest creative executions and evaluate campaign concepts. Today, focus groups are used to study knowledge, attitudes, and beliefs in a variety of marketplace situations. Researchers who study media, for instance, find focus group social interaction valuable for generating audience interpretations of media content and learning their opinions about the content. In addition, focus groups offer dynamics and ways not available in individual interviews of stimulating, eliciting, and elaborating audience interpretations. Focus groups are catalysts for individual expression of latent opinions, for the generation of group consensus, for free-associating to life, and for analytic statements about media. Turning away from traditional media influence and effects questions, media research today is concerned with how audiences interpret, make sense of, use, interact with, and create meaning out of media content and media technologies.[3]

A director of qualitative research at the Leo Burnett Advertising Agency in Chicago has this to say about focus groups:[4]

> Group interviewers must listen for patterns of how the product is mentioned. Even after 200 groups, patterns can remain similar and guide the researcher on trends and biases. Consumers have trouble dealing with the abstract—you must give them a concrete example first. Rather than saying "which words best describe this Kleenex—soft, clean, etc."—say instead: "What celebrity would probably use which Kleenex box among the ones represented here?" Consumers can only relate to objects, not abstract concepts.

Focus group facilitators often incorporate projective exercises (see Chapter 13) into sessions to uncover the underlying socially defined and shared meanings of the pictures or symbols being investigated. Observers of the process can then understand where social agreement shapes interpretation of a product or brand and what happens when there is no social verification for its significance, regardless of personal individual identification with it.

A case of nonstick cookware is an example of the usefulness of triangulating methods.[5] Managers believed that the observed 90 seconds consumers spend at the discount store shelf when purchasing a frying pan indicates an impulsive purchase decision moment with little room for thoughtful consideration of product attributes or brand significance. However, attitude and usage studies indicate clear priorities of importance on a wide range of benefits of pots and pans.

Focus groups were conducted to understand where the 90 seconds fits into a broader cultural and lifestyle context of family life and making meals. From that emerged a number of unspoken cues to decision-making behavior and the role of pots in household dynamics.

Researchers discovered that pots and pans "are my tools" for consumers and that choosing one begins weeks or months ahead of the 90-second purchase moment. It is an episodic process, whereby the need is identified and considerations take place in disconnected discussion and thinking. After the process, a consumer recognizes the right pot when he or she sees it. Lastly, in-depth, one-on-one interviews with a small sample were conducted in a kitchen with pots to expand and investigate the actual 90-second experience from within the consumer's consciousness. From this multitechnique approach, managers were able to rule out impulsive decision making as a purchase motivation.

Using Focus Groups

Formal focus groups range in size from 9 to 13 participants. Focus groups are the most popular form of qualitative research, preferred over other data collection methods for their ability to address a client's specific problems in a timely fashion. As part of the planning process for conducting focus groups, specific steps are necessary to ensure research success. The following are the most important steps.

Sample Selection

Purposeful in nature, focus groups require specific classes or types of participants. *Quota sampling* is the selecting of equal numbers of participants to represent the target population. Gender, race, age, usage levels, profession, and social class are variables used to construct groups. Previously gathered data identifies members of the desired population. Focus group participants must always be product category, media, or entertainment users to qualify. Because we are interested in a specific topic, only people who are familiar with that topic are selected.

From a developed list, potential participants are contacted by phone, solicited by mail, recruited from Internet chat rooms, or advertised for in newspapers. Invitations are followed by letters that contain the purpose, location, remuneration, and sponsor of the focus group. Often, the client's identity is withheld to avoid respondent bias.

Site Selection

Selecting the right place to conduct a focus group is crucial. Locations must be comfortable, convenient, noise free, and technologically appropriate. Research companies and advertising agencies often provide in-house focus group chambers equipped with video cameras and two-way mirrors behind which clients and marketing people may observe the action.

Facilitator Competence

Not everyone can conduct a formal focus group. Of primary concern is the ease with which participants and facilitators interact. Competent facilitators have the following skills necessary for achieving reliable results:

Familiarity with the respondents' idiomatic language

Ability to withhold personal opinions and remain objective about the topic

Listening skills

Summation skills

Membership in the target population

Facilitators are responsible for keeping the discussion on topic and making certain that all members are permitted to speak. Sessions begin with explanations of the group purpose and participant roles. Ground rules state that everyone should participate, that all ideas are equally valid, that there are no right or wrong answers, and that each person's view should be heard and respected. Once members introduce themselves, the group is ready to begin.

Potential Problems

As the saying goes, our best laid plans can go awry. The most common problem is participant no-shows. Always recruit double the amount of participants you need. Latecomers disrupt the group, so usually, tardy participants are not permitted to enter. By anticipating possible troubles in advance, problems are avoided. For instance, if you think people may have difficulty finding the location, include a map in your informational response letter. And remember to check that all technology is in working order before the group arrives.

For an example of a marketing focus group, see the guideline presented in Resource B.

Informal Focus Groups

One automobile manufacturer has adapted focus groups into its annual training sessions for executives and dealership owners. At one such conference, business women were invited to dine with marketing managers and company executives from Ford, Jaguar, Mazda, and Range Rover at the Four Seasons Hotel in Newport Beach, California. During this session, two female guests were seated with four corporate officers at six tables of six people each. Three groups of two questions were distributed among the tables, and dinner guests were invited to discuss the topics presented:

Group A:

What caused or would cause you to seek a new job or make a career change?

Do you make your vehicle purchase decisions relative to your business?

Group B:

What factors have influenced your career's upward mobility?

What corporate values must be present for you to do your best work and deliver your strongest business outcomes?

Group C:

How do you set the tone in your company to attract strong employees?

What values do you look for in corporate leaders?

After dessert, guests and executives came together to discuss similarities and differences in the group responses. A facilitator ended the session by asking each executive to say how the group discussion informed his or her forthcoming decisions. Ford Motor Company learned that women in Group A seek employment for flexible hours and opportunity for advancement. They select vehicles for reliability and personal needs rather than business needs, with high performance as the last consideration. B Group participants said that mentoring and support systems influenced upward mobility. Corporate values important for business outcomes are integrity and diversity. In Group C, women set the tone for their companies with passion and enthusiasm; they also valued integrity, diversity, and respect in their leaders.

Executives admitted that perceptions about issues important for women were enlightened by the group interaction and that the information generated in this session would be integrated into future hiring and automotive delivery services. Ford is one of many companies investing in qualitative research techniques to understand their target audience and address their specific needs.

Nominal Grouping Sessions

Conducting group sessions using the *nominal technique* is advisable when biases on the part of researcher and subjects threaten results. Touted by the developer as more valuable to marketing researchers than focus groups, grouping sessions "discover from and explore with targeted consumers the most important characteristics of the research problem rather than forcing discussions about particular characteristics."[6] Here, thought-listing techniques are incorporated into focus group sessions to produce a more democratic idea distribution system.

Nominal grouping session procedures are outlined in the following six steps:

1. Individuals are assigned to small groups of 6 to 10 participants based on chosen or common characteristics.

2. Group members silently and independently generate ideas about the topic under discussion.

3. Each participant presents one idea to the group without discussion in an iterative fashion until all ideas are offered. All ideas are recorded on a board.

4. Ideas are discussed for clarification, combination, and evaluation. Expressions of the importance of ideas are encouraged, but criticisms of others' ideas are discouraged.

5. Each member privately rates or ranks the pooled ideas in order of importance.

6. The group discusses the ratings until consensus is reached on them. The process generates the most important rating rationales.

Nominal grouping sessions are most effective for creating questionnaires and measurement scales. Recommended for service industry investigations, nominal grouping sessions were used to investigate the shopping intentions of private-passenger automobile insurance policy holders. Compared to focus group interviews, grouping sessions are better suited for obtaining numerical than narrative data.

Discovery

As we've just seen, interviewing data collection methods occur in two locations—in and out of the field—and in two styles, informal and formal. We can also bifurcate the discovery that results from interviews into two levels: description and disclosure. *Descriptions* are responses gathered during product-oriented focus groups or formally structured interviews where consumers readily share their thoughts about products, media, or performances. A professional stranger moderates interviews, and no personal connection exists between inteviewer and interviewee.

Disclosure, on the other hand, takes place in the presence of trust between interviewer and subject. Usually collected in the field or location chosen by the subject, disclosure occurs when subjects reveal their innermost thoughts and feelings without fear of reprisal or ridicule.

Self-disclosure is more than simple discussion, it is a revelation of one's private self. Disclosure has six levels of distinction: (a) self-presentation, (b) self-misrepresentation (lying), (c) self-description, (d) self-revelation (mistakes), (e) repetition, and (f) self-disclosure. Attributes of self-reference are truth, sincerity, intentionality, novelty, and privacy.[7] Varying degrees of attributes characterize each level of disclosure.

Of course, there are exceptions. All you have to do is listen to Oprah or one of her counterparts to hear the most intimate details shared with the multitudes. Or is something else going on? Sharing with Oprah may provide a person with cathartic experience because of its affiliation with celebrity or because of a need to publicly disclose personal tragedy. Focused interviews conducted with 29 respondents who had appeared on the Donahue Show revealed that an evangelical fervor underpinned their decisions to talk, overshadowing other concerns about disclosure in a public forum.[8] Mediated disclosures are part of performance.

Research is conducted to discover what we do not know about a consumer or a consumption experience, a viewer or viewing experience, an audience or performance experience. The research objectives dictate the level of discovery expectations. Knowing how consumers experience purchasing a refrigerator or listening to a newscast can be accomplished adequately from description. Understanding the emotions and attitudes of teenage mall rats requires a disclosure. Self-disclosure results from establishing a connection to the mall culture, building a relationship with the teens who hang out there, and conveying trust. These criteria enable members of that culture to share intimate details rather than just surface talk. Getting to the disclosure level has difficulties, but problems of discovery are present in most elicitation situations.

Structured Cybertools

Discovery online is a new technique for obtaining information about a culture that has no physical presence but which is a field of discovery none the less. Not only are we able to study virtual culture, we are also able to study E-commerce interactions in progress. Specifically, shopping can be studied in cyberspace. Research companies are establishing a variety of data collection functions based on qualitative techniques. Some of the tools available for online participatory interviews and groups are presented here.

Mystery shopping is conducted on line by several cyberbased businesses. The qualitative aspects of purchasing online are addressed the same way as face-to-face transactions are evaluated. Mystery shopping measures customer satisfaction, using researchers' experiences on E-sites as indicators. Target respondents with appropriate backgrounds are used to get customer opinions. People are assigned shopping tasks to be carried out online. Some of the E-site criteria assessed are product availability, shopping effectiveness, and overall purchase experience.

Concept testing is used to test creative ideas online using surveys and questionnaires to Web-based target markets. One company offering the service is www.Insightexpress.com.

Site usability tests identify functions that are pleasing and frustrating to shoppers. In this consumer-centered research, users are observed for nonverbal expressions while they use the site. Certain actions trigger questions about them from observing researchers (e.g., "Why did you just sigh?"). The human element is the most vulnerable tool of Web merchandising. This type of research fills the gap between understanding the way virtual shoppers think and the way they actually function.

Chat rooms serve as research sites for Internet marketing research firms. More than half of all major Web sites use some sort of chat function that provides long-running conversation-enabling formats for analysis. Discussion boards functioning within chat rooms use moderators to make sure that products are not promoted on the boards and to try to ensure that people posting messages have interesting conversations. Mighty Big TV has talk-back forums where visitors can discuss things such as Ally McBeal's hair (on the Hairiffic forum) and weigh in on their least favorite participant on "Survivor."[9] Mighty Big TV has a core of 150 to 200 people who keep the site on their screens all day, making this one of the most successful message boards on the Internet. Such discussion boards develop into strong communities; fostering community is the moderator's job.

At eDiets, an online weight-loss site where members pay monthly fees and can turn to one of 36 discussion boards for advice and support, moderators take charge of making certain all members get answers to their questions. Moderated chat rooms then provide a readable text for analysis by marketers for their insight into the forum's topic, from TV shows to dieting.

Chat Rooms Versus Focus Groups[10]

Online chat sessions, where one to dozens of prerecruited respondents type in responses to guided online discussion, can be used effectively to bring participants together from virtually anywhere. They discuss a client issue, activities, and experiences or provide feedback on products. Although the technology of Internet Relay Chat or Web chat makes it easy to conduct discussions, it does not necessarily replace the benefits of traditional off-line methodologies. Virtual groups do not allow for tactile experiences or capturing facial expressions of respondents as they are exposed to ideas and concepts. However, the depth of transcripts that can be derived from just an hour of discussion is powerful—often 20 to 30 pages of verbatim responses are available immediately.

The primary advantages of chat rooms are speed of recruitment, elimination of travel costs, respondent participation from home or office, and depth of information yielded. Although virtual groups will not always be able to replace in-person interviews, the benefits of speed and cost savings make them a very effective tool for researchers, especially for gathering Web site feedback with participants in that medium.

Online media offer several reliable and effective sampling strategies. Because the online user universe changes so rapidly, a difficult part is determining the sampling variables and their target proportions. Respondents can be recruited through a variety of methods, including client lists, research company databases, targeted Web site promotions, on-site intercepts, and online newsgroup posting areas. Passive recruitment is possible using opt-in, pop-up screens or banner ads on Web sites, provided that results are intended to represent visitors to that Web site.

The following companies take part in online focus groups and other qualitative data gathering methods:

e-Focus Groups (www.e-focusgroups.com/)

QualCore.com: a research company that offers traditional and Internet-based qualitative research services

Perception Research Services Web Marketing (www.prsresearch.com)

The worst problem that can occur in any of the aforementioned interview situations is reluctance of the participant to talk at all. To elicit a useful dialogue from consumers, interviewers may have to go beyond traditional probing techniques. The use of projective techniques is a proven method for prompting disclosure. The next chapter presents ways in which researchers employ projective techniques for both individual and group interviewing situations.

Summary

1. Respondent interviews are structured to obtain specific information; researchers may need to use probing techniques to elicit information.

2. Focus group interviews require a formal structure, monetary remuneration, and predetermined questions addressed to participants in a controlled setting.

3. Discovery has two levels, description and disclosure, that are determined by research objectives, and questions to elicit each are crafted by the interviewer.

4. Research tools, such as mystery shopping, concept tests, site usability tests, and chat rooms, enable qualitative researchers to obtain answers to specific marketplace questions.

5. Internet chat rooms yield fast results and high volumes of text for analysis, although they cannot take the place of focus groups for personalized data gathering.

Stretching Exercises

1. Structure the protocol for a formal group interview of females on how women use the Internet for purchasing products. Use the four types of probes described in this chapter. How would you modify the questions for use with a group of males on the same topic?

2. Listen to a friend interview someone for 5 minutes, recording the uses of probes. Critique the interview based on what you've learned from Chapters 11 & 12.

Recommended Readings About Formal Interviewing and Focus Groups

Barbour, R. S., & Kitzinger, J. (1999). *Developing focus group research: Politics, theory, and practice.* Thousand Oaks, CA: Sage.

Holstein, J. A., & Gubrium, J. F. (1995). *The active interview.* Thousand Oaks, CA: Sage.

Jones, S. (Ed.). (1999). *Doing Internet research: Critical issues and methods for examining the net.* Thousand Oaks, CA: Sage.

Krueger, R. A., & Casey, M. A. (2000). *Focus groups: A practical guide for applied research.* Thousand Oaks, CA: Sage.

Mann, C., & Stewart, F. (2000). *Internet communication and qualitative research.* Thousand Oaks, CA: Sage.

Morgan, D. L. (1997). *Focus groups as qualitative research.* Thousand Oaks, CA: Sage.

Case in Point: Tabloid Television and Network News—The Same or Different?[11]

Client: Television network news department

Problem: Accusations that consumers cannot distinguish between tabloid television shows and network news

RQ: How do viewers distinguish between televised drama and reporting?

Data Collection: Four focus group sessions of 9 males and females each were conducted, two in corporate conference rooms and two in the living rooms of participants to simulate normal viewing situations as closely as possible. Participants were heavy television viewers who relied on television for their primary source of news. Sessions averaged 90 minutes and were videotaped. The terms *tabloid* and *network* were not used in questions to participants to avoid bias. A television network news reporter assisted with developing question protocols and the questionnaire instrument.

Group sessions had two phases:

In Phase 1, participants watched a series of television news stories. After viewing each story, they completed a questionnaire designed to prove their thoughts about the stories' information value and to categorize them as either news or tabloid. By completing the questions individually, "group think" influence was eliminated.

In Phase 2, groups were shown video segments and engaged in a thought and opinion-sharing discussion. Stories were videotaped during regular broadcasts in the Los Angeles market over a 4-month time period; a total of nine stories were used for the study. Six of the stories were grouped into common segments for topic consistency. Segment A included coverage of the Oklahoma City bombing as broadcast by *CBS Evening News* and *Hard Copy*. Segment B covered the disappearance of millionaire Mrs. Levitz as featured by *Extra* and *NBC Nightly News*. Segment C featured the return of Magic Johnson to the NBA as reported by *NBC Nightly News* and *Extra*. The remaining three stories were of random, unrelated events: An *NBC Nightly News* report on the arrest of perpetrators of a telemarketing fraud ring, workers compensation insurance fraud reported on *Hard Copy*, and a *Current Affair* report on product liability of heat tape.

Story sources were masked from participants by blacking out program logos.

Data Analysis: Data from *group discussions* were coded, categorized, and abstracted into themes. Questionnaires were tabulated using descriptive statistics.

Results: The 36 participants consistently distinguished between tabloid television and network news reports. Questionnaire data revealed respondents were able to correctly identify the genre 78% of the time. Data indicate respondent preference for network coverage over tabloid presentation in all three segments by an average of 73%. Participants ranked the network stories higher than tabloids as most informative, most interesting, and most credible, 67% of the time.

Participants defined tabloid genre as entertaining, sensationalistic, subjective, emotional, and adjective laden.

> I enjoy tabloids. Yes, there is some news in it, but it's flashy. Lots of babies and heartbeats.

Techniques associated with tabloids include poor-quality video, background music, exaggerated vocal tones, outdated stories, and lengthy reports.

> . . . talking about delivery, well there's one thing about *Hard Copy,* they always put that sappy music, that dramatic music, behind the story, and instantly I know it's a fake. Peter Jennings wouldn't do that.

Stories with the highest percentage of error employed literary devices that crossed the genre boundaries participants had established.

Discussion: Dialogue generates an awareness by participants of tabloid cues:

> I judge it by the vocal tone. *Hard Copy* is more sensational. And their first presentation story, if it starts with a fact, I think it's news. If it starts with a gimmick, I would likely think it's a tabloid.

Credibility is a big factor in participant distinctions:

> When you see Dan Rather, you think he is credible. He's more professional.

When participants were asked to describe tabloids as cars, they suggested that Yugo and a beat-up Dodge described them most appropriately.

Responding to an industry quote that said audiences react best to sex and cats, one respondent comments,

> People who want news don't care about that stuff [sex and cats]. If they want entertainment, they skip the news completely.

Conclusion: The focus group revealed that television viewers interested in news can distinguish between genres of tabloid and network through a variety of clues. Network fears that viewers are unable to distinguish between news and entertainment are unfounded. Professionals wishing to maintain the integrity of traditional journalism may distance their product from the tabloid product by eliminating the tabloid devices identified in this study. By accepting the responsibility for maintaining the integrity of its product, the traditional news industry can separate itself from the tabloids.

Notes

1. From Lindlof, T. R. (1995). *Qualitative communication research methods* (p. 172). Thousand Oaks, CA: Sage.

2. From Stewart, C. J., & Cash, W. B. (1988). *Interviewing principles and practices* (5th ed.). Dubuque, IA: William C. Brown.

3. See Chapter 10 in Hansen, A., Cottle, S., Negrine, R., & Newbold, C. (1998). *Mass communication research methods.* Washington Square: New York University Press.

4. Quoted during an interview conducted by the author with Barbara Thomas at the Burnett offices in Chicago on January 14, 1987.

5. Reported by Chris Wright-Isak as part of a special topic session on qualitative methods presented to the annual conference of the American Academy of Advertising, 1995.

6. From Langford, B. E. (1994). A magazine of management applications. *Marketing Research, 6*(3), p. 47.

7. See Fisher, D. V. (1984). A conceptual analysis of self-disclosure. *Journal for the Theory of Social Behavior, 14*(3), 277-291.

8. From Priest, P. J., & Dominick, J. R. (1994). Pulp pulpits: Self-disclosure on "Donahue." *Journal of Communication, 44*(4), 90-96.

9. From an article by McGrane, S. (2000, June 22). On line might. *New York Times,* p. C2.

10. Based on FAQs on Online Research presented in *Marketing Research, 10,* a publication of the American Marketing Association, 1998, Winter.

11. Based on Teenor, K. (1996). *Tabloid television and network news: The same or different?* Unpublished master's thesis, California State University, Fullerton.

13 Projective Techniques

A problem common to interviewing in the field or in structured settings is getting people to disclose information, to talk to us. If eliciting information is the objective of marketplace research, then getting people to speak freely is not only necessary but also essential for successful results. Unencumbered talk is often facilitated best in situations where the subject is given a task to perform and where research questions can be answered indirectly.

According to the literature,[1] self-disclosure tends to be reciprocal. The concept of exchange reciprocity—you tell me and I'll tell you—is trust dependent. Research results are dependent on the willingness and honesty of respondents. Most of the time, a direct approach is successful. However, in some cases, indirect methods are warranted, as when respondents are reluctant to talk about the topic at hand because of real or perceived repercussions or the research topic is sensitive enough to warrant extra measures of anonymity for respondents. Indirect methods are also used to avoid respondent bias (trying to please or impress a researcher).

In cases where information is best gathered indirectly, projective techniques can be invoked. By getting subjects to talk about other people, asking them to solve other people's problems, or using other-directed reflection, researchers obtain very insightful information that may not be possible with traditional methods, such as focus groups and depth interviews. When researchers require intimate statements from subjects about themselves, they must adhere to psychological rather than sociological traditions for useful results.

For purposes of this text, a *projective technique* is defined as a situation-specific device created to elicit disclosure indirectly by asking people to discuss the preferences and feelings of others or to participate in an expressive activity.

Projective techniques have a long history of success in psychotherapy, where psychologists use them to learn about the inner self in order to prescribe treatment for troubled individuals. A discussion of the origins of projective techniques helps bring into perspective their role for marketing research.

168

From the Couch to Consumption

Projection is a term most commonly associated with personality assessment. Early psychological literature attributes projection to psychoanalytic theory, where it is used synonymously with rejection. Freud saw projection as a defense mechanism whereby the ego protects itself from a condition of anxiety by projecting or externalizing unpleasant feelings or elements of one's experience. Perhaps by seeing unpleasantness as external to self, a patient could eliminate its existence. Marketers, however, distance themselves from Freud's negative approach, preferring instead the notion that a projective technique is a process of "unwittingly attributing one's own traits, attitudes or subjective processes to others."[2] This process of transference is seen as helpful for understanding consumer attitudes.

Two names identified closely with the development of current projective techniques appropriate for marketing research are Gestalt and Rorschach. Cognitive psychology in the Gestalt tradition stresses a holistic nature of mental processes and emphasizes the creative aspect of the mind.[3] Rorschach tests (ink blots) also emphasize the need to consider a subject's response as a whole, shedding light on the personal and spontaneous elements that characterize true projective techniques.

Four techniques have been used to elicit disclosure from subjects. *Word-association* has respondents tell what first comes to mind when a word is mentioned. In *symbolic association,* respondents tell what a Rorschach inkblot looks like to them. For Murray's *thematic apperception test (TAT),* respondents tell a story about what they see in a painting or drawing. *Object-sorting technique* is a Rapaport test where subjects group items of like kind together. All forms of disclosure, these techniques have been known to the trade as methods for "reality testing."

According to L. K. Frank, projective techniques are characterized in the following ways:[4]

Constitutive, where the subject imposes structure on unstructured material, such as modeling with clay or plastic

Constructive, where subjects use structures such as building block materials to create reality

Interpretive, where subjects ascribe meaning to a stimulus situation, such as word association

Cathartic, which are play techniques

Refractive, used to assess expressive aspects of behavior

Verbal, visual, and concrete stimuli are appropriate elicitation devices for all of Frank's categories, which are still applicable to contemporary projective studies.

Projective tasks are presented in open-ended formats, with no correct response anticipated. They are classified according to the type of information they can yield—either diagnostic or descriptive. Whereas the intention of projective techniques for psychotherapy is most often therapeutic, their intention for marketing research is rich description—more specifically, self-disclosure. Similar to the objectives of therapists, marketing researchers want to understand the attitudes and feelings of consumers through verbal dialogue captured during disclosure.

Disclosure is often complicated by a need for confidentiality. Psychologists have established a de facto doctor-patient relationship that facilitates disclosure. Researchers, however, often rely on projective techniques to enhance confidentiality, especially when a topic is sensitive or subjects are reluctant to discuss their feelings.

Sensitive Topics and Reluctant Subjects

Sensitive topics can range anywhere from impotence to drug abuse. Market researchers may be asked to understand physical impairments among adults for promoting pharmaceutical products or to comprehend patient rationale for addiction in order to develop a strategy for promoting treatment. In such cases, Lee's treatment of sensitive topics is suggested reading for researchers who face delicate areas of study. (See recommended reading list at the end of the chapter.)

Reluctant subjects[5] are people who simply feel uncomfortable disclosing information that might damage their self-esteem or compromise their privacy. People who feel they have something to lose by sharing information also fall into this category. Or they may simply not trust the interviewer. Providing skilled interviewers can be difficult for researchers with limited budgets or time constraints. In an absence of skilled professionals, projective techniques may be useful tools for approaching reluctant subjects. An example of a study with reluctant subjects is presented in the video elicitation study discussed later in this chapter.

Studies comparing information gathered on sensitive questions using projective methods[6] show that projective methods yield much richer data closer in nature to self-disclosure than do questionnaires, randomized response surveys, depth interviews, and phone interviews. Reluctant respondents favor methods that maintain privacy; projective techniques offer this option without jeopardizing the richness of intimate disclosure.

Motivation Research for Marketers

During the 1940s and 1950s, many of the psychological techniques discussed earlier were used to explore marketing topics.[7] Marketing researchers determined that respondent disclosure can be affected by many circumstances and that respondents are expressive in relation to the nature of a stimulus and how they receive it. By asking indirect questions, we can facilitate disclosure. But what makes projective techniques so unique is in the interpretation of that disclosure. A researcher's understanding of the transcripts is the study's contribution. By its very nature, interpretation is subjective and situational. Lack of objectivity is often problematic for traditional researchers who use measures of reliability and validity to determine a study's worth. Before grappling with analysis, let's take a look at how advertising and consumer researchers are approaching information gathering since motivation research became an acceptable tool for marketing purposes.

In the 1990s, advertising agencies, such as Saatchi & Saatchi, hired psychologists to draw out and interpret people's subconscious ideas, and they used anthropologists and sociologists to study consumers' cultural environment. Marketing psychologists have now cast aside TATs and Rorschach tests because they focus on a person's problems or view, rather than on how a group feels or behaves.[8] Current techniques aim to wash out the individuals' idiosyncrasies and focus on how brands sit in consumers' minds.

Today, anthropologists on the Saatchi payroll hang out where real people do to understand the core values that shape brand choice and learn how a target audience likes to be perceived. The Young and Rubicam advertising agency hired an anthropologist to head up its research department in 1989, enabling new and exciting ideas to permeate marketing and consumer research from areas of expertise not previously valued in business disciplines.

Creative Approaches to Data Gathering

Asking direct questions about products and brands can cause respondent bias, forcing researchers to look for clever ways to disguise a study's true nature. Creativity plays a leading role in developing methods for gathering information from consumers without disclosing the purpose of the study.[9] Some of these methods are described for their applications to marketing and consumer research.

As early as 1964, *cartoons* were used to elicit information from women about birth control, often considered a taboo topic. Narrative balloons enabled sub-

Figure 13.1. Cartoon for KFC

jects to respond directly to an illustrated situation. Their responses would take on the illusion of a fictitious story rather than an incriminating personal admission. Market researchers often use cartoons as "pictured questions" to gather information on situational brand preference and attitudes toward retailers (see Figure 13.1).

Collages are assembled by consumers to represent their feelings about brands, stores, service, and so forth. They enable researchers to gather information on imagery and its meaning. In one collage study,[10] researchers looked at the nostalgia shoppers feel toward consumer products using magazine images, an alternative to TAT-type pictures. A combination of visual and verbal information about the perception and meaning of nostalgia showed marketers how to customize products for specific target audiences. Collages can be made individually or in groups to gather images that are more representative of varied demographic audiences. Subjects reveal their preferences by image placement and by image frequency. Using small groups of three or four people and dynamic visuals from magazines such as *Wired* and *Utny Reader* can enhance the task.

Role-playing is a viable method for eliciting truthful comments from subjects without putting them at risk. Bank managers considering the use of ATM machines wondered how customers would react to the absence of a teller during transactions. Using customers to role-play their interaction with ATMs during nonbanking hours, managers understood the value of round-the-clock access to funds for customers. The bank installed machines without fear of jeopardizing valued relationships. Other instances of role-playing successes are plentiful. Acting out how it feels to use or need a product resulted in award-winning radio commercials for Laughing Cow cheese. Psychodramas convinced one ad executive that detergent packages should have swirling, dynamic lines and that Mr. Clean should be asexual and nonthreatening to consumers.

Other methods incorporated into the routine of marketplace research include *sentence completion* ("Bud Light hosted a party last night and . . ."); *sketching* typical users of brands; *telling tales* about brands; *matching* products and companies with animals, places, colors, and types of music; *making clay models;* keeping consumer *diaries* about their relationships with certain products; and writing *obituaries* for brands and companies. When subjects eulogized one manufacturing company as "a distinguished citizen who died for not keeping up with the times," PR practitioners were able to reimage their company as vital and healthy.

Sketching, based on the psychological house-tree drawings,[11] helps advertisers to understand products in terms of their personalities. For instance, respondents of one study drew Marlboro's male consumers as hard workers and ladies' men and drew Michelin users as sophisticated, snazzy, briefcase-toting Porsche drivers. Pillsbury-cake-mix users were drawn as old-fashioned, dowdy, chubby, and bedecked in frilly aprons, whereas users of Duncan Hines mixes materialized as hip and with-it, in cocktail dresses with cleavage. Such personality profiles guide planners' and creative directors' strategic approaches to campaign development.

In a tradition of redefining the relationship between researcher and subject, photographic images have been used for decades as a form of information gathering.[12] Visual research with photographs as projective devices, used by anthropologists to study culture and visual sociologists to study group behavior, have been adapted by marketing researchers. Marketing research pioneer and professor Sidney Levy developed a *photoelicitation* technique called "auto-driving."[13] Researchers using this mode invoke photography and audio recording of informants to drive an interview, allowing consumers to see and hear their own behavior and then react to it. Visual techniques used in auto-driving are presented in more detail in Chapter 14.

Gray Advertising's *photo-and-tale* technique used for Playtex struck gold when consumer collages showed an association between their bras and full-breasted, overweight, old-fashioned women. They also used *photo-sorts* to obtain self-image portrayals of bra consumers. In photo-sorting, respondents work with a group of photographs, usually mounted on cards and arranged in a single stack. Subjects in the Playtex study were given a group of 40 photos of women of varying sizes and shapes, modes of dress, levels of occupation, and economic status. They were instructed to place the photos of women who were most likely to appreciate bra construction and appearance in one pile and photos of women who were unlikely to care about those features in another pile. By analyzing the similar responses of the 40 women in their likely-to-care piles, researchers found that their target audience cast themselves as intelligent, physically fit, well-dressed, independent women. In their replacement campaign, Grey featured a sexy, svelte, big-bosomed heroine and the tag line, "The fit that makes the fashion." Photo-sorts have also helped companies such as GE and Visa create campaign strategies from consumer feelings as expressed by photo selections.

Creative research allowed ad agency TBWA to uncover underlying values and anxieties of business people for a hotel client's campaign. They used verbal probes and narratives to discover that businessmen consider themselves warriors, and the job of a hotel is to care for the warrior while he relaxes and refuels.[14] *Stories, myths, and legends* are the stuff consumer research is made of, according to Sid Levy.[15] Stories may be solicited by showing crude or vague drawings of a shopping situation. Respondents are given a short scenario about what is happening between purchasers in a retail setting. For instance, two women are shown discussing boxed milk (vacuum packaged with a long shelf life); one woman is considering the product for the first time. The respondents are asked which one of the two women she might be and to tell a story about her. Then, the subject is asked to respond to the comments of the other woman. Forthcoming stories become vehicles to understand respondents' feelings about how they perceive other people might think about them for using the product, their attitudes toward feeding the product to their families, and reasons for and against using the product. Consumer stories often refer to origins of a family unit and explain what life was and is like. From these stories, researchers learn about values and preferences of consumers. In the box milk study, four profiles were constructed of purchasers.

Creative: A good cook who keeps all foods in stock

Practical, modern: A young mother who likes the convenience of milk that can be stored on the shelf

Lazy: A woman who likes to take the easy way out by using boxed rather than fresh milk

Underprivileged: An older mother who has to buy for her large family and for whom cost is a concern

This kind of marketplace storytelling can be analyzed as projective, likening consumers' household anecdotes to myths. A discussion of story analysis is presented in Chapter 15.

Figure 13.2. Projective Beer-Tasting Instrument

Instructions for filling out this survey: Please circle the beer that you think each person pictured above would drink. Then, fill in the bubble as to why you think this person would choose that particular beer.

SOURCE: Reprinted with permission from Emerson College, Boston, MA.

Figure 13.2 is an example of a projective technique designed by Belgian MBA students to characterize beer drinkers, who told stories about their favorite choices.

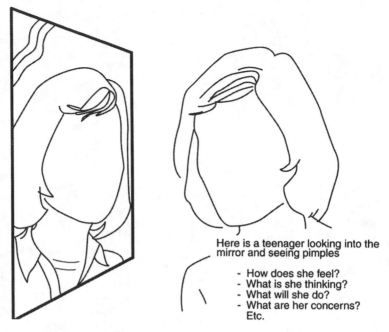

Here is a teenager looking into the mirror and seeing pimples

- How does she feel?
- What is she thinking?
- What will she do?
- What are her concerns?
  Etc.

Figure 13.3. TAT for Clearasil

SOURCE: Kanner (1989, p. 38). Reprinted with permission.

Winning Combinations

When consumers don't tell the truth, it's often because they don't know it. Projective techniques guard against subjects who say only what makes them appear smarter and more discriminating. A combination of TAT, sentence completions, and photo-sorts allowed Clearasil's agency to realize that tight-lipped teens think of their lives as a fast-paced social whirl that can grind to a halt because of a pimple. Consumer diaries helped Yuban understand how consumers feel about coffee. And brand personifications enabled N. W. Ayer to characterize pineapple juice as an appealing breakfast drink for nonusers. Ogilvy and Mather asked business travelers to "dream" about an airline and found their client's brand was lacking in perceived benefits. Advertising research also focuses on ways to quantify consumers' emotional bonds with products.

According to an executive at J. Walter Thompson advertising agency, it doesn't matter if a research technique seems far out, as long as it's used to try to understand what's important to people by tapping into their reality. Another method for tapping that reality is a technique called metaphor marketing, developed by Harvard Business School professor, Gerold Zaltman.

Zaltman Metaphor Elicitation Technique[16]

Because consumers may not know the truth of their preferences, Zaltman sought a technique to bring it out. He contended that our knowledge of what we need lies so deeply embedded in our brains that it rarely surfaces. "Most of what we say and do occurs below the level of awareness. We use projective techniques to get at hidden knowledge—to get at what people don't know they know," says Zaltman. His method, known simply as ZMET, combines neurobiology, psychoanalysis, linguistics, and art theory to try and uncover the mental models that guide consumer behavior. He even developed a bilingual phrase book to decode emotions, feelings, and fears.

In one ZMET study, consumers were asked to use magazines, catalogs, and family photo albums to capture their thoughts and feelings about a product. A week later, subjects discussed each picture during an intense 2-hour session with a trained interviewer-cum-therapist. The visuals doubled as windows into their minds. In another study, respondents were asked to describe their thoughts and feelings about coffee as a morning wake-up beverage. The research was a play in three acts—one: the pictures, two: the interview, three: the collage. Acknowledging that humans think in images rather than words, researchers invoked the *metaphor*—viewing one thing in terms of another—which is central to thought and crucial to uncovering latent needs and emotions. PhotoShop collages help subjects reveal their inner thoughts, and ZMET researchers are apt to receive *ahas*—answers to questions they never thought to ask.

In ZMET, the metaphor is a vehicle for making tacit knowledge emerge as explicit knowledge, using one domain to understand another. For instance, we say that *time* is (like) *money*. We understand tacitly that time is a scarce resource and express it explicitly, such as investing time, saving time, buying time, afford the time, and similar phrases that use both monetary and temporal words as metaphorical descriptions.

ZMET is concerned with metaphors as mental models that are based on the following assumptions:

Nonverbal and image communication predominates our conversation.

Metaphors are essential units of thought.

Metaphors are both deep and surface in nature.

Reason and emotion comingle in thought and expression.

Stories are metaphors that serve as models of understanding.

Figure 13.4 shows how mental models work.

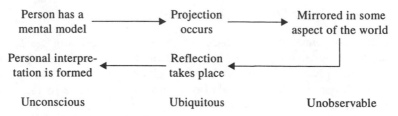

Figure 13.4. Mental Models[17]
SOURCE: Adapted from Olson & Zaltman (2000).

Researchers who use the Zaltman technique are able to uncover deep meta-phors through visuals that are produced and interpreted by the individuals under study. Here, the researcher is a facilitator who enables subjects to look outside of the frames of their visuals to analyze the context and potential of the brand or concepts under study.

One example is research on Nike. Consumers easily state their explicit under-standing of the product as "good design" and "speed." But by using ZMET, con-sumers are able to project their tacit knowledge and understand that the product's design is a metaphor for energy, that speed is a metaphor for achievement, and that the brand represents a journey, such as the journey to good health. Jour-ney is an example of a deep metaphor. Other common deep metaphors are bal-ance, force, nature, ideal, motion, time, container, and social relations. Deep metaphors connect researchers with deep meanings that consumers feel about brands.

Zaltman was one of the first researchers to recognize that emotion connects the consumer with a product, a strategy that will certainly predominate in new millennium advertising.

The Video Elicitation Technique[18]

The natural disasters of the late 1980s and early 1990s provided a canvas for creating techniques to understand the rebuilding phenomenon of people who had undergone traumatic loss. Insurance companies and retailers, anxious to serve disaster communities, needed information on how to provide services to consumers who were forced to replace all of their possessions.

A colleague who was a firestorm victim collaborated with this author to de-velop a device that would serve two purposes: (a) to collect information about the immediate and long-range needs of disaster victims and (b) to facilitate ac-quisition of the commodities needed to maintain and enhance the lives of these victims after suffering such a devastating loss. Using the Internet was not an op-tion at the time of this study.

Suburban retailers, including appliance centers, furniture stores, department stores, and home decorating centers, were interested in how they might market to resettled survivors who were not likely to respond to direct mail or other impersonal solicitations for business. Insurance companies also wanted to understand the needs of the disaster victims for future applications.

We faced several problems for data gathering, including invading the privacy of victims and reluctance among victims to speak with outsiders. A victim himself, my colleague asked for study volunteers during a meeting of survivors held several weeks after the firestorm. Once we had subjects, we set about developing a projective technique that could elicit honest and detailed information from victims without invading their privacy. Here are the six steps we took to develop what we call *video-elicitation.*

1. Survey: Using scaling techniques and multiple-choice questions, we surveyed the entire group of 350 households to determine their concerns about rebuilding. Two hundred and eighty three surveys were returned and statistically analyzed for significant issues. The results were used to construct questions for the next step.

2. Depth interviews: As a fellow victim, my colleague was viewed as an insider with access to victims who would not talk to me. Volunteers who had indicated on their returned surveys a willingness to talk with him were asked to elaborate on the issues revealed by the study. From his interviews, we learned of their feelings about loss, thoughts on how they might go about rebuilding and replacing their belongings, and to whom they would look for guidance and direction during the recovery process. Researcher bias kept us from using depth interviews for other than exploratory information used to prepare for the next step in our study, developing a video script.

3. Video production: We decided to attempt building parasocial relationships[19] between our video characters and respondents as a mechanism for eliciting an honest discussion. Using actors to portray a married couple typical of the victim sample, we created 14 scenarios in a 22-minute videotape. The actors talked about the problems they encountered after losing their possessions as if they were talking to a third party. Following their comments on the topic of each scenario, the tape was stopped, and an announcer asked paired respondents to comment on that same topic into an audio recorder. Respondents were told they could agree or disagree with the actors and were asked to elaborate on each topic.

4. Eliciting responses: Tapes and an audio cassette player were delivered to willing subjects who responded in the privacy of their homes. Because most households contained married or gay couples who would make joint decisions about rebuilding, respondents reacted to the tape in pairs. Materials were collected a few days later.

5. *Results:* The amount of disclosure received from the audiotapes was rich in description and emotion. We learned that respondents bonded to our actors from their vocal concern for them as fellow victims. We found out that most victims were purchasing more expensive models of their favorite brands of appliances than they had lost and were also upgrading their cars and electronics. They looked to contractors, architects, and friends for retail purchase recommendations. Women would be the primary purchasers, but men would play a significant role in selecting replacement objects.

6. *Outcome:* Learning that victims wanted information but not solicitation, we convinced retailers to present helpful seminars on topics such as how to select appliances for homeowner groups as a venue for marketing their products. Embracing our research results, retailers also targeted contractors and architects rather than victims for product and service solicitations. Insurance companies better understood the victim recovery process, enabling them to dispense funds that best addressed the needs of their customers.

Details of the video-elicitation technique and disaster studies appear elsewhere;[20] this brief overview is intended to illustrate the role of projective techniques in a study where self-disclosure could only be obtained without direct contact with respondents. Video-elicitation enabled reluctant respondents to project their feelings onto fellow actors-as-victims as they were portrayed in a real-life simulation. Privacy was maintained, and outcomes were beneficial for all members of the data sample as well as our retail and insurance clients.

Researchers should take note of this study's useful marriage of qualitative and quantitative techniques. Reversing the usual research procedure where qualitative techniques are used in exploratory stages and later validated with quantification, our study began with a survey and culminated with interpretive analysis. Projective techniques serve the user best when they are accompanied by multiple methods of information discovery. I invite readers and marketplace practitioners to discover the power of projective techniques for use in consumer research.

Summary

1. Projective techniques can be developed situationally as a method of information elicitation. Self-disclosure rather than self-description is possible, and limits are set only by the creativity of the researcher.

2. Practically speaking, projective techniques are unique ways to ask people questions about themselves and the products they use. People often express themselves more completely and naturally in informal dialogues than in structured or formal situations typical of other research methods.

3. Analysis is interpretive and dependent on the skill and perception of the researcher. The absence of structure and statistical data does not lend itself to scientific proof that is often expected from marketing research.

Stretching Exercises

1. Your client is a chain of sports bars that has experienced a decline in business over the past several months. Develop a cartoon with appropriate balloons to probe patron attitudes about the bar. Consider the target market, and make certain all segments of it are represented in your cartoon.

2. Your company is introducing a nonprescription version of Viagra and is anxious to know how men and women perceive users of penile dysfunction medication. Create an online method for obtaining self-disclosure from respondents of both sexes.

Recommended Readings About Projective Techniques and Sensitive Topics

Collier, J., Jr. (1967). *Visual anthropology: Photography as a research method.* New York: Holt, Rinehart & Winston.

Lee, R. L. (1995). *Doing research on sensitive topics.* London: Sage.

Rook, D. (Ed.). (1999). *Brands, consumers, symbols, and research: Sidney J. Levy on marketing.* Thousand Oaks, CA: Sage.

Semenoff, B. (1976). *Projective techniques.* London: Wiley.

Case in Point: Using George to Capture Entertainment Spending

Client: The Orange County Center for Performing Arts

Problem: Performance attendance declining among young adults

RQ: *How do county residents select and perceive their entertainment choices?*

Data Collection: Projective techniques are paired with ranking in this study. The sample are males and females 22 to 35 years old who have attended a performance of some type at some venue within the past 6 months. Rather than conduct structured interviews using directed open-ended questions, researchers devised a projective method for gathering information about performance attendance patterns of adult respondents.

Four researchers administered this technique to 40 male and 40 female subjects who were recruited at shopping malls and compensated them for the 30-minute interaction with free admissions to neighborhood cinemas, a cost of approximately $14 per subject.

Secondary data suggested that the average person in Orange County spends approximately $200 per month on entertainment activities. Using that figure as a benchmark, researchers gave subjects an imaginary $400 in cash at the onset of the interaction and told them that they must use the money to plan entertainment for the coming 2 months. They were directed to make selections from the Sunday calendar section of the regional metropolitan newspaper, which lists current and coming attractions and corresponding ticket prices for events being performed within a 50-mile radius of the city.

Respondents took about 10 minutes to peruse the paper before marking their selections on a tally sheet that listed categories of performance, including spectator sports, cinema, amusement parks, museums, zoos, theatre, opera, ballet, symphony, and popular music (rock, jazz, country groups, and single vocalists). Instructions asked them to write the nature of the activity in the appropriate performance column and the cost of the ticket(s) until they spent their $400.

Throughout the activity, researchers probed respondents for a rationale of their choices and some discussion about what kind of enjoyment the entertainment experience provided. Each interview was taped.

Data Analysis: Interviews were transcribed and sorted by sex for common themes and patterns. Analysis of ranking data provided descriptive statistics of entertainment preferences.

Results: Females 20 to 30 bought 223 tickets and spent $3,965.

Film tickets were highest for this group.

Males 20 to 30 bought 189 tickets and spent $3,825.

This group was second for sport and film tickets.

Females 30 to 40 bought 154 tickets and spent $3,983.

This group spent the most money on amusement park tickets.

Males 30 to 40 bought 223 tickets for $3,965.

This group bought the most sport and the most museum and zoo tickets.

Males and Females 40 to 50 bought 185 tickets and spent $3,995.

This group bought the most theater tickets.

Females selected theater, opera, symphony, or ballet more often than males. Both men and women chose amusement parks and movies, and men chose sports more often than women did.

Discussion: Narratives were rich in testimony about selecting and attending performances. Quotes were excerpted for the clients' report to provide the study with a high degree of authenticity. The biggest surprise was the difference sex made in the selection process. Men, who were delighted for an opportunity to select sports entertainment, made their ticket purchases without regard to other people who might join them or who may be left behind. They allocated single ticket prices to each selected event. Women, on the other hand, bought multiple tickets for spouses, boyfriends, or children. This difference resulted in fewer event options for female buyers, whereas males could include more events for the same amount of money.

Respondents of both sexes admitted that they rarely plan entertainment attendance more than a few weeks in advance, and most say they rely on the Calendar section of weekly newspapers for event listings. According to respondents, films and sports receive more of their attention than other forms of entertainment because of television promotion. They complained that performance arts promotions, except for occasional mentions in the calendar segments on public broadcast stations, are limited to newspapers and must be sought out.

Many respondents mentioned star power as attracting them to specific performances. Big names draw public audiences faster than famous titles of operas, plays, or ballets. In most cases, if a star is associated with a performance, subjects will select it above other performances of like kind.

From our report, the client understood its competition to be sporting activities and theme parks, and as a result, perceived competitor's venues as ideal for advertising the Center's coming events. The client also recognized the power of female buyers, allocating the largest percentage of future advertising and promotion dollars to women's media. And they planned to link a star's endorsement with every performance that featured no star of its own.

Conclusion: Projective techniques yielded descriptive information that was valuable to this client's strategic planning and marketing for their next performance season. Because of the success of this study, the Center hired a research coordinator to conduct regular projective studies with audiences and potential audiences.

Notes

1. See a review of disclosure literature presented in Derlega, V., Harris, M. S., & Chaikin, A. L. (1973). Self disclosure and reciprocity: Liking and the deviant. *Journal of Experimental Social Psychology, 9,* 227-294.

2. See English, H. B., & English, C. A. (1958). *A comprehensive dictionary of psychological and psychoanalytical terms.* London: Longman.

3. See Beloff, J. (1973). *Psychological sciences: A review of modern psychology*. London: Crosby Lockwood Staples.

4. Frank, L. K. (1948). *Projective methods*. Springfield, IL: Charles C Thomas.

5. The author makes a distinction between *reluctant subjects,* as discussed here, and *vulnerable subjects,* as described by FDA guideline 1.56: Vulnerable subjects are individuals whose willingness to volunteer in a clinical trial may be unduly influenced by the expectation of benefits associated with participation or of a retaliatory response from senior members of a hierarchy or institution in case of refusal to participate. Examples are members of groups such as medical, dental, and nursing students and persons in detention. Other vulnerable subjects include patients with incurable diseases, ethnic minorities, children, and those incapable of giving consent.

6. See Begin, G., & Boivin, M. (1980). Comparisons of data gathered on sensitive questions using direct questionnaire, randomized response technique, and a projective method. *Psychological Reports, 47,* 743-750. Also see Sayre, S., & Horne, D. A. (1997). Borrowing from Oprah, stealing from Freud: Video-elicitation for advertising research. In M. C. Macklin, Ed., *Proceedings of the 1997 conference of the American Academy of Advertising* (pp 67-72). Cincinnati, OH: University of Cincinatti.

7. For a review of motivational techniques for marketing developed during the 1950s, see Newman, J. W. (1957). *Motivation research and marketing management.* Boston: Harvard University Press; and Smith, A. (1954). *Motivation research in advertising and marketing.* New York: McGraw-Hill.

8. A direct quote from Paula Drillman, EVP and Director of Strategic Planning at McCann Erickson in 1989.

9. For more details, see Engel, J. F., & Wales, H. G. (1962, March). Spoken versus pictured questions on taboo topics. *Journal of Advertising Research,* 11-17.

10. See Havlena, W. J., & Holak, S. (1995). Exploring nostalgia imagery through the use of consumer collages. In K. P. Corfman & J. G.Lynch (Eds.), *Advances in Consumer Research, 13,* 35-41

11. Psychologist Shiela Crocker asked disaster victims to draw their destroyed homes so they might visually express their emotional reactions using an instrument called "House-Tree" (Oakland, California, 1989).

12. See Collier, J., Jr. (1967). *Visual anthropology: Photography as a research method.* New York: Holt, Rinehart & Winston.

13. Heisley, D., & Levy, S. J. (1991). Autodriving: A photoelicitation technique, *Journal of Consumer Research, 18,* 257-272.

14. Anecdotal materials used in the preceding pages are excerpts from Kanner, B. (1989, May 8). Mind games. *New York Magazine,* 34-40.

15. For more of Sid Levy's wisdom, read Rook, D. (Ed.). (1999). *Brands, consumers, symbols and research: Sidney J. Levy on marketing.* Thousand Oaks, CA: Sage.

16. From Pink, D. (1998, April/May). Fast company. *Marketing Science Institute Report,* 216-228. For more information on Zaltman's technique, see his 1995 article (with Robin Coulter) in the *Journal of Advertising Research* 35, pp. 36-51.

17. From Olson, J., & Zaltman, G. (2000, October). *Using projective methods in ZMET to elicit deep meanings.* Paper presented to the annual conference of the Association for Consumer Research, Salt Lake City, UT.

18. Sayre, S., & Horne, D. A. (2000). Self-disclosure and technology: The viability of video-elicitation for consumer research. In R. Belk (Ed.), *Research in Consumer Behavior, 9,* 147-172.

19. Parasocial relationships are formed between viewers of television dramas and drama stars, most commonly associated with soap opera actors and female viewers.

20. Discussions of video-elicitation and qualitative techniques used in disaster research can be found in the following three sources:

(a) Sayre, S., & Horne D. A. (1996a), *Earth, wind, fire and water: Perspectives on natural disaster.* Pasadena, CA: Open Door.

(b) Sayre, S., & Horne, D. A. (1996b). I shop, therefore I am: The role of possessions for self-definition. In K. P. Corfman & J. G. Lynch, Jr., (Eds.), *Advances in Consumer Research, 13* (pp. 323-328). Provo, UT: Association for Consumer Research.

(c) Sayre & Horne (2000). See Note 18.

Part V

TEXT ANALYSIS
AND REPORTING

O nce researchers collect reams of observational data and interview transcripts, they must decode it—make sense of it—and then explain it to someone else. Two types of textual data need our attention: visual and verbal. Visual
data help researchers ground analysis in a general way, review scenes from the
field, and point to areas of interest for further investigation. Chapter 14 deals
with interpreting photographs, videotapes, and material artifacts. An analysis of
field notes and interview transcripts follows in Chapter 15, where coding and
discourse analysis are also discussed. The chapter concludes with a list of computer tools useful for analyzing qualitative data. Writing up field stories and narrative reports is the focus of Chapter 16.

14 Analyzing Visual and Material Text

The uses to which photographs may be put are so numerous that we anticipate for it a very foremost place among the scientific applications.

—Photographic News, 1865

Sorting field notes and transcriptions is like organizing your closet—everything goes into piles of like kind; socks with socks, trousers with trousers, shirts with shirts, and so forth. After an initial sorting, each pile can be sorted again; dress socks from athletic socks, jeans from dress slacks, and T-shirts from tailored shirts. Sorting is obviously easy—unless someone from a tropical climate who is unfamiliar with clothing has the task. When the sorter is not familiar with the items, we must describe the sorting process in detail. First, we describe the item: a sock is a wool or cotton covering for feet; trousers are worn over the legs; shirts cover the upper body. Next, we list all the variations of each pile (call them *categories* from now on): patterned socks are for dress, cotton for sport, and so forth. We call this process *coding*. Coding allows a foreigner to sort items into categories in the same way you, the researcher, would sort them. Once sorted, we can tell a lot about the closet's owner.

Because qualitative researchers designate all data that come out of the field as *text,* we conceptualize the classification process as text analysis. Classification begins during the observation stage of data gathering. For instance, if you're trying to figure out what's going on at an outdoor cafe, you begin by describing all the possible groups you see: children, adults; eaters, drinkers, and readers; well-dressed, casually dressed, and so forth. Next, you notice that the clothing category can be sorted again: jogging costumes, business attire, beach wear, tennis, or golf casual. And you also notice the patrons engaged in various activities: getting coffee for their commute to work, socializing with friends after exercising,

189

reading the newspaper. You might even notice linguistic categories, such as accents (regional, international, surf slang), pitch (loud, shrill, whisper, mumbled), or topical (political, social, argumentative, gossip). Or you may see artifacts (coffee thermos, dog leash, keys, book, purse, cell phone).

Placing everything contained in a particular scene into categories enables us to "read" the text of a cafe culture. Visuals assist us by providing three essential tasks for field research: documentation, description, and disclosure. The use of photographs or videotape to record the major elements contained in a scene is called *documentation*. Anthropologists document their field finds the same way, as visual proof of their existence.

Cameras have also been employed as tools of *description*. By asking a consumer to photograph scenes from a typical shopping day, we have a visual expression of how they view shopping. We see what they see, what they deem important, and how they organize their experience. Visual description is a valuable tool for marketplace research.

Photographs and material objects or *artifacts* have value as tools for researchers to elicit disclosure from consumers. Photo-elicitation involves showing consumers photographs they have taken or were taken of them and asking for explicit details about what's going on in the picture. In the same way, objects from a consumer's collection or from a scene location help consumers recall memories and thoughts associated with items of material culture.

This chapter presents methods of analysis used for visual and material texts that document, describe, and disclose.

Analyzing Documentary Visuals

For decades, photographs have documented anthropological and ethnographic studies. With the advent of video and film, still photography has played a diminishing role in recording field information. For marketplace purposes, photography is important for its point of view. A discussion of postmodern documentary photography[1] begins with the idea that the meaning of a photograph is constructed by the picture taker and those who view the photograph. That is to say, the meaning of the photograph is context dependent. Viewing with colleagues demands a different type of viewing experience than viewing with friends.

Photographs focus on specifics, thereby eliminating from view all other details. Documentary photography may also glorify the obscene or beautify the ugly through style and focus. Marketplace researchers must keep in mind that we are not only gathering information with our photographs, we are also creating, organizing, and presenting information. By working from this assumption, we avoid creating visual images that unconsciously reflect our personal assumptions.

As documentary photographers, we appropriate images from the market-place, including mass media, and juxtapose these images to other objects of mass culture to serve as metaphor rather than analysis. In a study of international signage, I used documentary photography to record the presence of advertising images found in tourist locations and suburban areas of three European cities. To place the advertisements in context, long shots of the streets were included to show the relationship between the signage and the entire one-block space that became the data sample.

I conducted a qualitative content analysis, a selection and rational organization of categories to condense the meaning of image text, with a view to verifying an assumption. Here, the presence or absence of a theme may be measured but not the frequency with which it occurs in the data. Photographic texts were scanned into a computer and arranged to simulate the one-block areas in tourist and residential spaces. Images were compared for advertising language, content, and prominence within and between urban spaces. Lastly, tourist-area and residential-area photographs from all three cities were sorted into categories for similarities, differences, oppositions, and themes.

The outcome provides a reading of how advertising signage affects an American traveler entering two types of space—residential space, riddled with native language ads and unknown brands, and tourist space that contains global brands and English-language messages. In this case, the presence of advertising can provide the traveler with comfort and familiarity, regardless of its location. An absence of commercial messages designates "foreign territory" for the American tourist who is unaccustomed to ad-free areas.

The wider the camera's angle, the greater the image objectivity. Close-ups by their very nature imply intimacy and take on the aesthetics and interests of the photographer. According to traditional thought, a field photographer must approach documentaries completely from an observer's perspective to achieve an unbiased analysis.

In the spirit of immersion, however, ethnographic researchers may choose to abandon objectivity and work with marketplace members to photograph what is important to them. At this point, the photographs transcend the documentary stage and become more descriptive, admitting a point of view and capitalizing on it.

Analyzing Descriptive Visuals

Descriptive visual representations can be decoded with one of two types of analysis: symbolic and structuralist analyses.[2] Although both approaches attempt to address the meaningful aspects of images, structuralists borrow from literary methods. Images reveal what is socially significant to consumers in the marketplace. Rather than identifying isolated elements, as structuralists do, symbolic analysis strives to arrive at a full appreciation of the image by relating it to other marketplace arrangements. Borrowing from semiotics, symbolists believe that symbolism is the acknowledgment that one thing stands for another, one represents another. Our job as researchers is to establish the individual and collective meanings carried by those symbols (such as logos and brand names) and the logic of their patterning.

Symbolic Analysis

Meanings operate at several levels: *exegetical meanings* that come from informants, *operational meanings* established during observation, and *contextual meanings* that derive their relation to other symbols as part of a pattern or system.[3] For example, an informant may claim that wearing a designer label is simply a matter of individual choice (exegetical), but the field researcher may establish that particular designer clothes are only worn by members of particular social groups, such as yachtsmen. Here, the operational meaning differs from the exegetical meaning. A more comprehensive contextual analysis can reveal that, whereas designer yachting attire is appropriate in Newport, Rhode Island, its presence in the marketplace of Des Moines, Iowa, is a stretch.

We make sense of symbols by their reference to other symbols as communicated through language, the major symbolic system in human culture. In the marketplace, some symbols are clustered together as codes, such as fashion, gender, and so forth. Establishing what a symbol stands for may be difficult, because symbols may represent several things. For instance, the cross is a religious symbol for Christians, but for Jews, it is a historical icon. The marketplace is symbolically constituted and mediated. Actions, appearances, and artifacts all carry symbolic significance; hairstyles, flags, and logos all symbolize socially meaningful matters.

A hairstyle, for instance, communicates specific messages to viewers about the person wearing it. Dreadlocks worn by black rock stars are acceptable; a blond surfer may be construed as odd wearing such a hairstyle. Short hair is considered clean cut in certain business settings; facial hair is prohibited in some branches of the armed forces. Long hair can be a symbol of rebellion for the men wearing it; purple hair may signify belonging, to a punk rocker.

This is just one indication of how closely connected identity is to symbolic phenomena, as is the way we are perceived by others. We, like other consumers, establish various aspects of our identity through signs such as eye glasses, body language, clothing, body build, and so forth. This principle is used in photo-sorting. To match the type of person who might drive a BMW, photographs of men and women in varying sizes and shapes, wearing a variety of different attire, are sorted according to car brands. We analyze the BMW group of photographs by the identity signs of individuals who are chosen to represent that brand. If the resulting target group photos consist entirely of young women wearing tailored suits, we might assume that BMWs are for young, female professionals.

Consumer collages of images that portray nostalgia[4] are analyzed for patterns, repetitions, and omissions of visual representation of nostalgia. The results provide researchers with an understanding of how images from the past influence contemporary purchase behaviors.

Structural Analysis

Linguistic structuralism, such as semiotics, is the basis for image textual deconstruction. Structural analysis is a literary device developed to analyze text that has been adopted for visual analysis using similar semiotic techniques. Semiotic analysis holds that there is no link between a sound image, such as the word *tree* (the signifier), and the concept of meaning of this growing plant (the signified). The link between them is established by conventions of language. We must learn that the word *tree* is what we see pictured in a forest. So the meaning of a sign results from conventions that connect signifier and signified.

Ferdinand de Saussure, a linguist, identified two dimensions of the way signs are related to each other in language: syntagmatic and paradigmatic.[5] *Syntagmatic relations* are the way words are arranged in a sentence (we see meaning unfold in the statement, "A dog ate his bone"). *Paradigmatic oppositions* are the so-called vertical arrangement between signs (choosing *chewed* or *swallowed* over *ate* in the last example). To illustrate these dimensions further, I'll use a menu. Suppose you went to a restaurant and the menu choices were listed in a random fashion; soup with beverages, salads with main courses, and vegetables mixed in with desserts. Immediately, we are confused because what we've learned to expect on a menu is categories of foods that progress from appetizers through desserts in a linear fashion. The syntagmatic relations are out of whack! By reversing the order, we can quickly assess the range of offerings and cost from the paradigmatic opposition of choices on the menu.

Advertisements are decoded using semiotics to tell *how* visual signs convey meaning. Signs have a visual dimension, and it is important to understand which signs should be considered for analysis. Some signs appropriate for deconstructing an advertisement are color, size, spatiality, contrast, shape, and grain.[6]

In the Western world, *colors* generate different emotions. Red suggests passion, danger, heat; blue is cool and serene; violet is associated with royalty. *Size* elements and their relationship are also important within a sign system. A trip to

Las Vegas will provide an understanding of the relationship of signs to each other and to viewers of them. *Spatiality* is concerned with space within an advertisement. White space, for instance, is a sign of elegance. Cluttered ads connote a supermarket sale or other jumble of sales messages. Just as land meant wealth in the days of estates, empty space expresses quality in print product messages. *Contrast* refers to the shape and texture used in an ad for emphasis and usually consists of oppositions, such as light and dark, large and small, and so on. *Shape* plays an important role for generating meaning. We use hearts to signify love, diamonds to signify eternity, and guns to signify violence. *Grain* suggests amateurism in photographs, poor quality in newspapers, and documentary purpose in videotape. A soft focus suggests emotion, whereas clarity suggests technology and mechanism.

Although we seldom deconstruct advertisements in the field, signs and symbols are appropriate for analyzing descriptive photographs using a structural approach. Visual rhetoric—pictures speaking louder than words—enables researchers to use descriptive photography for understanding culture.

Visual Elicitation

By thinking of the photograph as field data, the unique character of images forces us to rethink traditional assumptions about how we move from observation to analysis. Photography within an ethnographic context seeks to redefine the relationship between researcher and consumer-as-subject by using photographs to generate conversation.

Here, the researcher uses marketplace photographs for informant discourse; the researcher becomes the listener. Sometimes, the consumer even directs the making of photographs before interpreting them.

The *consumer-directed imaging* technique was employed in a study of symbols of place. Residents of a Southern California county were asked to prepare a visual account of images that represented the county for them and for their guests. Using a disposable camera of 36 exposures, participants' photographed combined and sorted images with like content. Numeric totals revealed the most popular architectural landmarks to be the Crystal Cathedral, South Coast Performing Arts Center, and a life guard tower in a beach community. Entertainment categories included Disneyland, Knott's Berry Farm, movie theaters, a sports arena, and a baseball field. Natural settings of beaches, parks, and orange groves formed another category. In all, there were 27 categories of visual images.

After categories were established, participants got into small groups and discussed their selections. They were asked to select one image to represent an entire category and to give a rationale for their selection. Their discussions were taped. Individual group selections were then presented to the group as a whole for further consolidation and consensus. After collapsing several categories into one, 15 images were selected as the most appropriate for describing the county to strangers.

The consensus process facilitated a rich understanding of how residents conceptualized their county and how they would present the county to outsiders. By combining visual analysis with transcript analysis, we were able to provide the client with rich descriptions of consumer perceptions that might not have been possible with interviews alone.

Photo-elicitation is a technique that employs a researcher's photographs of consumption activities to stimulate consumer disclosure about what is happening in the photographs. Archival photographs may also be used as elicitation devices; high school or college yearbooks, photo albums, classic television shows, memorable advertising, and period films are a few of the visual materials available for stimulating consumer discourse and disclosure.

Material Culture

The field of material culture is one concerned with the relationship between artifacts and social relations. We use semiotics to deconstruct artifacts within their social context to understand the marketplace. As with visual data, the purpose of artifactual data is to document, describe, and elicit information about a consumption culture.

Analyzing Artifacts[7]

What consumers say and what they do are often contradictory. For instance, when consumers were asked how much bottled liquid (cola, wine, beer, juice, alcohol) they consumed in a week, their estimates were far short of their behavior. How do we know? We searched their trash for the evidence. We also used garbage as evidence to see what these consumers ate, drank, purchased, and discarded—valuable artifactual evidence indeed.

Researchers have also used residential artifacts to make assumptions about home dwellers. Decor is certainly a form of silent discourse about the people who own their homes. Office contents tell us a lot about the occupants, and refrigerator magnets provide a window for understanding household members.

The study of material culture allows us to explore multiple voices and interacting interpretations. Artifacts found in a culture can be interpreted relative to the context of their production, use, discard, and reuse. Unlike linguistic symbols, material symbols work through the evocation of sets of practices within individual experience. Material symbols tend to have abstract meaning through association and practice. For example, the ways in which certain types of music and sport are experienced are embedded within social convention and thus come to have common meaning.

There are two ways in which material culture has abstract meaning beyond primary utilitarian concerns: (a) through rules of representation and (b) through practice and evocation. Rules of representation, such as those used to categorize Egyptian hieroglyphics, are appropriate for problem solving. Practice and evocation, looking at what memories artifacts elicit, are best for pattern recognition. Material symbolism can be either representational or evocative; they are often closely related to one another. In other words, a souvenir seashell may represent a trip to the beach, whereas a matchbook may evoke memories of a first date. In both instances, objects can be symbolic of a consumption experience important for understanding a phenomenon.

People both experience and "read" material culture meanings. Taken out of context, a dried rose is simply a dead flower. But to its owner, the dried flower may convey memories of a high school prom. Through corsages, we may be able to read the prom culture. If you were asked what object you would include in a time capsule of the year 2000, what would you include? Perhaps a copy of the satiric film "American Beauty." But when the capsule is discovered, what will its viewers make of Kevin Spacey's cheerleader fantasy? Without understanding the context of the satire, the audience will miss the film's relevance to 20th-century social values.

An important assumption made by interpreters of material culture is that belief, idea, and intention are important to action and practice. In other words, it is possible to infer both utilitarian and conceptual meaning from material items. Eyeglasses, for instance, are important for practical reasons (seeing) and symbolic reasons (status, fashion). To understand the role of eyeglasses in a particular decade, a researcher must identify the contexts within which things had similar meaning (Buddy Holly's thick black plastic frames are similar in meaning to the country music popular in the 1960s). A researcher must also recognize the similarities and differences between eyeglass frames and musical expression. We may discover that Holly's glasses were less for style and more for vision, dispelling the analogy with music of that decade.

Object Elicitation

> *Boys don't make passes at girls who wear glasses.*
>   —Dorothy Parker, 1945

Table 14.1 Deconstructing Eyewear

Kind of Glasses	Meaning
Small wire rims	Egghead, nerd, techie
Extra large	Myopic or out of fashion
Round shape	Traditional, intellectual
Aviator type	Adventurer, sporty, show-off
Heavy plastic	Retro, cool
Titanium	Expensive, state-of-the-art
Rimless	Self-conscious, denies bad eyesight
Tinted	Mysterious, something to hide
Designer	Egotistic, outer directed
Antique	Nostalgic, makes a statement
Color-tinted	Eccentric, creative, rebellious

In addition to providing opportunities for analysis, objects of material culture act as devices for eliciting disclosure. Using a collection of eyeglasses worn during 40 years of her life, a consumer recalled four decades of memories about style and self-esteem while reliving experiences stimulated by these material objects.

To understand the role of eyeglasses in society, we must understand all the social and material implications of eyeglass wearing. The meaning of eyeglasses, like much material culture, comes about through use, and material culture knowledge is often highly chunked and contextualized. If we look at eyeglasses as text, we interpret various styles as signifiers and their meanings as signifieds. Table 14.1 illustrates how material culture in the form of eyeglasses can be read as text:[8]

Often, a single object serves to generate meaningful dialogue. Going back to his 30th high school reunion, another consumer reflected on the meaning of his class ring:

> I had to work extra hours in the drug store to afford this ring. Then I gave it to my girlfriend, and she had it until we graduated. My daughter wore it in junior high as a lark. The crest has a sailboat floating on black onyx. I guess this ring meant more to me than anything at the time. Now, it's just a piece of worthless jewelry.

As marketplace researchers, we care about material objects for the value they bring to reflection, discourse, and disclosure. Even a tennis shoe you find on the road has a story that may contribute to your understanding of a consumption culture. Collections, souvenirs, momentos—artifacts of cultures past and present—are valuable for marketplace researchers who strive to understand consumption experiences.

Last

The Internet provides resources for analyzing visuals.Visual-content analysis is explained online at content-analysis.de/qualitative. You can also experience visual analysis by completing the site's exercise that lets you work with photographs to establish and identify categories. HyperRESEARCH, a software product for Mac and PC users, provides a code and retrieval data analysis program for use with video, graphics, and audio sources. Go to www.researchware. com for information. VideoSearch is a tool for Mac users to locate and analyze video.

Once our textual data are collected and analyzed, we must translate our findings into readable narrative for clients or professors. The output is either a report, a thesis, or a journal article. The next chapter approaches the task of developing narrative reports on your study results.

Summary

1. All field data are texts, and text is analyzed by classification into structural or symbolic categories.

2. Moving and still images may serve as documentation, description, and disclosure mechanisms.

3. Documentation is based on traditional, objective visual image analysis.

4. Visual description is approached subjectively by the photographer (or film maker) and consumer to understand the consumption culture at exegetical, operational, and contextual levels.

5. Structural analysis uses semiotic techniques to deconstruct moving and still visual images.

6. Commercials and advertisements can be deconstructed semiotically, using visual signs as categories for analysis.

7. Visual elicitation uses photography and video to stimulate consumption memories.

8. Artifacts are useful as indicators of social meaning and as tools for elicitation.

Stretching Exercises

1. Take a roll of 18 exposures of your most valued possessions. Give the photographs to a friend and ask him or her to analyze the personality of the object's owner. Don't disclose your relationship to the photographs. What did you learn about your identity from his or her interpretation?

2. Have a friend take 18 photographs of a family ritual or holiday, such as Thanksgiving or Christmas. Analyze the photographic text for patterns, then have the friend explain each shot to you. What did you learn about holidays as consumption rituals?

Recommended Readings About Visual Analysis and Material Culture

Ball, M. S., & Smith, G. W. H. (1992). *Analyzing visual data.* Newbury Park, CA: Sage.

Berger, A. A. (1989). *Signs in contemporary culture: An introduction to semiotics.* Salem, WA: Sheffield.

Berger, J. (1988). *Ways of seeing.* New York: Penguin.

Collier, J., & Collier, M. (1986). *Visual anthropology: Photography as a research method.* Albuquerque: University of New Mexico Press.

Edwards, E. (Ed.). (1992). *Anthropology and photography.* New Haven, CT: Yale University Press.

Ewen, S. (1988). *All consuming images.* New York: Basic Books.

Tilley, C. (Ed.). (1990). *Reading material culture.* Cambridge, MA: Basil Blackwell.

Case-in-Point: Picturing Consumption

Client: Academic project

Problem: Definition of *consumerism* is changing and unclear.

RQ: *How is consumerism defined in 1999?*

Method: Photography

Data Collection: Thirty students used disposable cameras with 24 shots each to capture scenes depicting "consumerism" as they defined it. Graduate students in a California master's program and international masters' students studying in Brussels participated in the 2-week assignment. Written descriptions of the photographers' shots were also collected.

Data Analysis: Photographs from each site were arranged in categories that emerged from the data. Visual text was sorted by gender. Written text was thematically analyzed for commonalities. A comparative analysis was completed between cultures.

Results: Both written and visual text indicated a contextual definition of consumerism. U.S. students photographed signage and retail places of exchange. Belgian students photographed people transacting purchases. Written testimony exposed a purposeful and systematic approach to the definition for females and a random, cursory approach by males. Women were more personal in their descriptions, photographing the contents of their closets, refrigerators, and shopping bags. Men captured random occurrences of commercial venues. Entertainment, dining, shopping, tourism, and theme parks prevailed in photographs from students in both countries. Only three students used the dictionary definition of consumerism (advocacy) to inform the topic. Several students portrayed the effects of consumption: waste, vagrancy, and recycling.

Discussion: Visual definitions are culture based. U.S. consumers used their cars to shop at strip malls or location destinations. Branded retail outlets and entertainment venues were prominent. Outdoor advertisements and fuel distributors also played key roles in U.S. definitions. Commercialism is objectified by U.S. consumers of both sexes.

Belgian students portrayed consumerism more personally because open markets were part of that consumption experience. In the Belgian purchase process, personal exchange was meaningful and predominant. Public transportation and tourism were captured for their roles in promoting consumption.

Conclusion: Both gender and cultural differences influenced the visual description of consumerism. Few participants reflected the consumer advocacy definition in their visual or verbal responses. Evidence suggests that consumerism is no longer conceptualized as advocacy but as consumption. And consumption is conceived within the context of the prevailing culture.

Notes

1. From Harper, D. (1994). On the authority of the image: Visual methods at the crossroads. In N. Denzin & Y. Lincoln (Eds.), *The handbook of qualitative research* (pp. 403-411). Thousand Oaks, CA: Sage.

2. From Ball, M. S., & Smith, G. (1992). *Analyzing visual data.* Newbury Park, CA: Sage.

3. See Turner, V. (1967). *The forest of symbols.* Ithaca, NY: Cornell University Press.

4. See Havlena, W. J., & Holak, S. (1995). Exploring nostalgia imagery through the use of consumer collages. In K. P. Corfman & J. G. Lynch (Eds.), *Advances in Consumer Research, 13,* 35-41.

5. de Saussure, F. (1966). *Course in general linguistics* (C. Bally & A. Secheehaye, Eds.; W. Basking, Trans.). New York: McGraw-Hill.

6. From Berger, A. A. (1989). *Signs of contemporary culture: An introduction to semiotics.* Salem, WA: Sheffield.

7. From Hodder, I. (1994). The interpretation of documents and material culture. In N. Denzin & Y. Lincoln (Eds.), *The handbook of qualitative research* (pp. 393-402). Thousand Oaks, CA: Sage.

8. Adapted from Berger, A. A. (2000). *Media and communication research methods* (p. 49). Thousand Oaks, CA: Sage.

15 Analyzing Verbal Data

Everything that comes out of the field as notes or interviews is transformed into what we call data *text*. Text analysis is the primary concern in qualitative research. Text can be approached analytically or critically; our concern is with analysis rather than criticism. There are two approaches to analyzing textual data in qualitative research. One approach is philosophical; data are analyzed according to the philosophy in which the data are collected. The other approach is thematic analysis and code development. The philosophical basis for approaching consumption as text begins this chapter's discussion. Then, thematic analysis and code development are presented to explain how marketplace texts are analyzed for patterns to generate themes, or units of meaning. Concept development analysis appropriate for deconstructing documents is also explained. In this chapter, we focus on the variety of techniques available for analyzing and making sense of text, including computer programs for qualitative data analysis.

Approaching Consumption as Text

For each qualitative model, the process of classification for analysis is slightly different. Ethnography and phenomenology identify *units of meaning*. Case studies and life histories use categorical aggregation to establish patterns of *categories*. Grounded theory uses *open coding* to identify categories and properties found in text.

Of the five models we've studied, phenomenology occurs most frequently in marketplace research. To understand a phenomenon, researchers use consumer testimony about their consumption experiences for analysis. Phenomenology yields statements of meaning and *meaning units* (groups of statements) that are used to understand consumption patterns, motivations, and expectations.

Textual analysis for all models is grounded in philosophical assumptions made about how data are collected and organized. Before discussing analysis itself, I will outline the philosophical grounding options for qualitative data analysis. Of five assumptions identified by previous researchers,[1]—empiricism, socioeconomic constructionism, subjectivism, inerpretivism, and rationalism— three are most appropriate for text analysis within the framework of this book. Two extreme viewpoints, empiricism and rationalism, are omitted here because of their single-voiced reflection or creation of text. Instead, we will invoke analysis of text that is established through systemization, active reading, translation, or a combination of these.

Socioeconomic Constructivism

Socioeconomic constructivism is a strategy that assumes the world consists of a socially constructed and consensually validated common body of knowledge and that both the researcher and the text under investigation come from the same socially constructed world. To understand a particular social construction, ethnographic researchers immerse themselves in a culture and become one with that culture. Ethnographers *systemize text* so that when they interpret reality, it is from the perspective of one who shares that reality. In other words, the text can be translated into the primary experience of the researcher. Ethnographic data is analyzed for themes and patterned regularities. *This strategy assumes a social construction of reality.*

Marxism, which describes the transfer of knowledge from the social world to conscious thought, is often used to explore the structure and meaning within a material culture. Some individuals transfer a particular social group's worldview into cultural objects, such as films and songs. Charles Bukowski's screenplay for the film *Barfly* is an example of a portrayal of an alcoholic writing about an alcoholic's lifestyle. Marketing research seeking to document the patterns of social interactions that arise during consumption activities, or to analyze the social scripting of consumption through rituals and shared practices, are advised to consider ethnographic analysis.

Subjectivism

Subjectivism is akin to the phenomenological and existential philosophies of Sartre; we can characterize interpretive textual construction under these conditions as an *active reading*. Appropriate for cross-cultural research, subjectivism has an anthropological base. One consumer's experience of a consumption activity—flying on an airline—is an example. Using multiple consumers' recollections of a flying experience is another. *This strategy assumes an individual construction of reality.*

An application of subjectivism to consumer behavior phenomena is in hedonic and emotional responses that involve the whole consciousness: senses, thoughts, feelings, and values. Such experiences differ from the daily business of life—often consumers can't express themselves, saying "I can't explain it; you had to be there to understand."

Interpretivism

Interpretivism likewise assumes that the text under investigation is a product of social consensus; however, it also assumes that the researcher comes from a different primary culture or subculture. Here, the investigator acts as a *translator,* interpretively translating concepts from one context into those appropriate to another context. Included in this philosophical rubric are hermeneutics, semiotics, and structural criticism, which have recently been incorporated into consumer research studies. *This strategy assumes a linguistic construction of reality.*

Hermeneutics is a circular process by which an interpretation of the whole text guides the explanation of its parts, which, in turn, shape an understanding of the whole. It serves as a resolution of contradictions among and between elements and the larger whole of the text. *Semiotics,* the study of signs, focuses on a structure of binary oppositions as key to the recovery of meaning. *Structural criticism* looks at a symbolic system, including the consumption of everyday products, as text that can be interpreted using differences and contrasts. Using folk tales and mythical structures, fashion and advertising commercials can be deconstructed to reveal their meaning. Structural criticism is valuable for its insight into consumption symbolism, consumer behavior imagery, and business-related signs.

Interpretive Analysis

Interpretivism plays a significant role in understanding consumers within the marketplace. Consumer behavior and communication researchers use interpretation in a variety of forms to make sense out of text. As stated earlier, these processes are based on linguistic construction and require some knowledge of narrative structure on the researcher's part to be successful. However, exposure to this method may entice researchers new to the field to undertake interpretive analysis as a means of understanding consumers and consumption.

Hermeneutics

> *Anecdotes are sometimes the best vehicles of truth, and if striking*
> *and appropriate are often more impressive and powerful than argument.*
>
> —Tryon Edwards

Consumer stories are frequently collected for marketplace studies because of their power for understanding motivations and decision making. Formerly the responsibility of advertising and marketing practitioners, interpretive frameworks are now available to researchers for deriving insights from texts of consumer stories. The *hermeneutic framework*[2] provides a model for us to understand how consumers perceive products in relation to themselves. Consumer self-narratives reflect the personalized cultural meanings that constitute a person's sense of self-identity. In the hermeneutic model of meaning outlined in Figure 15.1, a person's life history is text. This perspective is used to contextualize the meaning of particular life events within a broader narrative of self-identity.

Interpreting consumer stories has two stages: (a) an initial reading to grasp a sense of the whole story and (b) additional readings to develop an understanding of the meanings within the text. Here, the researcher looks for patterns across different stories as well. Each reading of the text encompasses a broader range of considerations to arrive at a holistic interpretation. Hermeneutics assumes that a common frame of reference exists between the interpreter and the texts being interpreted. Here's where a researcher's personal experience and interest come into play, enabling a heightened degree of insight into the patterns of communication. A researcher-as-instrument metaphor captures the essence of this interpretivist approach.

There are five key aspects to the hermeneutic view, in which consumer narratives have these characteristics:

Plot lines that organize events and characters

Symbolic parallels among the meanings of different events and actions

Intertextual relationships where meanings of consumers' different stories become integrated into their personal histories

Existential themes about personal identity as reflected in consumption experiences

Draw from the cultural code of shared meanings and conventionalized viewpoints

A phenomenology of shopping experiences as told by three working women—Carol, Jan, and Cindy—all in their 30s, illustrates how consumer stories can be used to characterize this target audience in four steps.

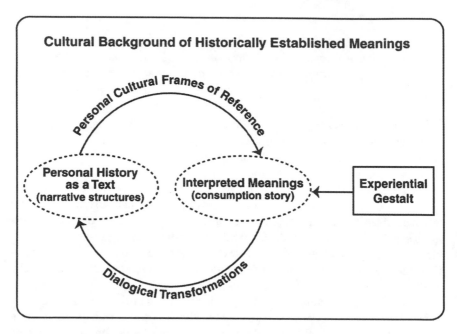

Figure 15.1. A Hermeneutic Model of Meaning Construction
SOURCE: Thompson (1997, p. 440). Reprinted with permission.

Step 1

Plot analysis, a key element in interpreting consumer stories, results from the organization of movement of events in order toward some goal.[3] Consumer narratives tend to move in a linear fashion from past to present to future; we are interested in this interrelationship. This consumer story illustrates how plot reveals Carol's emotion.

> The new PT Cruiser was hot, and I love the design. But the rear door had no window, so I couldn't put my easel in the car. If it had the window, I'd have bought the car right off, you know. But I got a Chevy Blazer instead because it had room for my art equipment, and it drove OK. But the Cruiser was so terrific, it looked like one of those 40s gangster cars. I really wanted a different look. Retro, you know. All my friends have RVs or SUVs. I wanted something special, but like, what would I do with my easel? And the Cruiser was even cheaper than the Blazer. You got leather seats and all sorts of extras for $22,000. The Blazer was a lot more money for just cloth seats and not even a CD player.

In the next story, *style* becomes a central feature in the future-driven narrative that revolves around carrying the artist's easel. As the story progresses, Carol buys the Blazer and encounters a variety of mechanical problems with the four-wheel drive. The story has a dissatisfying outcome.

> The Blazer was just in the shop most of the time. The four-wheel drive kept going out, and it had to be replaced after just a few months. You know, you spend a bunch of bucks on something and you expect it to work for a while. I ended up borrowing friends' cars so the Blazer could be fixed, and it was a nightmare. I'm really angry. I gave up the chance to have a really beautiful car, and now I have a bucket of problems instead. I could kick myself for not going with my instincts. Sometimes, it doesn't pay to be rational. I'm selling the piece of junk just as soon as it runs for a month. I've told all my friends and they were bummed. I'll never buy a Chevy product again.

She symbolically vindicates herself by swearing off of Chevy cars and spreading the word about her dissatisfaction. She blames her decision on ignoring her instincts.

These narratives bring out two factors: going with the best price and compromising on visual appeal. Although they're separate events, they were symbolically related to a consumer who blames her decision not to go with her instinctive choice. Here, narrative movement functions like a metaphor by linking events into an ongoing story.

Step 2

A second step in story analysis is *narrative framing,* the meanings through which an experience is understood as it is created among different consumption events. This next passage shows the way "eating out" is framed by a group of meanings related to the life of Jan.

> After I've been working all day, the last thing I want to do is come home and cook dinner. Or stop at the store and get some food. My family sits around the table like birds in a nest waiting for me to bring the worms and stuff them down their throats. Well, I want to fly away. I don't want to decide what to cook and deal with the dishes and cleaning up and all. I just want to have someone else do all that stuff. Just let me sit down and order a glass of wine and relax. Boy, that's for me.

For Jan, dinner is a chore that she must do for other people after she's been working hard. She framed the event around her responsibilities to both her job and her family. Here, we ask, what meanings render an issue important in this narrative? Her story revealed that cooking was a focal consumption experience related to a personally significant group of meanings.

> I used to watch my mom cook. She slaved over the stove and that was all she did. She had all day to do it. I have no time, and I'd rather not have to think about it.

Someone else should do this for me. I have so many duties. To my boss and my kids and my sister. They try to make me feel appreciated by flattering me. Saying they really love what I fix whenever I fix it. My kids really need some time with me, so I guess spending the time at the dinner table is good. Junior High is a tough time for kids, you know. And they like to complain to someone about how much they hate their teachers. And if they have junk for lunch or stop at McDonald's, I like to make sure they get one healthy meal a day. So I should cook. I mean, it's not that bad, just not wonderful.

This anecdote illustrates the symbolic relationship between a specific framing of an experience (cooking) and a consumer's narrative of a personal history. If we look at binary themes, oppositions, we can learn more about meanings. For instance, contrasts in this woman's narrative include eating out versus eating at home, being a responsible parent versus ignoring her kids, being together versus being apart, nurturing versus being nurtured, and giving pleasure versus receiving pleasure. If we apply these meanings, a theme emerges. The meanings she attributes to cooking can be interpreted as a theme of doing for others, doing for self. She balances the trade-offs of not liking to cook with giving her kids a nutritious meal.

Step 3

In this step, we interpret consumption stories from a perspective of self-identity. This perspective suggests that personal identity is continuously adapted through a person's actions. Self-identity is characterized as a process of negotiation between stability and change. This approach offers a means to articulate further the group of symbolic meanings brought out in the hermeneutic interpretation. In the next story, we see Cindy selecting a grocery store and its significance for her self-identity.

Well, they have a deli with imported cheese and meats, specially prepared foods, and a great wine selection. Of course, they're more expensive, but my friends and I think it's worth the price. Bristol Farms shoppers are more aware of what's good to eat and are willing to pay for quality. In the past, I had to make do with Safeway, but since I've been promoted, I can spend my money on things that matter.

This consumer's shopping transformation came about because her promotion enabled her to shop with people who "appreciate quality." Thus, Cindy's shopping self-image is consistent with her professional image that is reflected in the price she pays for food. Her self-discovery takes place later in the story when a consumption-oriented theme emerges in which Cindy interprets her earlier life stages as a process of being comfortable with an outer-directed identity.

I never used to care about where I shopped or what I was wearing. I did things pretty much for myself, you know. But now I realize that my friends are important, and I want to fit in. My real value is not what I think about myself but what other people think of me. After all, we're not alone in the world, and to be appreciated by friends is really important. Now, I buy the best clothes and eat the best food. My friends like me because I fit into the scene, I guess. But it's OK, 'cause that's also why I like them.

Cindy's consumption goals are linked to her identity. She shops in the places that fit an acceptable portrait of self. Choosing to shop at Bristol Farms reflects her self-identity as socially acceptable. Hermeneutic interpretation seeks to understand the pattern of meanings consumers use to construct an enhanced sense of self-esteem.

Step 4

Deriving a broader understanding of cultural, societal, or historical processes (or a combination of these) from the analysis of these stories is the final stage. A sociohistoric perspective is especially relevant to marketing interests because of the role that mass media, advertising, and public relations have played in shaping public perceptions of identity and lifestyle options. These aspects of communication offer consumers representations against which they can assess their lives. By becoming familiar with historical texts, such as archival records, diaries, and oral histories, we can make the comparison with relevant market segments. The goal is to develop a good working knowledge of the major social and historical themes that shape the cultural situation of a particular market segment. That's what we have done with these women's stories.

By analyzing the text's metaphors, common expressions, and distinctions in light of the historical considerations, we can gain insight into cultural myths in consumer interpretations of their experiences. We assume that consumer meanings are grounded in a collective cultural memory, so we can use those meanings for practical applications. Appeals to mythic themes are especially useful for positioning products and creating resonant promotional messages. The Jolly Green Giant is an example of a mythical character used to position vegetables.

Other strategic implications of hermeneutic analysis include assessments of consumer opinions of product quality and services that contribute to an understanding of how providers of those products and services can better address benefits to this market segment. Instinct, care giving, and self-image drive the narratives of three consumers. How those elements are incorporated into advertisements is another story, but we have certainly done the groundwork for a new campaign to thirty-something professional women.

Hermeneutics is more applicable to some types of marketplace research than others. A more conventional research paradigm is one where researchers have extensive knowledge of specific brand or product categories. To bring consumer stories to life, hermeneutic researchers must possess the background knowledge needed to recognize the relationships between narrative structure and the rich texture of consumers' self-identities and cultural contexts.

Critical Analysis and Semiotics

Textual analysis based on literary criticism has specific applications for advertising research.[4] Text, as we have said, can include pictures, sounds, movement, and so forth; virtually everything in the marketplace has been labeled "text," including consumers, products, and advertisements. In an attempt to make sense out of text, deconstruction researchers set forth textual boundaries of apparent meaning. The boundaries are crossed by seeking out what the text excludes—the space that exists between what an author says and what is not said. *Deconstructive analysis,* a form of critical analysis, uncovers gaps, aberrations, or inconsistencies in meanings that reveal an author's blind spots. Such readings bring out messages that had not previously emerged from the text. Deconstruction lets us take a closer look at the way interpretation has become privileged as a white, male, educated, middle-class undertaking. Such readings reveal culturally suppressed voices—of minorities and women—and remind us of what is unheard.

Semiotics is a tool used to identify signs and symbols through textual codes. Deconstruction uses semiotics to uncover deeper meanings in advertisements by rooting out multiple meanings, multiple reader contexts, and reader invention of absent contexts. Because readers put the meanings into advertisements, advertisements cannot assume that one message will mean the same thing to all readers. Text analysis can lead to a fuller understanding of the multiplicity of consumer meanings in advertisements.

Deconstructing a :60 Commercial[5]

An example of the use of semiotics to deconstruct an advertisement is found in an analysis of the famous television commercial based on Orwell's *1984* that announced Macintosh to the world during the 1984 Super Bowl without showing the product. In a study using potential computer buyers as audience, the commercial was shown, and 200 viewers were asked to describe the commercial and tell what it meant to them. Using a form of modified thought-listing, the viewers were also asked to identify the main characters of the commercial and tell what they thought the advertising message was. Their text was analyzed, and responses were coded by category determined by the message elements and oppositional structures. Words and phrases of identification and description were labeled as either intended or idiosyncratic meanings and themes.

A series of narratives emerged from the *1984*-style text, including David and Goliath, feminism, and science fiction scenarios. In the commercial, a young woman was the David who attacked the IBM Goliath, destroying the power of the giant. Other viewers saw the woman as a mythic heroine; one viewer saw a sexist image and referred to her as a "Hooters chick." Eighteen bipolar opposites were identified and viewers presented 137 concepts built on those oppositions.

The commercial message was only partially successful in transferring the metaphor of humanistic Apple Computer Company smashing its huge, technologically cold competitor. The narratives revealed a tendency toward eclectic and idiosyncratic meaning, particularly in the interpretation of certain message elements, such as Big Brother, the police, and the setting. Although over half of the viewers noted the product story, only one fifth of them had some sense of the conflict between friendly and unfriendly technology, which was the essence of the commercial's message. In spite of the variety of message interpretations, the commercial's artistry moved over 200,000 of the original viewers to purchase a Macintosh on the following Monday, its first day on the market.

Also employing semiotics, symbolic anthropology focuses not only on what consumers say and do but what their statements and actions mean symbolically. One approach is based on the concept of the "boundary"[6] for consumer research. According to this technique, boundaries have important implications for consumer behavior. Whenever a person crosses a major boundary (or life stage), the crossing symbolizes a new life. Brands and product categories that are important to self-image, such as liquor, clothing, and magazines, often change during border crossings. Beer advertising ("Miller time") tries to attach to beer all the favorite meanings associated with leaving work. The task of a qualitative researcher in this technique is to think creatively about what the key boundaries are regarding the product, what these boundaries mean, and how these meanings can be applied to the product through advertising, product naming, and packaging. Meanings are identified through consumer interviews and stories collected in the field and site-specific locations.

Thematic Analysis[7]

Thematic analysis is a way of seeing by perceiving a pattern or theme in seemingly random information. It can be used with most qualitative methods and models *and it allows for translation from qualitative information into quantita-*

tive data. Thematic analysis is a process of coding; a *theme* is a pattern found in the information to organize and interpret it. The benefit of this technique is its ability to facilitate the communication of findings and interpretations to others.

Like other techniques, this one has stages; they are previewed here. Sensing themes in data is foremost for mastering this technique. Recognizing what is codable is essential, and the skill is one that can be learned through training. Discipline is needed for developing themes or codes with consistency. Codes must be developed to process and analyze or capture the essence of observations. Lastly, researchers must interpret the information and themes in a way that contributes to the development of knowledge. It helps to have a theoretical grounding for this stage.

Coding Field Text

To undergo analysis, text must be broken down into manageable units; we call this *reduction.* Our first task is to read over all collected text to identify discernable patterns as they emerge naturally from it. The classification processes for collected data is often technique specific:

Field note text is classified by *sorting* observed occurrences.

Document text content relies on aesthetic or descriptive *classification* for analysis.

Interview transcriptions yield *thematic categories.*

Physically reducing the amount of information collected during interviews means sorting, categorizing, prioritizing, and interrelating data according to emerging schemes of interpretation. Once you have read over the transcripts, the repetition of key words and phrases will alert you to possible ways to sort the data. If you're looking at a shopping *process,* chronology of events might provide suitable categories (e.g., recognizing a need, looking for retailers, in-store experience, etc.). If *meaning* is a primary concern, pay attention to feelings and emotions described by consumers ("I loved it," "It made me laugh," "It was thrilling"). Underline these phrases for sorting and categorizing purposes.

Ideally, the concepts used in an analysis grow naturally out of an interaction between what happens in the field and what theories have said about that activity. Our task is to make sense of the way consumers make sense out of their own actions, goals, and motives. To explain consumers' actions and feelings, researchers begin by creating ordered concepts.[8] *First-order concepts* are member descriptions of how they explain their consumption experiences. *Second-order concepts* are fieldworker notions to explain the patterns found in first-order concepts. For instance, a man describes the way he purchases a tie: He looks at the colors, then feels the material, then holds one up to look at himself in the mirror with the tie (first-order concept). We interpret this report to mean that the shopper is very particular about design, texture, and appearance of the tie (second-order concept). Both are necessary to understand the tie selection phenomenon.

Order is invoked because we need some method of sorting these concepts to make sense out of our data. Classification is accomplished through a procedure of coding. Coding tools give us access to data content and are an integral part of interpreting the phenomenon under study. Learning how to code is the primary skill needed by marketplace researchers.

Analytic Coding

Identifying what is worth saving, how to divide it up, and how consumer discourse or behavior relates to other talk and behavior is our task. We begin by making several readings of the text, making marginal notes, and underlining repetitive or unique phrases. The first level of coding sorts out the obvious: actors, behaviors, settings, events, and activities. These simple, concrete, and topical categories let us begin the process of identifying more subtle categories.

Digging for meaning requires characterizing concepts, beliefs, themes, cultural practices, or relationships. This is best accomplished by keeping an eye out for implied or implicit:

Participant dramatizations

Puzzling or conflicted situations

Recurring elements

Action-evoking conditions

Key expressions

Consumption rituals

Your understanding of the culture and the phenomenon is needed at this point to tease out the categories from the mass of data. It's important to describe each coding category, especially when more than one person is doing the analysis. Qualitative coding allows us to tag segments of interest, not to achieve coder reliability as is typical in quantitative analysis.

The following is a coding example from a study on consumers who were forced to repurchase their possessions after losing them in a fire.

Category A. Concern about selecting retail locations (service, price, delivery)
Examples   Consumer concerned about a store that doesn't understand their plight
                   Consumer concerned about getting cheated

> Consumer concerned about buying now and getting the item after their new house is built
>
> Consumer concerned about a salesman taking advantage of them

Category B. Shopping behavior

Examples   Seeking help from professionals

Comparing prices

Shopping where fire victim discounts were offered

Purchasing upgrades of electronics and appliances

Taking trips with insurance housing funds

Category C. Brand decision influencers

Examples   Consumer seeks advice from architect

Consumer's neighbor recommends a brand

Consumer asks a neighbor

Consumer consults *Consumer Reports* magazine

Consumer uses Internet comparisons

Identified as one of the most influential descriptions of coding, the *constant comparative method*[9] is based on grounded theory and has explicit directions. A brief three-step explanation illustrates its advantages for analyzing marketplace text.

1. Comparing incidents applicable to each category calls for assigning data-text incidents to categories in the manner described earlier. With each new incident, categories are compared with those that exist to determine goodness of fit. Categories are built and clarified by going over the text several times.

2. Next, the analyst begins to integrate categories and their properties. This task changes the nature of categories from mere collections of coded incidents into constructs.

3. Identifying a theory at this stage brings scope to the phenomena.

Discourse Analysis

If it is not true, it is a happy invention.

—G. Bruno, 1585

The coding of interviews is a necessary step for discourse analysis. Texts derived during formally structured interviews can be coded for fast identification of elements such as description (W), definition (D), interpretation (I), **themes** (appear in bold), and <u>oppositions</u> (appear underlined). The excerpt that follows is from a study conducted by a performing arts venue to understand declining attendance rates.

> Q: What comes to mind when you think of performance arts?

D A: Uhhh, well, I think about **paying money** and going someplace where people are doing something active, like singing and dancing.

> Q: Singing and dancing?

D A: Yeah, you know . . . opera, ballet, that stuff. And maybe theater.

> Q: Tell me about your first experience with a performance.

W A: Ha (laughs). My girlfriend dragged me to a ballet in L.A. It turned out to be very long and boring . . . hardly anyone was there. She got free tickets. Even free was too high a price for that deal! (laughs again)

> Q: Boring?

W A: A woman in tights, slow music, darkness. No upbeat moments.

> Q: Was performance part of your childhood experience?

I A: Only what I **learned** about in music appreciation at school . . . you know, like

W Swan Lake. Like short, choppy steps. I was never very curious about dance except the kind I do myself.

> Q: Tell me about the places you and your family went for entertainment.

I A: Bowling.

> Q: Were there any times when you went to see a circus or concert?

A: Maybe a circus. Yeah, we went to stuff like the Ice Follies, amusement parks, stuff like that.

> Q: Describe an ideal performance.

D A: The ideal performance. A play. A musical play. A free musical play.

> Q: Why a musical?

W A: Because I like the singing. I like to be down in front so I can hear the different voices and see the people's faces, the actor's faces, that is. It's a **happy time.** Like, especially if I know the songs and all.

> Q: If you got free tickets to see any performance in New York City, what would you choose?

W A: A Broadway musical. They cost more than I can **afford.** So I'd take free

I tickets to bc on Broadway. It's a happening place. I think people go there because it's so exciting to be with all the **rich** people. And all the lights and sounds.

A quick overview of this transcript tells us that *money is a prime consideration* for this person's choice of performance. The *cost theme* prevails. He *contrasts* boring ballet with exciting musicals, free with ticket prices, and slow monotony with upbeat enjoyment. Three definitions characterize performance for him, and he describes the action that takes place during performance from his perspective. We learn that he has no appreciation for ballet and that he delights in musicals. Only two interpretive statements emerge: one acknowledging that he'd attend performance if it was free and the other that he did not have much performance experience as a child, and what he did have was not pleasant.

Notice the effective use of probes. The interviewer facilitated definition and description by repeating the respondent's words to expand or clarify his statements. By comparing this transcript with other transcripts of responses to the same questions, we may see a pattern emerge as themes become apparent. Discourse analysis is popular with practitioners to use with a series of interviews rather than in an extended field study.

Concept Development Analysis[10]

Concept development analysis is used to help develop or reposition product and service concepts word by word, line by line. This tool of analysis determines the range of reactions an audience has to a specific stimulus, addressing the following issue: What are the possible responses people have to the stimulus?

A sample of 18 to 20 phone interviews provides a good representation of the range of possible responses. Interview respondents are asked to look over, read, touch, feel, or hear the entire stimulus (an advertisement, product, direct mail piece, Web site, etc.) as a whole. Then, respondents discuss the stimulus, section by section. Normally, each set of stimulus material is divided into five sections. Respondents are then asked to go through each of the five sections by sentence, by word, or by part of visual material or sound. No questions are asked; rather, respondents are requested to talk about the stimulus and what comes to mind. Interviewers probe respondents to get a full language picture of what is going on in their minds about the stimulus.

Analysis consists of using psychiatric probing and semiotic techniques to analyze computer-readable text. Analysis determines what thought process respondents go through in reaction to the stimulus. Three forms of analysis are used:

Semantic analysis analyzes what ideas respondents have using computer retrieval programs that identify key words and phrases to determine what ideas co-occur in response to a stimulus. This form determines how respondents construct combinations of words to form ideas about the stimulus.

Syntactic analysis analyzes the order and grammar of the ideas that respondents create in thinking about the stimulus. It also tells us the degree to which they are intellectually interested, involved, or behaviorally motivated by the stimulus. The computer analyzes the subject, verb, and direct object of responses.

Pragmatic analysis analyzes the context or matrix (language response to the whole) in which the stimulus event occurs. The computer performs a contextual analysis to determine the kinds of situations the respondent places the product, service, or idea into.

Concept development analysis can be used to determine what changes can be made to the text, how motivating the message is, and what further development of the concept or the product needs to be made. The results provide the client with a full meaning of the message that the respondent got from the stimulus. The analyst then compares the client's intended message with the message received to determine how they compare, how believable they are, how motivated respondents are, and into what context the respondent places the stimulus. Here's an example:

After five years of flat sales, a lawn mower manufacturer learned from concept development analysis that mower users disliked the rigorous starting process of kicking over the engine and wanted a easy and quick-starting machine. Marketers recommended rephrasing the company's advertising slogan to, "Guaranteed to start on the fist pull or we'll fix it for free." As a result, sales increased 30% the first year and 50% the second year of using the new slogan.

Coding Disclosure

Pronouns are an indication of how much disclosure is contained in transcript data. Use of "I" and "we" indicate an in-group or personal discourse. "You" is familiar but projects distance on to the report—an out-group. "Your," "he," and "she" are unfamiliar, also part of an out-group. "They" is the ultimate out-out-group, indicating large distances between the speaker and the involvement. We use the presence of in-group pronouns to separate description from disclosure during analysis.

During transcription analysis, disclosure levels are coded in several ways. Self-reference is one way. Self-references appear in text when subjects refer to themselves, tell something about themselves, or refer to some effect they experience. One difficulty for researchers is assessing the level of clarity of subject statements. For instance, "I feel silly when I wear jeans that are out of style" is speaker explicit; "You feel silly when you wear jeans that are out of style" indicates some distance between the speaker and the concept. But speakers using "you" may still be referring to themselves.

There are three principle areas of difficulty for judging disclosure levels.[11] First, statements beginning with "I think" or "I know" may be evaluated either as a person expressing something about himself or herself or about someone else. Making this distinction is often problematic for researchers. Second, the use of reflective self-reference refers to usage where "you" may mean "I" and "people" may mean "me." Lastly, when a speaker omits who is experiencing the difficulty in statements such as "This is a difficult decision," deleted self-reference occurs. All three situations tend to obscure self-reference, causing some frustration for transcript analyzers.

Last

Qualitative data and transcript analysis can be enhanced with computer programs; however, no computer program will analyze your data. Computers don't analyze, people do. The main uses of computer software in qualitative studies are to collect and archive data in automatic and unobtrusive ways; do editing, coding, and storage tasks; keep available information in different logical fields; link data to form categories and networks of information; build theories and test hypotheses; and prepare reports. Software marketed by Sage for qualitative analysis is listed here.

ATLAS.ti is a powerful software package for the visual qualitative analysis of large bodies of textual, graphical, and audio text. An online support group is provided.

HyperRESEARCH enables you to code and retrieve, build theories, and conduct analyses of your data as text, graphics, audio, and video sources.

WinMAX is a straightforward, powerful tool for the analysis of text. It supports a grounded theory orientation code and retrieves analysis, combining both qualitative and quantitative procedures. Online demo and tutorial are available.

Ethnograph for Windows is designed to make the analysis of data collected during qualitative research easier, more efficient, and more effective. It creates and manages data file projects, easily codes data files, and expands search output display. Use it to analyze text from focus groups, interviews, diaries, transcripts, and so forth.

NUD*IST 4 opens a complete range of analytical possibilities, including the exploration processes by combining text searches and indexing.

SphinxSurvey helps you design, administer, process, and analyze surveys.

You may also consult a qualitative software discussion group: mailbase@ mailbase.ac.uk. For a list of other software products available and a discussion of their effectiveness, consult this Web site for software sources and online articles comparing analysis software: http://www.ualberta.ca/7Ejrnorris/qda.html.

Summary

1. All information collected in the field is seen as text.

2. Field text analysis is grounded in philosophical assumptions; three relevant assumptions for marketplace analysis are socioeconomic construction, subjectivism, and interpretivism.

3. Interpretivism allows researchers to extract meaning from consumer texts using hermeneutics, semiotics, and critical analysis.

4. Hermeneutic readings of consumer stories facilitate an understanding of consumers' motivations and decision-making processes.

5. Critical analysis uses semiotics to identify symbolic meaning consumers give to products.

6. Semiotics is a useful tool for deconstructing advertising messages for their symbolic meanings.

7. Thematic analysis and coding are useful for translating qualitative information into quantitative data.

8. Discourse analysis uses simplified coding to identify descriptions, definitions, interpretations, themes, and oppositions in consumer testimony.

9. Concept development analysis uses computers to interpret telephone interviews with semantic, syntactic, and pragmatic analysis techniques.

10. Disclosure levels are coded by self-references made in transcript text.

Stretching Exercises

1. Collect five consumer stories from young adults 20 to 25 years old about their experiences with having their car's oil changed. Analyze these stories using the hermeneutic method. What did you learn about the meaning of an oil change for this market segment?

2. Tape a 3-minute interview from television and transcribe it. Label the statements as descriptions, definitions, or interpretations; italicize the themes; and underline the oppositions. What does the interview tell you about the use of these elements for uncovering meaning?

Recommended Readings About Data Analysis and Report Writing

Boyatzis, R. E.(1998). *Transforming qualitative information.* Thousand Oaks, CA: Sage.

Hirschman, E. C. (Ed.). (1989). *Interpretive consumer research.* Provo, UT: Association of Consumer Research.

Lindlof, T. R. (1995). *Qualitative communication research methods* (Chapter 7). Thousand Oaks, CA: Sage.

Richards, L. (1999). *Using Nvivo (Nud*ist) in qualitative research.* Thousand Oaks, CA: Sage.

Riessman, C. K. (1993). *Narrative analysis.* Newbury Park, CA: Sage.

Silverman, D. (1993). *Interpreting qualitative data.* London: Sage.

Case in Point: Sparkle Dog Food— A Concept Development Analysis

Client: Sparkle Dog Food

Problem: Female shoppers are skeptical of the product's claims.

RQ: *How do we revise the product claims to appeal to our target market?*

Method: Concept development analysis

Twenty individual telephone interviews were transcribed and processed through a series of computer programs.

Claim: *A revolutionary new kind of dog food that makes your dog more comfortable and easier to live with*

Analysis: Women associate the word "revolutionary" with an advertising ploy. They think it must have added medicine or chemicals to do the job it claims. Women miss the idea of their dog being "easier to live with and more comfortable." Many think that their dog is already easy to live with and that the claim offers nothing new.

Claim: *Dogs love the taste.*

Analysis: Women think this is advertising and not very valuable. Women want their dog to love the taste, but they say that all dog foods claim to have a taste dogs love. This statement detracts from rather than adds to the concept.

Claim: *Sparkle helps your dog's teeth and coat sparkle, and even your dog's eyes will sparkle.*

Analysis: The overuse of the word "sparkle" causes this claim to end on a weak, skeptical note. Women are skeptical about what is in the product; they don't want additives that can hurt their dogs, and the idea of chemicals is not something they want.

Recommendation: The ordering of ideas in the concept should be changed to reflect the logic and thought process of the woman shopper. The ordering should be as follows:

It has no fillers, just the protein necessary for being healthy and energetic.

This food is more digestible than food with filler, so your dog gets no gas pains and is more comfortable.

It has better absorption, so your dog gets more out of its food with less waste, which means stools are firmer and smaller.

Blocks: Things that demotivate women from product trial:

Advertising claim

Unhealthy food

Added chemicals

Overuse of the word "sparkle"

Gaps: Things that are missing from the concept:

New dog food is dry and better than current dry foods.

New dog food has no added fillers.

The food is good because of what is not in it, not because chemicals are added.

Results: New concept slogan was recommended and is being tested for credibility among female dog owners.

Notes

1. See Hirschman, E., & Holbrook, M. (1992). *Postmodern consumer research.* Newbury Park, CA: Sage.

2. From Thompson, C. (1997). Interpreting consumers: A hermeneutical framework for deriving marketing insights from the texts of consumers' consumption stories. *Journal of Marketing Research, 34,* 438-455.

3. To learn more about plot analysis, see Stern, B. (1995). Consumer myths: Frye's taxonomy and the structural analysis of consumption text. *Journal of Consumer Research, 22,* 165-185.

4. Presented by Barbara Stern as part of a special session on qualitative methods at the annual conference of the American Academy of Advertising, 1995.

5. See Sayre, S., & Moriarty, S. E. (1993). Technology and art: A postmodern reading of Orwell as advertising. In Braden, R., Baca, J., & Beauchamp, D. (Eds.),

Art, science and visual literacy: Selected readings. International Visual Literacy Association.

6. See Durgee, J. (1986, Winter). Richer findings from qualitative research. *Journal of Advertising Research,* 36-44.

7. From Boyatzis, R. E. (1998). *Transforming qualitative information.* Thousand Oaks, CA: Sage.

8. From Van Maanen, J. (1979). The fact of fiction in organizational ethnography. In J. Van Maanen (Ed.), Qualitative methodology [Special issue]. *Administrative Science Quarterly, 24,* 535-550.

9. See Glaser, B. G., & Strauss, A. L. (1967). *The discovery of grounded theory: Strategies for qualitative research.* Chicago: Aldine.

10. A method called Q'cept has been developed by Charles Cleveland for Communication Development Company, West Des Moines, Iowa.

11. From Chelune, G. J. (Ed.). (1979). *Self-disclosure: Origins, patterns and implications of openness in interpersonal relationships.* San Francisco: Jossey-Bass.

16 Writing Field Stories and Narrative Reports

I should like my writing to spare other people the trouble of thinking. But, if possible, to stimulate someone to thoughts of his own.

—Ludwig Wittenstein, 1958

Just when you think it's safe to conclude your study, you're hit with a startling realization: You must tell someone what you did and what you learned. The two aspects of the writing task are approached with these questions: Who is your audience? and What is the purpose of the report?

Who you are writing for is of paramount importance for determining your communication style. A client requires a business presentation, whereas a professor demands scholarly prose. Journal article audiences are used to a format compatible with the journal's purpose. Whether you have a single or multiple audiences is another reader-oriented consideration. Once you identify the primary audience for your report, ask yourself what this audience expects or needs from this document.

Clients expect professional, informative communication that addresses the research problem in lay terms. Brevity and economy are two considerations here. You must balance their need to know with your need to justify the fee they paid for the research. In this case, try to "bottom line" your report, letting the reader know exactly how the results will benefit their business or affect their decision-making process. You will tell a marketplace story with a purposeful narrative that is both interesting and informative.

Academic audiences, however, require a bit more detail and rigorous delivery. Professors and thesis committee members need a demonstration from you that you used the correct methodological approach and conducted appropriate data analysis and that your results make a logical connection to theory. Formats similar to the ones presented in the Case in Point sections at chapters' ends are modified for journal audiences as specified by the publication's style and presentation requirements.

What I'm trying to say is, no one format is appropriate for all reports, and no style suits every situation; your writing must be adapted to fit the expectations and needs of your reader(s). So why bother with this chapter at all, you ask. Because writing up the results is a very important aspect of research. Rather than leaving you in limbo to flounder on your own, I will suggest a few models for writing reports to get you started.

Writerly Roles[1]

Writers of qualitative reports often think of themselves not as researchers but as authors of cultural description. Field studies are reported in a narrative fashion to present an unknown to strangers. Whether you are explaining an audience culture or a national one, the purpose is the same—telling an informative story about the marketplace. As authors of field research, you function as an artist, a translator-interpreter, or a transformer.

As an *artist,* you apply sensibilities to the form and style of the written presentation. You might even be mistaken for a journalist, a fiction writer, or—even worse—a poet. By seeking imaginative connections between events and people, you bring delightful interpretive information to your readers. There are no rules that say reports must be boring!

As you work to understand the marketplace culture, you act as an *interpreter* of that culture for others. You *translate* the consumer's language into marketing strategy. You may be translating the teen-speak of mall rats to shopping center owners or interpreting a Belgian flea market negotiation strategy to antique buyers; in both cases, audience comprehension depends on your ability to communicate that culture vividly and with flavor. Drawing on your own experiences, knowledge, and disposition, you present your understanding of the consumption experience to readers. Inference and conjecture is the bedrock of the interpretive process. You are shaped by your field experiences, your sponsors, your theoretical positions, and your observational perspectives. And often, you craft your reports to fit the needs of the audience. These and other forces shape our interpretations. By being aware of these influences, you serve the needs of research.

In the role of *transformer,* you persuade others that your research brings new insight to a phenomenon or subject. You want readers to identify with your problems and your discoveries about marketplace interaction. Called an *intellectual exorcism,*[2] good reporting takes the perspective of the consumer, getting us out of ourselves and into the world we are studying.

Developing Form and Style

> Tell me a story, tell me a story,
> Tell me a story and then I'll go to sleep.
>
> —Nursery rhyme, 1864

Our field reports should be communicated as awesome stories or field tales. Field studies rely on five conventions of the *tale:* realism, confession, impressionism, criticism, and formal tales.[3] The author takes a position of authority for *realist tales,* being an omnipotent observer. Thick description of people's lives, using quotations to portray the native point of view, are key for realism. Ethnography, phenomenology, and grounded theory are presented as realist tales.

The author of *confessional tales* views fieldwork as an interpretive act and is very present in the text. Here, the point of view is of interpreter, not native; we are presenting rules we learned in the field. This section is found in the Description section of the IMRD (Introduction, Methods, Results, Discussion) report format discussed later. Case studies, histories, and biographies are confessional tales.

Writers of *impressionist tales* make use of dramatic recall, artistry, and literary standards. You make the audience experience what you have experienced in a very colorful way by developing and naming characters with real needs, emotions, and motivations. Researchers using all models of qualitative study may present their field reports as impressionistic tales, but they lend themselves best to self-narratives or personal life histories of consumption activities.

Occasionally, we become critics, drawing on neo-Marxist perspectives by demonstrating concern for the oppressed of a capitalistic society. *Critical tales* bring out a writer's crusading spirit. Authors of critical tales are focused on theory, using the field as a laboratory to answer research questions. Grounded theory studies often are written as critical tales.

Field writing that conforms to ethnographic conventions is useful for understanding market segments, niche, markets, or global markets that require a researcher's extended immersion. If, however, you have not been in the field for any length of time, you may wish to approach report writing in a more conventional way. In either case, use your proposal as a guide. A comprehensive proposal is the best blueprint you can have to direct the focus of your field study or business report.

Organizing and Writing
Qualitative Reports

Nothing really has happened until it has been described.
—Virginia Woolf

Considering the report early in the research process enables writers to organize material in a storytelling fashion that can later be adapted for special applications. Reports are often approached as cases because they can be segmented into specific readable sections. An outline is presented here as one approach to report organization.

1. *Preview:* This mini-story will get readers into the scene by introducing the situation, location, and time of the investigation.

2. *Purpose and method:* Your audience may already know the purpose and is ambivalent about your methods, but it's wise to restate the study objectives and include a *brief* explanation of how you went about accomplishing them. You might also summarize the issues involved in the case and your role in the research process.

3. *Narrative:* An extensive story narrative describes and defines the case and its context. Without interpreting what you're reporting here, present a body of uncontestable description to bring the reader farther into the story. Controversial information can be presented in the form of interview testimony, second hand so as not to appear biased.

4. *Issues:* Develop a few key issues so the reader understands the case's complexity. Here, you may draw from past research or your own understanding of other cases to make your point and elaborate on the issues.

5. *Description:* Some issues need additional probing. Include documents, quotations, and triangulated data to provide detailed descriptions.

6. *Assertions:* If your reader is to reconsider his or her knowledge in favor of the illumination the case yields, you must, provide enough information to make your point. Interpretation and summation is the essence of this section, a very crucial one for making an argument or claim about research results.

7. *Postview:* It's always a good idea to close with a reminder that this case is only one of many and that the report is written from your personal encounter with the marketplace situation.

Narrating the Report

The title, client, and author of the study appear first. To separate each section, headings—formal or descriptive—help the reader focus on topics; they are also visual indications of topic transition. Additional visuals, such as charts, graphs, and tables, break up the narrative and provide readers with an abbreviation of the material presented. Using this format, here is a very abbreviated case report form to give you an idea of the flow of story narrative with descriptive headings, prepared for the New Zealand Kiwifruit Authority (NZKA).

The Case of New Zealand Kiwifruit[4]

A study conducted for the New Zealand Kiwifruit Authority by John Jones

Fruitful Introduction for Kiwi

(Preview)

> Kiwifruit was virtually unknown to the western world 35 years ago: It was an exotic fruit produced and consumed in New Zealand (NZ). First introduced in England in 1952, kiwis were shipped with lemons and were an immediate hit. Australians also liked the fruit, providing two positive market tests for product launch. By the end of the 1980s, kiwi exports exceeded 46 million trays of fruit worldwide. Kiwi developed some identity problems over time, requiring the association to reposition the fruit in the marketplace.

Unpeeling the Advertising Message

(Purpose and method)

> Although New Zealand has enjoyed much success with the marketing of its kiwifruit, NZKA is reevaluating several aspects of its marketing program. Accepting the fact that fruit does not lend itself to special promotions (you either like it or you don't), consumer advertising is the most important factor in determining the success of marketing kiwis. This case study analyzes three alternative creative themes for its consumer advertising by evaluating the context within which the advertising message will run and the competitive messages in the marketplace and analyzing consumer perceptions about kiwifruit. This researcher is a consultant hired by NZKA to conduct the study because of his familiarity with perishables and advertising expertise.

Furry Fables

(Narrative)

> Kiwifruit is widely known as New Zealand's odd little hairy berry. Originating along the border of the Yangtze River Valley in China, the fruit was called the Chinese Gooseberry. The name *kiwi* was first used in 1959 to capitalize on the value of a brand name that was associated with New Zealand, the world's largest producer and exporter of kiwifruit.

Enjoying the benefits of health awareness

> Among its attributes, kiwi is healthy. In the past decade, we've seen an increased consumer interest in eating more fruits. Table 1 [tables are not included here]

shows the worldwide per capita consumption trends of fruits between 1990 and 2000. Notice that the U.S. per capita consumption of kiwi is 40 times greater now than it was 10 years ago. Kiwifruit has only 34 calories each, has no pit or stone, can be eaten with a spoon by itself or in salads, and is an attractive topping for all foods.

Price follows the demand curve

As demand increased, so did the price of kiwi fruit. Table 2 shows the average annual wholesale market price per tray for selected major world markets in 1987 and 1997. The centralized buying of supermarkets and their aggressive marketing strategies account for an increasing proportion of exotic fruit sales.

Competitive threats

As kiwifruit developed into an accepted fruit by world markets, other countries experimented with growing it. By 1987, almost half of the world's production of kiwifruit came from countries other than New Zealand. Italy, which benefits from EEC free trade, is a serious threat to New Zealand's dominance of the European market. Chile is gradually taking over the market share in the southern hemisphere.

Working together for success

In spite of the rise of strong competition, the NZ kiwifruit industry is one of the country's major sources of income. NZKA was established in 1977 to promote the interest and welfare of the NZ kiwifruit industry. NZKA controls the overseas promotion activities and collects fees from its growers and exporters for this purpose.

Generic branding strategy fails

Many fresh fruits and vegetables are branding themselves with adhesive name labels or printed logos. Unfortunately for New Zealand, kiwifruit has become a generic term used by all producers of the fruit. Consumer testimony validates this notion:

> I thought all kiwis came from the same place. (Mary, 36)

> Doesn't Sunkist or Dole produce kiwi? (Fred, 42)

> Is there a difference between one country's kiwi and another's? (Alice, 20)

Sowing Kiwi Seeds

(Issues)

Promoting perishables has proven troublesome for many growers over the years. Chiquita created a Latin dancer in the shape of a banana who sang to us on television. Sunkist was the first to use ink branding directly on its citrus. Both companies called attention to themselves using a variety of integrated marketing communications. One issue for NZKA was how to effectively promote the kiwi and to call attention to the brand, New Zealand Kiwifruit.

NZKA worked closely with food editors of magazines and journals to increase their knowledge of kiwi and to supply them with ideas for serving the fruit. Other promotional activities included point-of-purchase (POP) materials, trade articles, specialty advertising, premiums, and advertising. POPs have proved to be one of the most important forms of promotion for kiwi, improving sales in every instance of their use.

Advertising's role is a second issue. Using print, broadcast, and outdoor media, NZKA has advertised throughout the world with varying success rates. Because New Zealand no longer owns the kiwifruit market, its competitors use the "buy local" strategy to keep kiwi sales in the countries of origin.

Creating Airwave Appeal

(Description)

Three themes were proposed by the advertising agency retained by NZKA to develop a campaign to increase brand awareness and position New Zealand as the best kiwi grower in the world:

1. *Buy NZ kiwi because they are healthy, nutritious, and tasty.*

   This generic theme focuses on the fruit's main selling features. No differential advantage is included.

2. *Buy NZ kiwi because it is the original and best on the market.*

   Associating kiwi with exotic and beautiful New Zealand may create an image for kiwi that reflects the country's attributes.

3. *Buy NZ kiwi because of its distinctive personality.*

   A brand character (a "fuzzy, ugly but cute fruit") was selected for use with this theme to characterize the fruit and capitalize on its distinct taste and appearance.

Themes were tested in four countries for viewer recall and creating favorable attitudes. Results show that no single theme was appropriate for all four countries; they differed in their ability to promote recall or to create a favorable attitude toward New Zealand kiwifruit. The dilemma of whether to create a local campaign based on test results for each country or to adopt a single theme for a global campaign was hotly debated among members of the Authority. At this writing, no decision had been made. Meanwhile, the New Zealand kiwi continues to lose market share worldwide.

Make Kiwi the "Real Thing"

(Assertions)

If you may recall, Coke's "Real Thing" slogan established them as a global power, not because the slogan was sent to a single global audience but because they gave it local appeal. NZKA must create a global awareness with a single brand idea—perhaps the brand character—while conforming to local perceptions of health and taste for a truly successful worldwide presence. As reflected in the literature, brands cross borders better than slogans. Visuals communicate faster and better than words. Using those considerations, the NZKA will do well to follow the Coke example.

Ugly Is Beautiful

(Postview)

> As the VW Beetle has proven, ugly can be beneficial for marketing unique shapes
> to a sympathetic public. The idea of a self-conscious fruit in the Woody Allen sense
> is very appealing to many Western countries. For others countries, perhaps a ma-
> cho kiwi character kicks off the campaign. If we are to remember New Zealand
> when we think of kiwifruit, we must be entertained by the idea of a beautiful para-
> dise boasting about its ugly little taste sensation.

The IMRD Structure of Qualitative Reports[5]

Typically, students and researchers write up qualitative reports in a four-section
format of Introduction, Methods, Results, Discussion—thus, the IMRD structure. The Discussion section is the lengthiest, especially when quotations are
used to illustrate emerging themes. The generic approach of the IMRD structure
lends itself to a variety of uses and can be easily adapted to journal or thesis requirements. The content of each section is briefly described here.

Introduction: Readers want to know in a very short time why this topic is of
interest and what you hope to accomplish by conducting the research. Relevant
literature and the topic's importance for your field are also expected here. You
supply your readers with a sense of context and background to help them understand the nature of the report and its importance.

Methods: Because not all marketplace researchers or clients are familiar
with qualitative methods, it's a good idea to ground them in your model and rationale for using it, as well as an explanation of each technique of data gathering
and analysis. Provide the assumptions qualitative researchers have toward research and naturalistic inquiry, followed by nontechnical definitions of the
terms used in the report.

Results: This section's only concern is with *what* you found, not why. If you
identified four themes, state them. If you have numeric data (from a corresponding quantitative study or content analysis), present them in tables or charts. Con-
fine your remarks to the bottom line—what happened during the study.

Discussion: This is the meat of your report, the *why* of your results. This section is what distinguishes qualitative research from quantitative because it contains detailed evidence to support and elaborate on what you found. Confessional tales (described earlier) are contained in this section. You can explain
what was unexpected or surprising as well as compare your study with what
other researchers have found in the past. Research usually produces unanswered
questions; these can be proposed for future research in this section.

Last

Don't be fooled by the brevity of this chapter; it does not reflect the length of reports you will need to produce about your research outcomes. My advice is to take a look at qualitative journal articles in the *Journal of Consumer Research,* at masters' theses, and at Harvard Business School case studies. Writing reports can be a very cathartic experience; take advantage of it.

Summary

1. Two vital determinants of report writing are the audience or reader and the report's purpose.

2. An ethnographic writer can approach field reports as tales of realism, confession, impressionism, criticism, or formalism.

3. A seven-part organizational scheme can be used for writing case studies and organizational narratives.

4. The IMRD format can be adapted for academic or professional reports on qualitative studies.

Stretching Exercises

1. Locate an article from the *Journal of Contemporary Ethnography.* Identify one type of tale that the article reflects, and explain your choice.

2. From an article you locate in the *Journal of Consumer Research,* explain the usefulness of the Discussion section for understanding the marketplace phenomenon studied.

Recommended Readings About Report Writing

Creswell, J. W. (1994). *Research design: Qualitative and quantitative approaches.* Thousand Oaks, CA: Sage.

Glesne, C., & Peshkin, A. (1992). *Becoming qualitative researchers: An introduction.* New York: Longman.

Moch, S. D., & Gates, M. F. (Eds.). (1999). *The researcher experience in qualitative research.* Thousand Oaks, CA: Sage.

Case-in-Point: Mmm! What a Tan— Presenting Beach Lore to Minnesotans

Client: 3M Company, Personal Product Division

The Brand: *Mmm! What a Tan*

Audience: Marketing manager and national sales managers

Purpose: 3M developed the first suntan lotion with numbered screen designations. In preparation for a test market, they commissioned a study to determine what promotions were appropriate for the San Diego lifestyle. The researcher's job was to study the relationship between the beach culture and suntan lotion and present the results in an interesting and informative field narrative. The client was a Minnesota company with little knowledge about beach culture.

What follows is the process of developing a *video report* of a study conducted to develop concepts for product promotion.

Medium: 15-minute videotape

> **Author's role:** Author as interpreter, presenting a confessional tale of the beach culture of young adults during a typical summer season along the California coast.

Background: In the early 1980s, 3M wanted a very splashy rollout promotion for their newly developed suntan lotion. The task is to conduct field research and create appropriate promotions for test market events. To understand the beach culture, the researcher spent 3 months observing, interviewing, and recording beach activity. Here's what she found out:

> San Diegans hang out at beaches nurturing tans, playing Frisbee and volleyball, and of course, surfing. To characterize Southern California for Minnesotans, she condensed 27 hours of surfside lifestyle into a quarter-hour upbeat videotape.

Video Narrative: The tape begins with a long shot of the Del Mar beach: surfers catching waves, swimmers coming out of the water, sun bathers of all shapes and sizes, and dogs leaping in the air for Frisbees thrown to them at water's edge.

A voice-over narrates the scene: "Welcome to California where the sun always shines and a tan is the culture's most prized possession." Segments from interviews with sun bathers feature discussions of their favorite lotions and their lifestyles. Young girls want an oily lotion, surfers like lotion that stays on in the water, and moms like sun block to protect their children from sunburn. With a hand-held microphone and video crew, the researcher captures beach activity and consumer commentary.

Beach Boys music continues throughout the tape, and the voice-over describes the blare of radios, proliferation of group sporting activities, and tanning rituals. The researcher interprets beach slang, explains the meanings of tan shades for their social significance (dark is beautiful, white is ugly), and translates fashion symbolism.

Reception: In Minneapolis, the clients sit around a conference table and the researcher begins the presentation by handing out visors with the new product logo, T-shirts, and small vials of beach sand labeled "California gold." The video plays to an enthusiastic audience. An exhaustive ethnographic written report accompanies the tape to answer questions and describe research methods. Ultimately, the tape is made available for distributors and retail accounts to generate excitement for the product rollout and test market the following season.

Results: From the research, the researcher was able to prepare a promotional schedule to take full advantage of the activities identified as important to culture members. In the spirit of a popular television show called *Mod Squad,* the researcher recruits three young college women to act as beach ambassadors, calling them the "Tan Squad." Clad in logo-emblazoned yellow visors, sandals, tank tops, and shorts, the Tan Squad arrives at San Diego beaches in a special yellow Mazda van for beach parties sponsored by different radio stations each week. Tan contests are held at each beach location, and winners receive a variety of prizes. To enter the contest, participants purchase the lotion and receive an *Mmm! What a Tan* decal to affix during exposure to the sun. Contests are judged by the crowds who gather to dance to music provided by a radio station's mobile van and drink free Pepsi. Everyone receives a free *Mmm! What a Tan* visor.

Promotional sponsors include Mazda, Pepsi Cola, and Jantzen Sportswear, who provide prizes for our tan contest winners. Tan Squad members appear in local commercials and in newspaper accounts of each event. Their beach role was to hand out product samples to beachgoers and invite them to participate in the next tanning contest.

At summer's end, *Mmm! What a Tan* had gained a market share second to Coppertone, the leading lotion in national sales. As a result of the product's success, 3M commissioned another study for the San Francisco market the following summer.

Notes

1. From Glesne, C., & Peshkin, A. (1992). *Becoming qualitative researchers: An introduction* (Chapter 8). New York: Longman.

2. From Shweder, R. (1986, September 1). Storytelling among the anthropologists. *New York Times Book Review, 21,* p. 38.

3. See Van Maanen, J. (1988). *Tales of the field: On writing ethnography.* Chicago: University of Chicago Press.

4. From a case prepared by C. Patti and S. Liangdeng for presentation to the annual conference of the American Academy of Advertising, 1992.

5. From Berger, A. A. (2000). *Media and communication research methods* (Chapter 16). Thousand Oaks, CA: Sage.

Resource A: Protocol
for a Structured Interview

Client: Fieldstrom Department Stores

Purpose: Determine the value of store gift certificates to female consumers

Time of Interview:

Date:

Place:

Interviewer:

Interviewee:

        (Briefly describe the project)

Questions:

1. When you are buying gifts for family and friends, how often do you consider purchasing a gift certificate?

2. Under what circumstances would you purchase them?

3. How many have you purchased in the past? In what amounts?

4. What has been your experience with gift certificates?

5. How do the recipients of your gift certificates react?

6. How would this reaction be different from a reaction to a specific object as a present?

7. What do you think people who receive gift certificates feel about the giver?

8. Have you ever received a gift certificate?

9. What were your thoughts about the giver?

10. Will you continue to give gift certificates in the future? Why?

(Thank them for their participation and assure them of confidentiality of responses and potential future interviews.)

Resource B: Protocol for Focus Group Discussion

Focus Group Discussion Guide: In-Ground Watering Replacement[1]

Client: Toro Irrigation Division, for launching retail expansion

Purpose: To gather opinions and attitudes about needs, shopping for, purchasing, installing, and using in-ground sprinkler systems to water lawns and gardens

Sample: Twelve men and women who have recently purchased any brand of sprinkler system for their homes

1. Describe Needs

How did you originally decide you wanted or needed an in-ground sprinkling system? (PROBE: better looking lawn, convenience, water savings, replacement)

- What were your considerations in the purchase? (female)
- What was important to you? (male)

From the time you first considered a sprinkler, how long did it take before you purchased it? What finally made you go for it? Describe the steps in your decision process. (WRITE ON BOARD)

Were there times when you thought you would not go through with the purchase? Please describe. (BARRIERS TO PURCHASE)

2. Information Review/Shopping Process

How would you rate your knowledge of sprinkling systems?

(Scale 1 to 10; 10 is expert)

WRITE: When you think of these systems, what part first comes to mind?

Which piece is important? (PROBE: timer, valve, pipes, heads)

What different types of stores did you visit in selecting sprinkler system components? (PROBE: large format hardware, lawn & garden specialty, small hardware, other type)

Finish the sentence: "Shopping for sprinkling systems is like . . ."

Conduct differential exercise.

3. Brand/Purchase

How many brands of sprinkler systems did you notice in the stores?

What brands do you know in these types of products?

(LIST ON BOARD)

(PROBE: HydroRain, Lawn Genie, Champion, Orbit, RainBird, Toro)

Conduct price/quality exercise.

(DISCUSS RESULTS)

Conduct purchase influencer exercise.

Test relationship between brand, price, features, product quality, availability of information, and ease of installation.

(DISCUSS RESULTS)

How do you determine quality in sprinkler system products? Is there much difference between the various brands available?

(USE PRODUCT SAMPLES FOR REVIEW)

Is it helpful to know that the brand you're buying is used by professionals?

Do you have a price in mind or preconceived notion of cost?

4. Point of Sale

Did you purchase your system parts on your own or get help from someone in the store?

Was there a display in the store you visited?

(SHOW DISPLAY SAMPLES)

Did they help your selection?

Was there any information available at the point of purchase to help you?

Please describe. Did you use it? When you use a company's information, do you more often stay with that brand or go to others?

(SHOW COMPETITION SAMPLES)

How about the package? Was the information clear? Helpful? Please talk through the process. What did you want to know that wasn't on the package? Compare boxed versus open versus blister pack.

(PACKAGE REVIEW)

(PROBE: Information needs, 800 number)

5. Installation

When did you discuss the installation? Before, during, or after purchase?

How did you find your installer?

Did you install it yourself? How could the process be made easier?

6. Results

> Overall, how pleased are you with the results (1 is not at all satisfied and 10 is extremely satisfied)
>
> What kept you from rating a 10?
>
> Did you experience any problems or surprises?
>
> How would you rate your knowledge of these systems now? (10 = expert)

7. Positioning

> There are several different ways to think about sprinkling systems. The statement you have in front of you talks about these products in different ways. I'm going to read the statement aloud. As I read along, please underline in green the parts of the statement that provide information that is appropriate or helpful to you. Underline in red the parts that are not helpful.

8. Future

> If you could make your systems work differently, more efficiently, how would you change them?
>
> (PROBE: radio/auto control, moisture probes, monthly control versus weekly control, add-on/delete flexibility)
>
> What about the idea of being able to use a demo kit or some kind of test kit so you could try out different types of sprinkler heads?
>
> (SHOW KIT IDEA)
>
> (PROBE: Potential reaction, benefits, problems, etc.).

Note

1. Based on a study conducted in 1995 by Fitch, Inc., of Worthington, Ohio.

Resource C: Additional Text
Recommendations by Chapter

Chapter 2

Angrosino, M. V. (1989). *Documents of interaction: Biography, autobiography and life history in social science perspective.* Gainesville: University of Florida Press.

Chapter 4

Armer M., & Grimshaw, A. (Eds.). (1993). *Comparative social research: Methodological problems and strategies.* New York: Wiley.

Chapter 5

Booth, W., Colomb, G., & Williams, J. (1995). *The craft of research.* Chicago: University of Chicago Press.
Denzin, N. (1988). *The research act.* New York: McGraw-Hill.

Chapter 7

Denzin, N. (1984). *The research act.* Englewood Cliffs, NJ: Prentice Hall.
Feagin, J. R., Orum, A. M., & Sjoberg, G. (1991). *A case for the case study.* Chapel Hill: University of North Carolina Press.

Chapter 9

Rogers, M. (1983). *Sociology, ethnomethodology and experience.* Cambridge, UK: Cambridge University Press.
Spradley, J. P. (1979). *The ethnographic interview.* London: Harcourt Brace Jovanovich.

Chapter 10

Glaser, B. G., & Strauss, A. L. (1967). *The discovery of grounded theory: Strategies for qualitative research.* Chicago: Aldine.
Lindzdey G., & Aronson, E. (Eds.). (1985). *Handbook of social psychology: Vol 1. Theory and method.* New York: Random House.
Spradley, J. P. (1980). *Participant observation.* New York: Holt, Rinehart & Winston.

Chapter 11

Robbins, K. (1996). *Into the image: Culture and politics in the field of vision.* New York: Routledge.
Star, S. L. (Ed.). (1995). *Culture of computing.* Cambridge, MA: Blackwell.

Chapter 12

Hansen, A., Cottle, S., Negrine, R., & Newbold, C. (1998). *Mass communication research methods.* Washington Square: New York University Press.
Stewart, C. J. & Cash, W. B. (1988). *Interviewing principles and practices* (5th ed.). Dubuque, IA: William C. Brown.

Chapter 15

Chelune, G. (1979). *Self-disclosure: Origins, patterns and implications of openness in interpersonal relations.* San Francisco: Jossey-Bass.

Chapter 16

Glesne, C., & Peshkin, A. (1992). *Becoming qualitative researchers: An introduction.* New York: Longman.

References

Angrosino, M. V. (1989). *Documents of interaction: Biography, autobiography and life history in social science perspective.* Gainsville: University of Florida Press.

Arnould, E., & Price, L. (1996). Conducting the choir: A strategy for multimethod consumer research. *Advances in Consumer Research, 13.*

Ball, M. S., & Smith, G. (1992). *Analyzing visual data.* Newbury Park, CA: Sage.

Beaudrillard, J. (1985). The ecstasy of communication. In H. Foster (Ed.), *Postmodern culture.* London: Pluto.

Begin, G., & Boivin, M. (1980). Comparisons of data gathered on sensitive questions using direct questionnaire, randomized response technique, and a projective method. *Psychological Reports, 47,* 743-750.

Belk, R., Wallendorf, M., & Sherry, J. (1991). The sacred and the profane in consumer behavior: Theodicy on the odyssey. In Belk, R. (Ed.), *Highways and buyways: Naturalistic research from the consumer odyssey* (pp. 59-101). Provo, UT: Association for Consumer Research.

Beloff, J. (1973). *Psychological sciences: A review of modern psychology.* London: Crosby Lockwood Staples.

Berger, A. A. (1989). *Signs of contemporary culture: An introduction to semiotics.* Salem, WA: Sheffield.

Berger, A. A. (2000). *Media and communication research methods.* Thousand Oaks, CA: Sage.

Booth, W., Colomb, G., & Williams, J. (1995). *The craft of research.* Chicago: University of Chicago Press.

Borsook, P. (2000). *Cyberselfish.* New York: Putnam.

Boyatzis, R. E. (1998). *Transforming qualitative information.* Thousand Oaks, CA: Sage.

Boyder, J. (1987). *The silent minority: Non-respondents on sample surveys* (p. 143). Cambridge, MA: Polity.

Bym, N. K. (1995). From practice to culture on Usenet. In S. L. Star (Ed.), *Cultures of computing* (pp. 29-52). Cambridge, MA: Blackwell.

Chadwick, D. W. (1996). A method for collecting case study information via the Internet. *IEEE Network, 10*(2), 36-39.

Chelune, G. J. (Ed.). (1979). *Self-disclosure: Origins, patterns and implications of openness in interpersonal relationships.* San Francisco: Jossey-Bass.

Cole, A. (1994). *Doing life history research in theory and practice.* Paper presented to the American Educational Research Association, New Orleans, LA.

Collier, J. (1967). *Visual anthropology: Photography as a research method.* New York: Holt, Rinehart & Winston.

Correll, S. (1995). The ethnography of an electronic bar: The Lesbian Café. *Journal of Contemporary Ethnography, 24,* 270-298.

Creswell, J. (1998). *Qualitative inquiry and research design: Choosing among five traditions.* Thousand Oaks, CA: Sage.

de Saussure, F. (1966).*Course in general linguistices* (C. Bally & A. Secheehaye, Eds.; W. Basking, Trans.). New York: McGraw-Hill.

DeLorme, D., & Reid, L. (1999). Moviegoers' experiences and interpretations of brands in films revisited. *Journal of Advertising, 28*(2), 71-95.

Denzin, N. (1970). *The research act.* Chicago: Aldine.

Denzin, N. (1984). *The research act.* Englewood Cliffs, NJ: Prentice Hall.

Denzin, N. (1988). *The research act.* New York: McGraw-Hill.

Denzin, N. (1989). *Interpretive biography.* Newbury Park, CA: Sage.

Derlega, V., Harris, M. S., & Chaikin, A. L. (1973). Self disclosure and reciprocity: Liking and the deviant. *Journal of Experimental Social Psychology, 9,* 227-294.

Durgee, J. (1986, Winter). Richer findings from qualitative research. *Journal of Advertising Research,* 36-44.

Edings, J. (1994). *How the internet works.* Emeryville, CA: Ziff-Davis.

Elliott, S. (1993, August 23). Advertising column. *New York Times,* p. B8.

Engel, J. F., & Wales, H. G. (1962, March). Spoken versus pictured questions on taboo topics. *Journal of Advertising Research,* 11-17.

English, H. B., & English, C. A. (1958). *A comprehensive dictionary of psychological and psychoanalytical terms.* London: Longman.

Evans, W. (1990). The interpretive turn in media research. *Critical Studies in Mass Communication, 7*(2), 145-168.

Featherstone, M. (1990, February). Perspectives on consumer culture. *Sociology, 24,* 5-22.

Fetterman, D. (1989). *Ethnography step by step.* Newbury Park, CA: Sage.

Fetterman, D., & Pitman, M. (Eds.). (1986). *Educational evaluation: Ethnography in theory, practice, and politics.* Beverly Hills, CA: Sage.

Fisher, D. V. (1984). A conceptual analysis of self-disclosure. *Journal for the Theory of Social Behavior, 14*(3), 277-291.

Form, W. (1973). Field problems in comparative research: The politics of distrust. In M. Armer & A. Grimshaw (Eds.), *Comparative social research: Methodological problems and strategies.* New York: John Wiley.

Fortini-Campbell, L. (1992). *Hitting the sweet spot: How consumer insights can inspire better marketing and advertising.* Chicago: The Copy Workshop.

Frank, L. K. (1948). *Projective methods.* Springfield, IL: Charles C Thomas.

Frederick-Collins, J. (1993, April). *The workingman's constant companion: The pin-up advertising calendar and sexual harassment in the workplace.* A paper presented to the annual conference of the American Academy of Advertising, Montreal, Canada.

Garton, L., & Wellman, B. (1995). Social impacts of electronic mail in organizations: A review of the research literature. In B. R. Burleson (Ed.), *Communication Yearbook 18* (pp. 434-453). Thousand Oaks, CA: Sage.

Geertz, C. (1973). Deep play: Notes on a Balinese cock fight. In C. Geertz (Ed.), *The interpretations of cultures: Selected essays.* New York: Basic Books.

Glaser, B. G., & Strauss, A. L. (1967). *The discovery of grounded theory: Strategies for qualitative research.* Chicago: Aldine.

Glesne, C., & Peshkin, A. (1992). *Becoming qualitative researchers: An introduction* (Chapter 8). New York: Longman.

Gold, R. L. (1958). Roles in sociological field observations. *Social Forces, 36,* 217-223.

Gourgey, H., & Smith, E. B. (1996). Consensual hallucination: Cyberspace and the creation of an interpretive community. *Text and Performance Quarterly, 16,* 233-247.

Guba, E., & Lincoln, Y. (1989). Competing paradigms in qualitative research. In N. Denzin & Y. Lincoln (Eds.), *Handbook of qualitative research* (pp. 105-117). Newbury Park, CA: Sage.

Haire, M. (1950). Projective techniques in marketing research. *Journal of Marketing, 145,* 649-656.

Hammersley, M. (1990). *Reading ethnographic research: A critical guide.* London: Longman.

Hansen, A., Cottle, S., Negrine, R., & Newbold, C. (1998). *Mass communication research methods* (Chapter 10). Washington Square: New York University Press.

Harper, D. (1994). On the authority of the image: Visual methods at the crossroads. In N. Denzin & Y. Lincoln (Eds.), *The handbook of qualitative research* (pp. 403-411). Thousand Oaks, CA: Sage.

Havlena, W. J., & Holak, S. (1995). Exploring nostalgia imagery through the use of consumer collages. In K. P. Corfman & J. G. Lynch, Jr., (Eds.), *Advances in Consumer Research, 13,* 35-41.

Haysom, I. (1988). *A case study of effects of e-commerce on customer service.* Unpublished master's thesis, California State University, Fullerton.

Heisley, D., & Levy, S. J. (1991). Autodriving: A photoelicitation technique, *Journal of Consumer Research, 18,* 257-272.

Hirschman, E. (1986). Humanistic inquiry in marketing research: Philosophy, method and criteria. *Journal of Marketing Research, 23,* 237-249.

Hirschman, E. (1992). The consciousness of addiction: Toward a general theory of compulsive consumption. *Journal of Consumer Research, 19,* 155-179.

Hirschman, E., & Holbrook, M. (1992). *Postmodern consumer research.* Newbury Park, CA: Sage.

Hirschman, E., & Stern, B. (1998). Consumer behavior and the wayward mind: The influence of mania and depression on consumption. *Advances in Consumer Research, 25,* 421-427.

Hirschman, E., & Thompson, C. (1997). Why media matter: Toward a richer understanding of consumers' relationships with advertising and mass media. *Journal of Advertising, 26*(1), 43-60.

Hodder, I. (1994). The interpretation of documents and material culture. In N. Denzin & Y. Lincoln (Eds.), *The handbook of qualitative research* (pp. 393-402). Thousand Oaks, CA: Sage.

Huff, C. W., & Rosenberg, J. (1989). The on-line voyeur: Promises and pitfalls of observing electronic interaction. *Behavior, Research Methods, Instruments & Computers, 21*(2), 166-172.

Jones, J. (1998). *How advertising works: The role of research.* Thousand Oaks, CA: Sage.

Kakutani, M. (2000, June 27). When the geeks get snide. *New York Times,* p. B1.

Kanner, B. (1989, May 8). Mind games. *New York Magazine,* 34-40.

Kassarjian, H., & Sheffet, J. E. (1975). Personality and consumer behavior: One more time. In E. Mazze (Ed.), *Combined proceedings* (pp. 324-327). Chicago: American Marketing Association.

Kent, P. (1994). *Ten minute guide to the Internet.* Indianapolis, IN: Alpha.

Langford, B. E. (1994). A magazine of management applications. *Marketing Research, 6*(3), 45-59.

Lasswell, H. (1964). The structure and function of communication in society. In L. Brown (Ed.), *The communication of ideas* (p. 37). New York: Cooper Square Publishers.

Lavin, M., & Archdeacon, T. (1989). The relevance of historical method for marketing research. In E. Hirschman (Ed.), *Interpretive consumer research.* Provo UT: Association for Consumer Research.

Lee, R., & Renzetti, C. (1990). The problems of researching sensitive topics: An overview and introduction. *American Behavioral Scientist, 33,* 510-528.

Levy, S. (1981). Interpreting consumer mythology: A structural approach to consumer behavior, *Journal of Marketing, 45*(3), 49-61.

Lincoln, Y., & Guba, E. (1985). *Naturalistic inquiry.* Beverly Hills, CA: Sage.

Lindlof, T. R. (1995). *Qualitative communication research methods.* Thousand Oaks, CA: Sage.

Lindlof, T. R., & Shatzer, M. (1998). Media ethnography in virtual space: Strategies, limits and possibilities. *Journal of Broadcasting and Electronic Media, 42*(2), 170-190.

Manning, P. K. (1987). *Semiotics and fieldwork.* Newbury Park, CA: Sage.

Maxwell, J. (1996). *Qualitative research design: An interpretive approach.* Thousand Oaks, CA: Sage.

McGrane, S. (2000, June 22). On line might. *New York Times,* p. C2.

McQuarrie, E. F. (1998). *Customer visits: Building a better market focus.* Thousand Oaks, CA: Sage.

Morgan, G. (1983). *Beyond method: Strategies for social research.* Beverly Hills, CA: Sage.

Moustakas, C. (1994). *Phenomenological research methods.* Thousand Oaks, CA: Sage.

Myers, D. (1987). Anonymity is part of the magic: Individual manipulation of computer-mediated communication contexts. *Qualitative Sociology, 10,* 251-266.

Newman, J. W. (1957). *Motivation research and marketing management.* Boston: Harvard University Press.

Olson, J., & Zaltman, G. (2000, October). *Using projective methods in ZMET to elicit deep meanings.* Paper presented to the annual conference of the Association for Consumer Research, Salt Lake City, UT.

Paccagnelli, L. (1997). Getting the seats of your pants dirty: Strategies for ethnographic research on virtual communities. *Journal of Computer Mediated Communication, 3*(1), 347-356.

Patti, C. (1995). *Case studies: Understanding and expanding their purpose.* Proceedings of the 1995 conference of the American Academy of Advertising, p. 216.

Petronio, S., & Bourhis, J. (1987). Identifying family collectives in public places: An instructional exercise. *Communication Education, 36,* 46-51.

Phillips, J. (1993). History from below: Women's underwear and the rise of women's sports. *Journal of Popular Culture, 27*(2), 129-146.

Pink, D. (1998, April/May). Fast company. *Marketing Science Institute Report,* 216-228.

Press, A. (1996). Toward a qualitative methodology of audience study: Using ethnography to study the popular culture audience. In J. Hay, L. Grossberg, & E. Wartella (Eds.), *The audience and its landscape.* Boulder CO: Westview.

Priest, P. J., & Dominick, J. R. (1994). Pulp pulpits: Self-disclosure on "Donahue." *Journal of Communication, 44*(4), 90-96.

Raman, N. (1997). A qualitative investigation of web-browsing behavior. *Advances in Consumer Research, 24,* 511-516.

Robbins, K. (1996). *Into the image: Culture and politics in the field of vision.* New York: Routledge.

Rogers, M. (1983). *Sociology, ethnomethodology and experience.* Cambridge, UK: Cambridge University Press.

Rook, D. (Ed.). (1999). *Brands, consumers, symbols, and research: Sidney J. Levy on marketing.* Thousand Oaks, CA: Sage.

Sayre, S. (1986). *Leader communication and organizational culture: A field study.* Doctoral dissertation, University of San Diego, CA.

Sayre, S. (1999). Using introspective self-narrative to analyze consumption: Experiencing plastic surgery. *Consumption Markets & Culture, 3*(2), 99-128.

Sayre, S. (2000). *Tourism, art stars and consumption: Wyland's whales.* Paper presented to the annual meeting of the Association of Consumer Research, Salt Lake City, UT.

Sayre, S., & Horne D. A. (1996a). *Earth, wind, fire and water: Perspectives on natural disaster.* Pasadena, CA: Open Door.

Sayre, S., & Horne, D. A. (1996b). I shop, therefore I am: The role of possessions for self-definition. In K. P. Corfman & J. G. Lynch, Jr., (Eds.), *Advances in Consumer Research, 13* (pp. 323-328). Provo, UT: Association for Consumer Research.

Sayre, S., & Horne, D. A. (1997). Borrowing from Oprah, stealing from Freud: Video-elicitation for advertising research. In M. C. Macklin (Ed.), *Proceedings of the 1997 conference of the American Academy of Advertising* (pp 67-72). Cincinnati, OH: University of Cincinatti.

Sayre, S., & Horne, D. A. (2000). Self-disclosure and technology: The viability of video-elicitation for consumer research. In R. Belk (Ed.), *Research in Consumer Behavior, 9,* 147-172.

Sayre, S., & Moriarty, S. E. (1993). Technology and art: A postmodern reading of Orwell as advertising. In Braden, R., Baca, J., & Beauchamp, D. (Eds.), *Art, science and visual literacy: Selected readings.* International Visual Literacy Association.

Schau, H., & Gilly, M. (1997). Social conventions of a fast food restaurant: An ethnomethodological analysis. *Advances in Consumer Research, 24,* 315-321.

Schensul, J. J., LeCompte, M., Nastasi, B. K., & Borgatti, S. (1999). *Advanced ethnographic methods.* Walnut Creek, CA: AltaMira.

Schouten, J., & Alexander, J. H. (1993). Market impact of consumption subcultures: The Harley-Davidson mystique. *European Advances in Consumer Research, 1,* 389-393.

Scotte, J. W. (1989). History in crisis? The other's side of the story. *American Historical Review, 94,* 680-692.

Shweder, R. (1986, September 1). Storytelling among the anthropologists. *New York Times Book Review, 21,* p. 38.

Sieber, J., & Stanley, B. (1988). Ethical and professional dimensions of socially sensitive research. *American Psychologist, 43,* 49-55.

Smith, A. (1954). *Motivation research in advertising and marketing.* New York: McGraw-Hill.

Smith, L. M. (1994). Biographical method. In N. K. Denzin & Y. K. Lincoln (Eds.), *Handbook of qualitative research* (pp. 286-305). Thousand Oaks, CA: Sage.

Smith, M. (1993). *Voices from the WELL: The logic of the virtual commons.* [Online]. Available: Smithm@nicco.sscnet.ucla.edu.

Snyder, J. (1997). Groupware: Colonizing new ground for industrious networks. (www.Techweb.com /se/directlink.cgi?NWC19960315).

Spradley, J. P. (1979). *The ethnographic interview.* London: Harcourt Brace Jovanovich.

Spradley, J. P. (1980). *Participant observation.* New York: Holt, Rinehart & Winston.

Stake, R. E. (1989). Case studies. In N. Denzin & Y. Lincoln (Eds.), *Handbook of qualitative research* (pp. 236-247). Newbury Park, CA: Sage.

Stake, R. E. (1995). *The art of case study.* Thousand Oaks, CA: Sage.

Stephanie, S. (1999, October 14). A life more ordinary, all the better for these anthropologists. *Los Angeles Times,* p. A6.

Stern, B. (1995). Consumer myths: Frye's taxonomy and the structural analysis of consumption text. *Journal of Consumer Research, 22,* 165-185.

Stewart, C. J., & Cash, W. B. (1988). *Interviewing principles and practices* (5th ed.). Dubuque, IA: William C. Brown.

Sudweeks, F., & Rafaeli, S. (1995). How do you get a hundred strangers to agree? Computer mediated communication and collaboration. In T. M. Harrison &

T. D. Stephen (Eds.), *Computer networking and scholarship in the 21st-century university* (pp. 115-136). New York: SUNY Press.

Teenor, K. (1994). *Field observations.* Unpublished paper, California State University, Fullerton.

Teenor, K. (1996). *Tabloid television and network news:The same or different?* Unpublished master's thesis, California State University, Fullerton.

Tesch, R. (1990). *Qualitative research: Analysis types and software tools.* New York: Falmer.

Thompson, C. (1997). Interpreting consumers: A hermeneutical framework for deriving marketing insights from the texts of consumers' consumption stories. *Journal of Marketing Research, 34,* 438-455.

Thompson, C., Locander, W., & Pollio, H. (1989, September). Putting consumer experience back into consumer research: The philosophy and method of existential-phenomenology. *Journal of Consumer Research, 16,* 133-146.

Thompson, C., Pollio, H., & Locander, W. (1994, December). The spoken and the unspoken: A hermeneutic approach to understanding the cultural viewpoints that underlie consumers' expressed meanings. *Journal of Consumer Research, 21,* 432-452.

Tuchman, G. (1994). Historical social science: Methodologies, methods, and meanings. In N. Denzin & Y. Lincoln (Eds.), *Handbook of qualitative research* (pp. 306-323). Thousand Oaks, CA: Sage.

Turner, J. (1985). In defense of positivism. *Sociological Theory, 3,* 24-31.

Turner, V. (1967). *The forest of symbols.* Ithaca, NY: Cornell University Press.

Van Maanen, J. (1979). The fact of fiction in organizational ethnography. In J. Van Maanen (Ed.), Qualitative methodology [Special issue]. *Administrative Science Quarterly, 24,* 535-550.

Van Maanen, J. (1988). *Tales of the field: On writing ethnography.* Chicago: University of Chicago Press.

Vorderer, P., & Groeben, N. (1992). Audience research: What the humanistic and the social science approaches could learn from each other. *Poetics, 21,* 361-376.

Weick, K. (1985). Systematic observation methods. In G. Lindzdey & E. Aronson (Eds.), *Handbook of social psychology: Vol 1. Theory and method.* New York: Random House.

Wellman, B., Salaff, J., Dimitrova, D., Garton, L., Guilia, M., & Haythornthwaite, C. (1996). Computer networks as social networks: Collaborative work, telework, and virtual community. *Annual Review of Psychology, 22,* 213-229.

Wolcott, H. (1994). *Transforming qualitative data: Description, analysis, and interpretation.* Thousand Oaks, CA: Sage.

Workman, J. P. (1992). Use of electronic mail in a participant observation study. *Qualitative Sociology, 15,* 419-425.

Index